Financial Institutions, Gardener

GW01325944

Banking in the New Europe

Also by Edward P.M. Gardener

BANK STRATEGIES AND CHALLENGES IN THE NEW EUROPE (*with P. Versluys*)

BANKING AND SECURITISATION (*with J.R.S. Revell. H. Minsky, M. de Cecco and E. Montanero*)

CHANGES IN WESTERN EUROPEAN BANKING (*with P. Molyneux*)

CREDIT INSTITUTIONS AND BANKING (*with B. Moore and P. Molyneux*)

EFFICIENCY IN EUROPEAN BANKING (*with P. Molyneux and Y. Altunbas*)

EUROPEAN SAVINGS BANKS: Coming of Age? (*with P. Molyneux and J. Williams*)

INVESTMENT BANKING: Theory and Practice (*with P. Molyneux*)

STRATEGIC CHALLENGES IN EUROPEAN BANKING (*with J. Fazon*)

THE FUTURE OF FINANCIAL SYSTEMS AND SERVICES

UK BANKING SUPERVISION: Evolution, Practice and Issues

Also by Philip Molyneux

BANCA ASSURANCE (*with N. Genetay*)

EUROPEAN BANKING: Efficiency, Technology and Growth (*with J. Goddard and J. Wilson*)

FINANCIAL INNOVATION (*with N. Shamroukh*)

GERMAN BANKING (*with D. Maude*)

PRIVATE BANKING (*with D. Maude*)

Also by Barry Moore

EAST ANGLIA IN THE 1990S ECONOMIST INTELLIGENCE UNIT (*with K. DiDonato*)

GEOGRAPHICAL VARIATIONS IN INDUSTRIAL COSTS AND PRODUCTIVITY IN THE UK (*with J. Rhodes and P. Tyler*)

METHODS OF MEASURING THE EFFECTS OF REGIONAL POLICIES (*with J. Rhodes*)

REGIONAL POLICY IN THE UK (*with J. Rhodes and P. Tyler*)

THE IMPACT AND EFFECTIVENESS OF INTERNAL MARKET INTEGRATION ON THE BANKING AND CREDIT SECTOR OF THE EUROPEAN UNION (*with E.P.M. Gardener and P. Molyneux*)

THE IMPACT OF REDUNDANCIES ON LOCAL LABOUR MARKETS: A Study of the Ravensburg Closure (*with D. O'Neill*)

THE IMPACT OF REDUNDANCIES ON LOCAL LABOUR MARKETS AND THE POST REDUNDANCY EXPERIENCE (*with D. O'Neill*)

URBAN LABOUR MARKETS: A Review (*with Peter Townroe*)

Banking in the New Europe

The Impact of the Single European Market Programme and EMU on the European Banking Sector

Edited by

Edward P.M. Gardener
Director of the School for Business and Regional Development
University of Wales
Bangor

Philip Molyneux
Professor of Banking and Finance
University of Wales
Bangor

and

Barry Moore
Assistant Director of Research and Fellow in Economics
Downing College
Cambridge

First published 2002 by
PALGRAVE MACMILLAN
Houndmills, Basingstoke, Hampshire RG21 6XS and
175 Fifth Avenue, New York, N.Y. 10010
Companies and representatives throughout the world

PALGRAVE MACMILLAN is the global academic imprint of the Palgrave
Macmillan division of St. Martin's Press, LLC and of Palgrave Macmillan Ltd.
Macmillan® is a registered trademark in the United States, United Kingdom
and other countries. Palgrave is a registered trademark in the European
Union and other countries.

ISBN 0–333–96434–9

This book is printed on paper suitable for recycling and made from fully
managed and sustained forest sources.

A catalogue record for this book is available from the British Library.

Library of Congress Cataloging-in-Publication Data
Banking in the new Europe : the impact of the single European market
programme and EMU on the European banking sector / edited by E.P.M.
Gardener, P. Molyneux, and Barry Moore.
    p. cm.
  Includes bibliographical references and index.
  ISBN 0–333–96434–9
   1. Banks and banking—Europe. 2. Economic and Monetary Union.
 3. Europe—Economic integration. I. Gardener, Edward P. M. II. Molyneux,
Philip. III. Moore, Barry, 1941–

HG2974 .B356 2002
332.1'094—dc21

                       2002074830

10 9 8 7 6 5 4 3 2 1
11 10 09 08 07 06 05 04 03 02

Printed and bound in Great Britain by
Antony Rowe Ltd, Chippenham and Eastbourne

Contents

List of Tables

List of Figures

Preface

The twelve chapters of this book explore the impact on individual country credit sectors of the EC Single Market Programme (SMP) and EMU (Economic and Monetary Union). The SMP and EMU comprise the most significant credit sector regulatory events in modern European history. The SMP was the essential precursor to EMU and, in this context, might be viewed as the regulatory and expectations-changing 'bridge' from the old world to the 'New Europe'. Both of these regulatory events are undeniably of unparalleled significance. The economic gains sought through these deregulatory and integrative moves are those accruing from greater competition, including lower prices, more innovation, a greater responsiveness to market needs and higher output.

The impact of these regulatory events on credit sectors is of particular economic significance. Credit sectors play a singularly important role in economic development. Their importance is heightened by the potential economic benefits that may accrue to other sectors which use financial services delivered from a more efficient credit sector. At the same time, a more efficient and flexible financial system is a better conduit for macro monetary and other policies. The potential economic gains that accrue from these different functions conspire to enhance the particular economic importance of credit sectors. This latter role is again re-emphasised when the impact of deregulation and associated integration (or globalisation) policies on economic systems are considered. Little wonder, then, that policymakers are particularly concerned with the impact of their economic reform strategies on credit sectors. If you get the latter wrong, then the overall reform may be seriously compromised.

This volume comprises eleven country chapters written by acknowledged banking and credit sector experts in each of these countries. The countries covered are Belgium, Denmark, France, Germany, Greece, Ireland, Italy, the Netherlands, Portugal, Spain and the United Kingdom. The selection of countries and the use of country experts are explained by the origin of this volume. The book arose from a major research project commissioned by the EC from Economic Research Europe Ltd, Cambridge, and was directed by Barry Moore (Cambridge) and Professors Ted Gardener and Phil Molyneux (Institute of European Finance, University of Wales, Bangor); the project reported in 1997. The project explored the impact of the SMP on the EU credit sectors. Many of the same country experts in the current volume also worked on this latter project.

This project comprised one of the biggest research projects of its kind ever undertaken on the EU credit sectors. It deployed a variety of research techniques, including case studies, an extensive postal survey, and statistical and econometric analyses. The research built from a firm institutional context, rather than a theoretical one. The use of country experts from the respective countries has the obvious advantage that each country is being covered by someone who has 'on the ground' knowledge of the sector and the institutional context in which it operates. This confluence of expertise can be particularly important in analysing and understanding credit sectors.

The countries included in this book are those covered in the EC project from which the book emanated. This allows the volume to build directly from the major research that has already been undertaken within the project. It allows the same data, case studies and survey work to underpin the present volume. As a result, the present volume does not cover all important EU credit sectors and the new member countries. Nevertheless, it encompasses the biggest and most of the more important credit sectors.

Each country chapter, then, builds on the data and results that flowed from the EC (1997) study. The latter has set the pattern and format of each of the country chapters. Authors were encouraged to adopt a similar approach in their individual country chapters. This facilitates comparative analyses. Of course, a lot has happened since the EC study reported in 1997, not least of which was the launch of EMU! Authors were commissioned to update and develop their analyses used in the 1997 research (which focused primarily on the impact of the SMP). Each author explores the following areas:

- Market Structure and Performance
- Regulatory Framework
- Impact of the SMP
- Bank Preparations for EMU

The volume, therefore, is a comparative survey of institutional developments and the respective strategic impact of the SMP and EMU. It is impossible generally to isolate the specific strategic impact on credit institutions of regulation from other important strategic drivers like competition and technology. The present volume recognises this practical fact of banking life and attempts to set regulation in the context of other important strategic drivers.

Our task as editors and co-authors of this volume has been helped enormously by the help and cooperation of our fellow authors; we thank all of our contributor authors, the 'country experts' in this volume. We must also thank Emily Smith and Christine Owen in the Institute of European Finance, who managed key stages of what turned out to be a complex project. We are grateful to the publishers and referees for supporting this project. Our thanks go also to the EC who commissioned from us the project that formed the genesis of this volume. We thank all of these key 'stakeholders' in the present book. It goes without saying that any errors and omissions that remain are ours alone.

TED GARDENER
PHIL MOLYNEUX
BARRY MOORE

Synopses of Contributions

1 Introduction

Barry Moore

At the end of an extensive legislative programme which preceded the entry into force of the Single Market in 1992, the Council of Ministers asked the European Commission to present in 1996 an *ex post* analysis of the impact and effectiveness of the legislation which had been put in place. The Banking and Credit Sector was one of some fifteen sectors analysed in depth to assess the impact and effectiveness of the legislation. This volume has its origins in that research programme and several of the authors were involved in supporting and undertaking desk research, case studies of banks, and survey research which provided the basis for the initial report on the impact of the Single Market Programme (SMP) on banking and credit institutions in twelve EU countries (ERE, 1997). The research underpinning this earlier assessment has now been significantly updated. The results are presented here in separate country chapters rather than incorporated in thematic chapters on a cross-country basis as in the 1997 report. This approach enables the authors to bring out more clearly the country-specific impacts and to explore in more depth the institutional structures which help shape the impact of the programme in each country.

2 Belgium

Rudi Vander Vennet

The Belgian banking sector has undergone significant changes, but still faces a period of substantial restructuring. It is equally clear that the SMP and EMU are dominant and mutually dependent causes of this trend. However, it remains difficult to isolate the specific impact of SMP because its implementation coincided with a number of other important structural developments, especially in the technological field. Nevertheless, the SMP has certainly intensified bank competition and further increased foreign entry. It has induced a shift from regulatory capture and collusive behaviour towards a more market-based pricing of products and services. These trends have caused a substantial narrowing of the traditional interest margin. In terms of bank strategy, the SMP has provoked a shift from a predominant supply-side approach to a post-deregulation demand-based strategy. One of the effects of the SMP has been to increase the operational productivity and the overall risk return efficiency. In general it can be stated that deregulation, internationalisation and increased competition have rendered the Belgian banking markets more contestable. Although the exact impact of the SMP is difficult to assess, it is clear that the major forces in reshaping the banking environment have been the regulation-induced intensification of functional diversification and the focus on operational efficiency. Faced with this changing environment, small and large banks have adapted their strategies accordingly.

3   Denmark

Morten Balling and Anders Grosen

The Danish regulatory framework concerning financial markets and institutions has been continually adjusted to EU Directives and regulations since Denmark joined the European Community in 1973. After so many years of amendments created with a clear European integration perspective, there are very few barriers left. The deregulatory aspects of the SMP have contributed to an intensified competition by opening up the financial system to new players. This means that an increasing number of institutions are providing financial services and products. Surveys carried out on a sample of Danish financial institutions indicate that they have been used to exposure to international competition for decades: therefore, they do not expect major revisions in their business activities and strategic reactions due to EMU. Indeed, the majority of the respondents expect that the prospects of the euro will accelerate the reality of a single European banking market.

4   France

Dominique Plihon

The structure and operating conditions of the French banking system have undergone far-reaching changes since the mid-1980s. One of the most significant of these developments has been a transformation of shareholder structures and a gradual return of banks to the private sector. The banking industry has also been marked by liberalisation, which has been boosted by the SMP, and booming capital markets, which have contributed to greater competition against a background of slower economic growth in the early 1990s. This new context has led to a sharp decline in traditional intermediation business, which has been offset by accelerated growth of trading activities through the rapid growth of banks' securities portfolios and off-balance-sheet transactions. Another effect of liberalisation has been a steadily growing volume of international activity, both on capital markets and through the development of foreign investment. The new environment has given rise to an unprecedented wave of financial restructuring in the world economy, an area in which continental Europe seems to have lagged behind. There is a strong probability that EMU will accelerate banking restructuring. The attempt to merge three large French banks, BNP, Société Générale and Paribas in March 1999, with a view to create the largest bank in the world by balance sheet size, is an illustration of this deep transformation.

5   Germany

Günter Lang

The creation of a single European currency is affecting German banks more significantly than the SMP, because the latter is more or less a harmonisation-driven change within the regulatory framework. It is no easy task, however, to separate the effects of the SMP, EMU, and other changes in the market environment, such as growing disintermediation or technical progress. The reason for this difficulty is that, in many ways, these forces work towards the same direction: growing competition within the banking sector, and between banks and non-bank financial institutions. EMU will further speed up structural change in German and European banking. Large, stock-traded German banks, especially, are currently under pressure because of their relatively low profitability. To maintain or enhance profitability in an environment of decreasing margins, all banks must increase their efforts to reduce costs. The reduction in capacity, especially in the number of branches and banks, will continue.

6   Greece

Christos Gortsos

In addition to adapting their operations to the requirements imposed by the introduction of the euro, Greek banks will have to reappraise their strategies for survival in the single European financial market. In the years to come, some of them will retain a domestic orientation by exploiting the comparative advantages of their local presence. Since Greece's ratio of consumer and housing loans to the gross domestic product is the lowest among the member states of the EU, the expected growth in these markets will provide opportunities for Greek banks to grow and profit. Some Greek banks, however, will attempt to compete on a European scale by penetrating the markets of other member states and/or resist the increased competition from other EU-based banks in Greece (which may choose to provide services in Greece only on a cross-border basis). The structure of the Greek banking system and the performance profile of financial intermediaries operating in this system will be definitively different from what has been described in this paper.

7 Ireland

Ray Kinsella and Philip Bourke

The Irish financial system, at the heart of which are credit institutions, has experienced a period of unprecedented expansion and structural change since the mid-1980s. There was a broadening and deepening in the key services provided by banks, both domestic institutions as well as those from other EU countries and from outside the European Economic Area , in intermediation, deposit taking and money transmission, financial and investment services, and portfolio management and related services. This change process has been accompanied by institutional (including regulatory) and structural change. The SMP contributed substantially to the further liberalisation of what, since the late 1960s, had ostensibly been a relatively open banking market. Global competitive pressures reinforced the effects of the SMP and thereby contributed to the process of deregulation of credit institutions and also to the emergence of bancassurance as the dominant institutional structure. The prospective impact of the introduction of the single currency on the Irish banking system, and the wider financial services sector, is difficult to assess. What can be said is that the single currency, coming on the top of the SMP, has transformed Irish banking.

8 Italy

Franco Bruni, Andrea Balzarini and Daniele Fox

To assess the impact of the SMP on Italy's banks and to evaluate their competitive strengths and weaknesses, somewhat sophisticated measures are needed of their technical and scale efficiency, which are more informative than the usual indicators of profitability. After some brief comments on the comparative profitability of Italian banks, this chapter describes various measures of efficiency. The results of efficiency calculations are then shown for Italian banks and compared with corresponding institutions in Germany, France and Spain. An analysis of the evolution over time of the efficiency of Italian banks is then presented. Finally, some conclusions follow on the strategic response of the Italian banking system to the increased competitive pressure coming from the Single Market for banking services and from the European currency unification.

9   Netherlands

Harald A. Benink and Jacques J. Sijben

The Dutch banking sector represents an interesting case study since the Dutch market has been, well before the adoption of the EU regulations related to the SMP and the Europe 1992 target date, relatively small, open, liberal and efficient. At the same time, the SMP has had a profound impact due to bankers' anticipatory reactions to internal market legislation. Moreover, the introduction of the euro is likely to have significant consequences for the banking system in the Netherlands. This chapter presents an overview of the Dutch banking sector in terms of market structure and performance. Attention is paid to the main players and market positions, the degree of competition, the entry barriers, and the banking performance and condition. It goes on to describe the regulatory framework for banks in the Netherlands, both before and after implementation of the SMP and then analyses how the SMP has affected the strategic behaviour of Dutch banks. Special attention is paid to the strategy of the ING Group, based on interviews with high-ranking officials of ING. Using key results of the Economic Research Europe report, empirical evidence on the Single Market's impact on Dutch banks is presented. Section 5 deals with the preparations by Dutch banks for the planned introduction of EMU with a common currency, the euro. The combined effect of the Netherland's relatively small size and high degree of concentration makes it difficult for foreign financial firms to enter the Dutch banking market. A postal survey conducted among five Dutch banks concludes that the introduction of the euro is likely to change this situation by opening up possibilities for increased market integration, greater uniformity in market practices, and more transparency in pricing.

10   Portugal

Paulo Soares de Pinho

This chapter aims to evaluate to what extent the Single European Act of 1986 affected the Portuguese banking industry and to analyse the preparations made by this industry to face EMU. It is not a simple task. Being a highly regulated and protected market just ten years prior to the implementation of the Single Market legislation, the country's banking sector had to be deregulated at a very fast pace in order to allow for a smoother transition to the new European environment. Thus, in most cases, it is impossible to distinguish between the specific effects of the domestic deregulation of the early 1990s and the specific effects of the Single Market legislation. There is, however, one point on which most observers agree. Without the need to comply with the Single Market legislation, domestic banking deregulation would have been slower and most probably less extensive. Therefore, although their individual economic effects are indistinguishable, it is arguable that most domestic banking legislation passed between 1985 and 1992 had the Single Market in mind. And, therefore, most of the economic changes that this market has recently experienced are either directly or indirectly a consequence of the Single Market Programme in banking.

11 Spain

José M.Pastor and Javier Quesada

Well before Spain joined the Common Market, a group of economic sectors was concerned over how to adjust to the new conditions successfully. The financial sector in general, and especially the banking sector, was the clearest exponent of a rapid and continuing adjustment to the new atmosphere imposed by the new competitive panorama. This reaction accelerated over recent years as the Spanish banking system became involved in multiple processes of change, namely the introduction and adjustment to new technologies, liberalisation, internationalisation, globalisation and deregulation. These processes were sometimes pushed by the authorities, following EC Directives, as well as by the banks themselves. Different strategies including, among others, mergers and acquisitions and the establishment of cooperation agreements, were followed in order to adapt institutions to the new conditions imposed by the SMP. The old strict regulatory framework presented a serious obstacle to free competition for two reasons: first, it was an 'entry barrier' to foreign banks and, second, it was an 'exit barrier' because it precluded many non-performing banks from going into bankruptcy. The consequence of these circumstances was a lack of innovation processes proposed by private initiatives. This situation has changed substantially in recent years due to the SMP and to successive Directives. Section 2 describes the impact on market structure and performance. Section 3 describes the regulatory framework, with emphasis on those deregulation processes that most affected the banks' behaviour and highlighting the main remaining barriers. Section 4 presents the areas in which the SMP had most consequences, differentiating, where possible, the effects caused by the SMP from the effects caused by generic trends common to all banking systems. Section 5 summarises these effects.

12 United Kingdom

Edward P.M. Gardener and Philip Molyneux

The changing features of the UK banking system have mainly been a consequence of the changing market environment and also a result of various domestic regulatory reforms. While the SMP appears to have influenced the strategic positioning of UK-based banks in relation to cross-border provision of wholesale banking services, there appears to have been little material impact on the domestic commercial banking scene. European banks from outside the UK have no significant presence in retail financial services or banking to small and medium-sized enterprises. Although the presence of continental European banks in the UK has grown post-SMP, their activities are almost solely confined to wholesale investment banking and securities activities based in the City of London. The introduction of the single currency from the 1 January 1999 and the creation of a single European monetary policy have acted as a strong fillip to create an integrated European capital market. The recent spate of alliances between major European stock markets and derivatives exchanges is clearly a precursor to full integration. The full impact of EMU on UK bank strategy has hardly been realised. Current forces, however, suggest that irrespective of whether the UK is 'in' or 'out' of the eurozone, the main banks are almost certainly going to engage in substantial cross-border eurozone deals within the near future.

1 Introduction

Barry Moore

1 INTRODUCTION

At the end of an extensive legislative programme which preceded the entry into force of the Single Market in 1992, the Council of Ministers asked the European Commission to present in 1996 an *ex post* analysis of the impact and effectiveness of the legislation which had been put in place. The Banking and Credit Sector was one of some fifteen sectors analysed in depth to assess the impact and effectiveness of the legislation. This volume has its origins in that research programme and several of the authors were involved in supporting and undertaking desk research, case studies of banks, and survey research which provided the basis for the initial report on the impact of the Single Market Programme (SMP) on banking and credit institutions in twelve EU countries (ERE, 1997).

The research underpinning this earlier assessment has now been significantly updated. The results are presented here in separate country chapters rather than incorporated in thematic chapters on a cross-country basis as in the 1997 report. This approach enables the authors to bring out more clearly the country-specific impacts and to explore in more depth the institutional structures which help shape the impact of the programme in each country.

Since the 1997 ERE report, attention has also switched somewhat from the impact of the SMP and has focused increasingly on the implications of EMU for the banking and credit sector. Much of this research (Dermine, 1998) has been concerned with the implications for investment and wholesale banking, and there is something of a dearth of literature on the implications for retail banking. However, with the onset of EMU, the impact of the SMP on the retail end of the market could be significantly enhanced. White (1998) has referred to the euro as a catalyst for change with potentially profound implications for retail activities. The SMP is part of an ongoing process and the introduction of EMU is integral to the ultimate objectives of securing a competitive and efficient banking system in Europe. Authors were therefore asked to express their views on this in their individual country contributions.

1

Section 2 of this introductory chapter presents a brief profile of each of the country contributors and Section 3 discusses the implications of EMU for the retail financial services sector at a pan-European level.

2   AUTHOR PROFILES

Morten Balling is Rector (Vice-Chancellor) of the Aarhus School of Business (ASB) in Denmark. In April 2001 he returned to his permanent position as Professor of Finance at the ASB. Balling is a member of the supervisory board of a number of Danish foundations and companies, including institutions in the financial sector. He is also a member of the managing council of the Société Universitaire Européenne de Recherches Financières, SUERF. He has published articles and books on monetary policy, the management of financial institutions, and corporate financial management. In 1998 he was co-editor of a book entitled *Corporate Governance, Financial Markets and Global Convergence* (Kluwer Academic Publishers, Dordrecht/Boston/London).

Andrea Balzarini graduated in 1995 from Bocconi University and then worked there as a research Fellow. In 1997 he joined the economic research department of Pirelli SpA, the global tyre and cables manufacturer. He is now working at the Basle branch office of Pirelli Finance (Luxembourg) S.A. in the Financial Planning Department.

Harald A. Benink is Full Professor at the Rotterdam School of Management at Erasmus University, Rotterdam, where he holds a chair of 'Institutional Design of Integrating Markets'. Professor Benink is also chairman of the International Master of Science in Business Administration (IMScBA) Programme at the Rotterdam Schools of Management and Economics, Erasmus University, Rotterdam, and senior associate to the Financial Markets Group of the London School of Economics. He received his PhD in finance and economics from Maastricht University: the thesis was entitled *Financial Fragility*. His research focuses on banking and finance, and on European financial and monetary integration. He has published in various academic journals, including *The Journal of Finance*, and has also published two books. He is also founder and chairman of the European Shadow Financial Regulatory Committee (ESFRC), a group of 15 professors and experts from ten European countries and the US. During the period 1989 to 1996, Professor Benink was adviser to the banking and financial services group Ernst & Young in the Netherlands.

Philip Bourke is currently Irish Banks' Professor of Banking and Finance, and Dean of the Faculty of Commerce in the Graduate School of Business at University College Dublin. He has held the professorial appointment since 1989, prior to which he was Director of the Australian Centre for Banking and Finance at the University of New South Wales, Sydney. His previous appointment was as Director of the Centre for the Study of Financial Markets at University College Dublin, an appointment that he combined with a position in the Department of Banking and Finance. Professor Bourke has published extensively in the field of banking, finance and investment: his publications appear in international and domestic journals and in book form, and he has also presented conference papers in Europe, Asia and Australia. He has lectured widely to business organisations and to universities and academic institutions in Europe and throughout the world on financial topics, and has also consulted widely with banking organisations in Europe. His academic research and consulting have focused on bank management issues, including profitability and strategy, and his university teaching has been mainly at the postgraduate level.

Franco Bruni is Full Professor of International Monetary Economics and Director of the Department of Economics at Bocconi University, Milan. He is editor of the *Giornale degli Economisti e Annali di Economia*, Scientific Director of ISPI (Milan's institute for research in international relations), President of the Société Universitaire Européenne de Recherches Financières (SUERF) and a member of the European Shadow Financial Regulatory Committee (ESFRC).

Daniele Fox graduated in 1998 at Bocconi University where he then served as a research assistant. He worked at the Treasury Department of Banca Commerciale Italiana, received the European Postgraduate Degree in Fund Management, and is now working for Europlus Research and Management in Dublin.

Edward P.M. Gardener is Professor of Banking and Finance, co-director (with Professor Molyneux) of the Institute of European Finance, and Head of the School of Business and Regional Development (SBARD) at the University of Wales, Bangor. He is also a Visiting Professor at Queen Mary and Westfield College and the University of Malta. He has published over 200 articles, books and reports on banking topics. Recent publications include, as co-author, *Efficiency in European Banking* (John Wiley, 1996), *Investment Banking: Theory and Practice* (Euromoney),

European Savings Banks: Coming of Age? (Euromoney), and *Strategic Challenges in European Banking* (Macmillan, 2000). Since 1996 he has (working with colleagues from the Institute of European Finance and Cambridge University) co-directed two major banking projects: one was for the European Commission (DG XV) and was published as *Credit Institutions and Banking: The Single Market Review* (Kogan Page) and the other was for HM Treasury within the March 2000 Cruickshank Report on competition in UK banking services.

Christos Gortsos is Associate Professor of International Financial Law at the Panteion University of Athens and is Legal Counsel of the Hellenic Bank Association. He studied law and economics in the Universities of Athens, Zurich, Geneva and Pennsylvania (Wharton Business School) and holds a PhD from the Graduate Institute of International Studies, University of Geneva. Dr. Gortsos is a member of the Athens Bar Association and the author of books and articles on international, European and Greek monetary and banking law.

Anders Grosen is Associate Professor of Finance and Head of the Department of Finance at the Aarhus School of Business. He is also an officially appointed member of the Danish Pensions Council. He has published more than one hundred articles, books and reports on banking and insurance topics. Recent publications include 'Valuation of Early Exercisable Interest Rate Guarantees' (*The Journal of Risk and Insurance*) and 'Fair Valuation of Life Insurance Liabilities: The Impact of Interest Rate Guarantees, Surrender Options, and Bonus Policies' (*Insurance Mathematics & Economics*).

Ray Kinsella is Professor of Banking and Financial Services at the University of Ulster and Visiting Professor of Banking and Insurance at University College Dublin Graduate School of Business, where he established and is Director of the Centre for Insurance Studies. He has worked as an economist with the Central Bank of Ireland and as an economic advisor to the Irish Government. He has written extensively in the fields of banking, finance and insurance, and his publications include: *Internal Controls in Banking* (Wiley, 1997); (with Professor Vincent McBrierty) *Ireland and the Knowledge Economy: the Techno-Academic Paradigm* (Oak Tree Press, Dublin, 1998) and *The EMU: Operational and Policy Constraints: A Central Bank for Europe*, 11th Lothian Conference (London, 2000).

Günter Lang is Associate Professor of Economics at the University of Augsburg. He received his doctoral degree in 1993 for his work in industrial economics. His research interests include industrial organisation, regulation, and environmental and resource economics. He has published empirical papers on many topics in the German banking industry.

Philip Molyneux is Professor of Banking and Finance and co-director (with Professor Gardener) of the Institute of European Finance at the University of Wales, Bangor. He also holds the Special Chair of Financial Services and Financial Conglomerates at Erasmus University, Rotterdam. His main area of research is on the structure and efficiency of banking markets and he has published widely in this area, including recent papers in the *Journal of Banking and Finance, Journal of Money, Credit and Banking, Economica, Journal of Post-Keynesian Economics* and *Applied Economics*. He has authored/co-authored a variety of books. The most recent include: *Banking: An Introductory Text* (Macmillan); *Efficiency in European Banking* (John Wiley, 1996); *Private Banking* (Euromoney); *Investment Banking* (Euromoney); *Banking in Germany* (Financial Times); *Credit Institutions and Banking: The Single Market Review* (Kogan Page); *Bancassurance* (Macmillan, 1998); *Financial Innovation* (John Wiley); and *European Savings Banks: Coming of Age?* (Euromoney). He has acted as a consultant to the New York Federal Reserve Bank, the European Commission, the World Bank, Citibank, Merrill Lynch, and many other commercial and government organisations.

Barry Moore is an applied economist and an internationally recognised authority on the evaluation of government regional and urban policies. He joined the Department of Applied Economics in the University of Cambridge in 1970 and in 1985 he became an assistant director of research in the Department of Land Economy. In the late-1980s he was involved in setting up the ESRC Centre for Business Research in Cambridge. He was a special adviser on regional policy to the OECD for more than ten years, and one time adviser to the House of Commons Select Committee on Welsh Affairs. He has been an adviser and consultant to a number of government departments in the UK and to the European Commission. In the mid-1990s he directed a major cross-country evaluation of the impact of the Single Market Programme on the banking and credit sector of the EU, and was a consultant to the recent HM Treasury study of competition in UK banking (Cruickshank Inquiry). He is a Fellow in Economics at Downing College, Cambridge, and has published widely across a broad range of subjects.

José M. Pastor is Graduate and PhD (with extraordinary award) in economics from the Universitat de València (1996) where he is currently Lecturer in Economic Analysis. Professor Pastor's fields of speciality are banking and regional economics. He has received scholarships from institutions as diverse as the Consellería de Educación de la Generalitat Valenciana, the Fundación Caja de Madrid and FIES, and has been visiting researcher during 1996-97 at Florida State University in the Finance Department. He has jointly published many books and articles in Spanish journals, including *Investigaciones Económicas, Revista Española de Economía Aplicada,* as well as in international specialised journals (*Applied Economics, Applied Financial Economics, Economics Letters, Transportation, European Journal of Operational Research, Regional Studies,* among others). He has been consultant to the World Bank and currently is Associate Researcher in the National Research Plan.

Paulo Soares de Pinho is Assistant Professor of Banking and Finance and Director of Executive Education at Universidade Nova de Lisboa. He is also a consultant to banks and companies involved in project finance. His research has focused on the competitive structure of Portuguese banking, and on bank asset and liability management. He has published articles in many academic journals and contributed chapters to books on European banking.

Dominique Plihon is Professor in the Department of Economics at Paris-Nord University (France) where he directs a Master Programme (Diplôme d'Etudes Supérieures Spécialisées) in banking and finance. He was Dean of the Department of Economics from 1995 to 1997. He graduated from Paris University with an MA in Economics in 1969 and from the State University of New York, Albany, with a PhD in economics in 1974. He worked at Banque de France from 1974-83 and at the Commissariat du Plan from 1983-88. He became full-time Professor in 1988. He has undertaken consultancy for Banque de France (1992-95) and the Banking Commission (1996-98). Professor Plihon has published widely in the fields of banking, international finance and European economics. Among his recent publications are: *Risk Management by Credit Institutions: Macroeconomic Modelling Attempts* (in collaboration with J. Cordier and P. Jacquinot) in *Economic Modelling at the Banque de France* (Routledge, 1996); *The Banks, New Strategies,* a book published (in French) in 1998 by Documentation Française; and *Exchange Rates,* a book published (in French) by La Découverte in 1999.

Javier Quesada graduated in Economics from the Universitat de València and holds a Doctorate in Economics from the University of Cincinnati, Ohio. He is a Full Professor of Economic Analysis at the Universitat de València. His main field of research is in financial and monetary economics. He has jointly published two books: *Economìa Española 1960-1980: Crecimiento y Cambio Estructural* (Blume, 1982) and *Dinero y Sistema Bancario: Teoria y Análisis del Caso Español* (Espasa-Calpe, 1991). He has written articles in *The Changing Face of European Banks and Securities Markets* (St. Martin's Press, 1994) and *The Recent Evolution of Financial Systems* (Macmillan, 1997), both edited by J. Revell; in *The Competitiveness of Financial Institutions and Centres in Europe* (edited by D.E. Fair and R J. Raymond); and in *Banking Cultures of the World* (edited by L. Schuster), as well as in specialist journals including *Applied Economics, European Journal of Operational Research, Investigaciones Económicas, Moneda y Crédito* and *Zeitschrift für Wirtschafts-und Sozialwissenschaften.* From 1985-86 he was a visiting scholar at Harvard University.

Jacques J. Sijben is Full Professor of Money, Credit and Banking at the Department of Economics, Tilburg University. He is also director of the Master in Financial Economics (MFE) Programme of TIAS Business School, Tilburg University. He holds both a Master's and a PhD in Economics from Tilburg University. Professor Sijben's research focuses on monetary economics, financial stability and banking. He has published in various academic journals (including *Kredit und Kapital, Revue de la Banque* and *Jahrbücher für Nationalökonomie und Statistik*) and has also published two books. He has served as adviser to various financial institutions and corporates.

After completing a Master's degree in finance, **Rudi Vander Vennet** obtained his PhD in economics in 1994 from the University of Ghent with a study on European bank mergers. Currently he is professor at the University of Ghent and chairman of the Financial Economics Department. He is the author of various articles on banking issues in academic journals, including the *Journal of Money, Credit, and Banking* and the *Journal of Banking and Finance*, and is co-editor of two books about European monetary union. He is also a member of the board of directors of a number of Belgian financial services companies.

3   EMU AND RETAIL BANKING IN THE EU

In a brief overview of the results of the research programme assessing the impact of the SMP, Monti (1997), referring to the research on the retail banking sector, concluded: 'Generally then, the single market's impact on banking has been positive but not startling. Though barriers remain, the chief of which are the differing tax rates and regimes which persist around Europe, most bankers surveyed in the research have their minds fixed on the next target in European integration: monetary union. "Without this", one of them said, "the single market is like Hamlet without the Prince"'.

Certainly, the EU's retail banking sector has been judged as one of the sectors least effected by the SMP, and an important question addressed here is whether the introduction of EMU will catalyse the legislative changes now in place as a consequence of the SMP. Most importantly, EMU reduces some of the competitive advantages enjoyed by local banks as a result of currency risk, lack of price transparency and local expertise on national monetary policy. It thereby provides banks with enhanced opportunities for exploiting greater market integration derived from the SMP and other factors such as developments in telecommunications and computer technologies. Perhaps more importantly it also reinforces bankers' perceptions that the European banking industry is in the midst of a period of unprecedented change, with increased contestability in all markets. This is not to deny that the response lags by both banks and customers to these changes may be long and that the full implications for the structure and performance of European retail banking will take time to emerge.

Although the introduction of EMU will intensify competition in all financial product market segments, the pace of change and the impact will vary by country, by product and between the personal sector and small and medium-sized enterprises (SMEs). Like its forerunner, the SMP, the impact of EMU on banking is complex and the initial conditions and institutional structures in each country will exert a powerful influence on the scale and timing of its impact. In particular, the impact of EMU on the competitiveness of the retail banking sector (and indeed of other forces for change such as the SMP and technological advances) turns critically on the potential for customers to switch from one financial service provider to another. If significant switching costs exist, or if there are institutional, cultural, legal or other impediments to switching, effective competition is impeded. Thus, although EMU removes an important barrier to cross-border trade and improves the ability of customers to make intra-country and cross-country price comparisons, from the perspective of the personal and SME customer the impact is mediated by switching costs in the short to medium term. In these circumstances, consolidation and efficiency improvements by banks may raise shareholder value but there may be limited benefits to customers in those market segments where switching costs are high (or perceived to be high).

A final theme addressed here is that for all countries the current period of turbulence and change will give rise to increased tensions and dilemmas for policymakers. For example, enhanced competition may ultimately improve consumer welfare but increased rationalisation of the supply side may increase monopoly power in selected product market areas, with potentially adverse welfare implications for consumers (White, 1998).

3.1 Forces for change in European retail banking

The major forces that have been shaping the structure and performance of retail banking in the EU are well known and will be discussed only briefly here. Figure 1 identifies five major sources of change influencing the retail banking sector in the EU: regulatory changes, demography, EMU, market factors and technology. Arguably, the most important of these forces are developments in the use of computing and telecommunications technologies, and changes in the regulatory and policy environment within the EU and globally.

The forces for change identified in Figure 1 provide the context within which the potential effects of EMU must be considered and they critically influence how this new factor will impact on the retail banking market. Several recent contributions have explored these changes, including the European Central Bank (1999), White (1998), Gardener *et al.* (1999), Vives (1998), and Economic Research Europe (1997). The broad conclusion reached is that retail banking in the EU will continue to experience increasing competition, leading to further consolidation and restructuring as banks respond to their new strategic environment. EMU will accelerate this transformation of the retail banking sector. However, most banks will seek to exploit domestic opportunities before turning to cross-border opportunities and, although EMU will also result in further bank consolidation, it will be a slow process.

(a) Technology
There is little doubt that developments in the use of new computing and telecommunications technologies are having a major impact on retail banking and their application is affecting all aspects of banking operations, including the customer-bank interface, business management, core processing, and support and integration. Customer-facing technology is

the most visible sign of change and has advanced considerably over the last decade. The growing use of ATMs, cash dispensers and bank cards, and the effecting of automatic transfer payment and retrieval of basic account information by customers have also become common practice. In addition, EFTPOS (electronic funds transfer at the point of sale) and home banking developments have also grown in importance. The broad embrace of new customer-facing technologies is forcing banks to provide multi-channel delivery systems where banking services are offered via the branch, telephone, mail, internet and interactive TV. This has led some commentators to talk about the evolution of the 'network bank' where multi-channel delivery systems are fully integrated with back-office and middle-office activities/systems with the ultimate objective of providing lower cost and higher quality customer service (Gandy, 1999).

Another area indicating the extent of technology development in the retail payments area relates to the growing use of electronic money or e-money. 'Card-based e-money' refers to e-money as stored value on cards or prepaid card products that allow customers to make (small-value) transactions whereas 'network e-money' refers to e-money transactions conducted via telecommunications networks, primarily the internet (European Central Bank, 1999). The internet is also being increasingly used as an alternative delivery channel for established banking services, most often as an additional channel to meet the requirements of more sophisticated customers. To date, the size of the internet banking market is relatively small in Europe and, according to Morgan Stanley Dean Witter (1999), 'Only MeritaNordbanken in Finland states that it has significant internet penetration among its total customer base, of some 18%, whereas other banks' rates are in the very low single digits'. Recent research by Moody's Investor Service (2000) foresees fundamental changes arising from the use of the internet, with new developments such as wireless internet WAP (wireless application protocol) based on the use of mobile telephones becoming an important medium for on-line banking.

The development and integration of effective customer relationship management (CRM) systems has been, and continues to be, an important feature of many bank IT developments. CRM systems aim to provide banks with information on the lifetime value of a customer and the ability to segment actual and prospective customers by needs, behaviour, propensity to buy, and other characteristics. In short, they provide banks with the ability to price and cost customer relationships across a broad range of market segments such as product, customer, and geography.

Business management technologies include systems that aim to

Figure 1.1 Forces of change in European retail banking

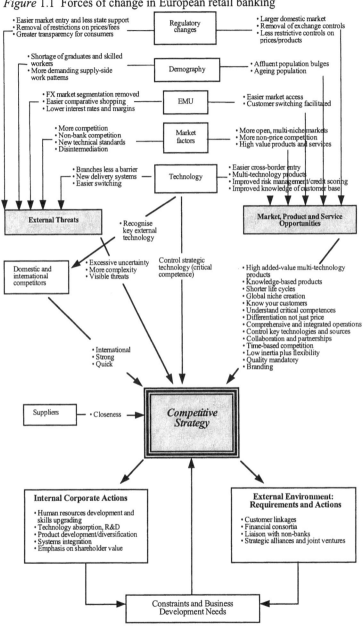

enhance the organistion and flow of information within firms in order to enhance managerial decision-making. Such technologies include data warehousing, data mining, middleware, and credit and risk management systems. The cross-selling of financial services is often quoted as the major driver for banks to develop their business management systems. However, evidence suggests that this is not happening on the scale required to justify large IT spends in this area.

Core processing technologies involved with cheque processing, statement issuance, interest and charging systems are, in most large banks, typically run by mainframe computers that provide information resources for the large branch networks and customer bases (see Gandy, 1999, pp. 21-26). These systems were well developed for UK and European banks but in recent years they have not evolved as rapidly as expected given the constraints imposed by the Y2K problem and the conversion to the euro. The recent trend towards the outsourcing of core processing activity is, at present, not a major current option for many of the big European banks, although new entrants typically use outsource providers to do all their processing. A recent survey by DataMonitor (1999) notes that UK banks will be the biggest spenders on external technology solutions over the next five years. The study also reports that the IT outsourcing market is growing rapidly, which may suggest that there will be a push for some of the larger UK banks to outsource more of their core processing business.

These and other developments in the application of new computing and telecommunications technologies have a number of important implications for European retail banking, and potentially influence the impact of EMU on the retail banking sector in the following ways:

- they contribute to the reduction of the costs associated with the management of information (collection, storage, processing and transmission) by replacing paper-based and labour-intensive methods with automated processes
- they modify the ways in which customers have access to bank services and products, mainly through automated channels ('remote banking') (European Central Bank, 1999), whilst at the same time reducing the need for extensive branch networks
- they undermine traditional 'relationship' banking and commodify financial products by facilitating their unbundling and rebundling and separable delivery
- they enhance the potential for much greater transparency of prices and value for money comparisons for the more 'standardised' financial services across different providers

- they erode traditional barriers to entry in selected niche markets by making markets more contestable (Gardener *et al.*, 1999)
- they enhance the importance of strong and trusted branding in underpinning banks' franchise value as products are commoditised and distribution is disintermediated (Moody's, 2000)
- they contribute greatly to improved risk management by banks and market segmentation
- they open up the possibility of a longer term trend towards EU-wide and global markets for certain financial products.

The pace of change in the introduction and application of new technologies varies throughout Europe and reflects a wide variety of factors operating in different countries. For example, a major constraint in developing core processing technology relates to the sheer size of customer bases. A recent TCA (1999) survey found that there are no technology providers currently supplying systems that can work effectively at the scale of the main UK banks in terms of processing volumes and numbers of customers. Consequently, UK banks cannot easily replace out-dated systems and therefore have to evolve their existing systems. Indeed, the extent and success with which new technologies can be integrated with legacy systems is inversely related to bank size and complexity.

A similar problem arises with the introduction of customer relationship management (CRM) systems. Organising a multi-product bank around customer segments at the same time as building data-driven marketing and customer management capabilities creates extraordinary complexities for systems, processes and human resources. To a certain extent the motivation for implementing such systems has been driven by the success of the US mono-line providers such as MNBA and Charles Schwab. These firms tend to have a narrower product focus compared with traditional banks and use more advanced CRM systems to compete effectively. The success of these and other new entrants illustrates the competitive advantage that advanced CRM, as well as other, systems can provide.

The effects of these technological changes suggest that the prospective impacts of EMU will be to make regional and local markets more contestable, but at the same time to strengthen the information advantages enjoyed by local banks. Nevertheless, the different types of European banks face competition from specialist lenders that have taken advantage of technological developments and are providing lower cost services (Gardener *et al.*, 1999). EMU will also facilitate and encourage internet and other forms of cross-border direct banking, particularly in those areas where it has the effect of producing a much greater standardisation and transparency of financial products and institutional market features.

(b) The regulatory environment

The regulatory framework within which retail banking in the EU operates today bears little resemblance to that which existed a decade ago when banks and credit institutions in the majority of EU countries conducted their business in a protected and sheltered national environment. The dismantling of this protective regulatory structure occurred earliest at the wholesale end of the market and the main challenge for the SMP was to recast regulations and remove restrictions which permeated the retail market.

The cornerstone of the SMP for liberalising banking services is the Second Banking Directive, which was adopted in 1989 for implementation in 1993. By radically altering the framework for banking in the EU it had implications for the structure, conduct and prudential supervision of the industry. The Directive's importance in removing barriers derives from several major changes leading to a single market or 'single passport' for banking services and these are summarised below:

- it establishes conditions for the free provision of banking services by adopting the principle of mutual recognition of a single banking licence or passport, which eliminates the need to get a local banking charter from the host country for branches and products that are permitted in the home country
- it establishes the principle of home country control whereby bank branches from another member state are subject not to the host country's regulatory supervision and control but to that of the home country
- it harmonises key supervisory standards relating to minimum capital requirements, requirements with regard to the major shareholders of the credit institution, and bank limitations to participation in the non-financial sector
- it abolishes requirements for branches to maintain a minimum level of endowment capital which hitherto had presented an obstacle to free establishment of branches in other countries.

It should be pointed out that Article 21(5) states that the host country has the power 'to take appropriate measures to prevent or punish irregularities committed within their territories which are contrary to the legal rules they have adopted in the interest of the public good'.

In addition to this process of deregulation, a parallel process of re-regulation has been taking place, with Own Funds and Solvency Ratio Directives being the most important. These legislative changes have been accompanied by other major policy initiatives such as interest rate deregulation and the abolition of capital controls. Concurrently, in key supervisory areas like capital adequacy, the EU regulatory system has developed in line with international convergence objectives and criteria.

Thus, by the late 1980s and early 1990s EU banking and credit sectors had embarked on a significant process of legislative implementation aimed both at fostering more liberalised domestic banking markets and creating a single European banking market.

Banking still remains a highly regulated industry but legislative changes in the past decade have put an increasing emphasis on establishing a regulatory framework to encourage rivalry and efficiency whilst not compromising the need to maintain financial stability and protection for depositors. Moreover, as the chapters of this volume will show, the pattern and pace of change has differed widely across countries. At the beginning of the 1990s Germany, the UK, the Netherlands and Denmark were generally less regulated than the other members of the EU, and Portugal, Spain, Greece and Belgium were arguably the most regulated. However, by the beginning of 1993 a new regulatory environment was largely in place in all EU countries, although currently certain barriers still remain to be removed before a genuine single European banking and credit market is achieved.

3.2 The implications of EMU for the structure and competitiveness of retail banking in Europe

The main outcome of changes in the regulatory environment and the application of new computing and telecommunications technologies have been to push forward the process of market integration in the EU and, in particular, to change radically the competitive environment within which banks operate. EMU represents a further step in the process of market integration and introduces a significant additional factor with the potential to facilitate and strengthen competitive pressures. A first observation, therefore, is that the introduction of EMU will give an added impetus to structural change and the performance of banks, reinforcing developments already under way as a consequence of other forces for change. Secondly, because product prices will be quoted in the same currency, and given the advances in technology noted above, it should be easier for customers to compare product prices and assess value for money from financial services offered by banks and other providers in the different countries of the EMU. Whether customers will be able to respond by switching their provider depends on the perceived costs and ease of switching.

The internationalisation of banking is one important source of restructuring and enhanced competition likely to be given a stimulus by the introduction of EMU. The past decade has witnessed growing internationalisation of banking, mainly in investment and wholesale banking but also at the retail level (White, 1998). Moreover, it is argued that internationalisation could intensify competition significantly at the retail level if customer loyalties to 'local' banks could be eroded and customers' preferences could be shifted away from traditional branch banking in favour of on-line transactions. In some retail markets, such as personal credit cards, this is happening and there is evidence of customers switching to globally branded names but the degree of market penetration, although growing, remains small (Cruickshank, 2000). However, for other financial products such as chequeing accounts and personal secured loans, there is little evidence of increasing competition from international sources in either the personal sector or the SME sector. Thus, notwithstanding developments in selected retail markets, it is difficult to disagree with the conclusion of White (1998) that in continental Europe, 'retail banking services continue to be overwhelmingly provided by 'national' corporate entities', a conclusion also reached in the ERE (1997) study.

However, although cross-border activity in the retail segment is currently quite limited, the introduction of EMU is taking place in a period when such activity is beginning to grow. The ERE (1997) study indicated that trade in financial services increased across a range of financial markets in the post-SMP period, although admittedly the greatest increases were in off-balance sheet activities, investment management, and in the corporate loan segments rather than in the retail sector. Time series data from Eurostat also provide evidence of growing internationalisation and data on the establishment of cross-border branches compiled by the 'Groupe de Contact' of the EU banking supervisory authorities show an increase of 58% in cross-border establishment in the three years after 1992. In addition, the Commission received from 11 EU member states 43 notifications of establishment or acquisition of subsidiaries as credit institutions (from third countries) during the first three years of the internal market. Cross-border acquisitions also increased sharply after 1985, as did cross-border joint ventures and strategic alliances.

These developments are likely to be reinforced by EMU but may have only a limited impact on the competitiveness of European retail banking in the short to medium term. This is primarily because there are significant constraints (information shortfalls, search costs and switching costs, limited transparency of price and non-price factors) to retail customers switching providers. The recent Cruickshank Report (2000) provides strong evidence of significant switching barriers even within countries where arguably information, confidence and trust in alternative 'local' providers may be greater than might be the case for less familiar banks from other EU countries and elsewhere. In addition, restrictions continue on the financial products which can be offered by new entrants from overseas through the opt-out clause (in the interests of the 'general good') in the Second Banking Directive. In these circumstances the potential benefits of market enlargement both for customers and providers are likely to be slow to emerge.

In a number of EU countries, national consolidation and restructuring of retail banking is gathering momentum and EMU should give a further fillip to this process. Walter (1999) suggests that in a number of respects the present situation in Europe is not unlike that in the US at an early stage of its financial restructuring at the beginning of the 1980s. Since then the US has experienced a substantial reduction in the number of banks and a wave of mergers. From 1980 to 1994 there was an average of 423 mergers a year (Vives, 1998). In Europe, domestic mergers have also accelerated and in many countries the number of banks has declined (see, for example, ERE, 1997 and White, 1998). Small savings and cooperative banks (building societies in the UK and Ireland) serving customers at a local, and often rural and provincial level, have been the most likely to merge, partly to exploit economies of scale and scope but also to safeguard their competitive position and avoid falling victim to takeover by larger, nationally- or regionally-focused banks.

Another interesting feature is that in most EU banking systems (with the notable exceptions of Belgium, Denmark, France and the UK) the number of bank branches has also increased while the total number of banks has fallen, suggesting an increased consolidation within the sector. In Italy branching restrictions were removed in 1989 and this subsequently led to an increase in branches, but the increases experienced in other systems are more difficult to explain. They are possibly a reflection of increased competition through market share, a form of non-price competition. In contrast, the major UK banks are engaged in a substantial drive to reduce costs by rationalising their branch networks.

The ERE case studies (1997) revealed that, in several EU countries, one of the important consequences of the SMP has been increased 'defensive' merger activity in the expectation of a more competitive banking market. EMU, because it removes an important source of cross-border market segmentation, namely that caused by different currencies, should reinforce this defensive response by banks and stimulate increased domestic merger activity. Moreover, although there have been many more domestic than cross-border mergers and acquisitions, the latter should also be stimulated as banks seek to penetrate and benefit from the enlarged 'domestic' market arising from EMU. Evidence presented by Hughes *et al.* (1996 and 1998) identifies significant benefits for US banks when the degree of geographic diversification increases. How quickly these benefits will materialise is difficult to judge and, while there may be good reasons for consolidation to continue, it is clear that there are constraints on the pace of change in different national banking systems and national authorities will continue to play an important role in influencing the consolidation process. For example, in France, although privatisation and the reform of the savings bank system is under way, hostile takeovers are regarded as undesirable by some regulators. Consolidation in Germany is also constrained. By contrast, in Italy the restructuring of the banking sector is gathering momentum and some 54 mergers took place in 1998.

3.3 The implications of EMU for prices of retail financial products

More informed cross-border comparisons of prices by those purchasing financial products should increase price and non-price competition. Benefits derived from price reductions were a central focus of the assessment of the impacts of the SMP and it is instructive in speculating on the possible impact of EMU to review research on the SMP addressing this issue.

The potential benefits to the consumer from the augmentation of the SMP by EMU are likely to emerge according to the earlier rationale set down in the Cecchini (1988) *ex ante* study and the *ex post* study by Economic Research Europe (1997). These studies claimed that substantial economic benefits would arise from the integration of the European market in financial services as prices of financial products and services would tend towards the respective lowest prices. These price reductions and respective price convergence assumptions were the basis of the Cecchini microeconomic model of consumer surplus gains and, under these assumptions, substantial consumer surplus gains were estimated from the greater integration of the European financial services sectors. The process is summarised thus:

'Cecchini envisaged that the productive effects of greater competition from the elimination of barriers to trade, would be to eliminate economic rents (the margin of excess profits or wage rates that result from market protection), reduce X-inefficiencies (for example, the costs of over-manning, excess overhead costs and excess inventories-inefficiencies not related to the production technology of the firm's investments) and allow firms to gain the benefits of economies from restructuring (scale and scope economies). Within this vision, Cecchini also envisaged a substantial increase in both cross-border trade and cross-border mergers and acquisitions in banking, as banks sought to exploit economies of scale and scope' (ERE, 1997).

By removing the market segmentation arising from currency differences and facilitating easier cross-border price comparisons, EMU will also reduce barriers to trade and set in motion a similar process to that adumbrated above.

Although the *ex ante* analysis suggested the potential for significant price effects and economic benefits, the *ex post* analysis identified relatively modest price adjustments by banks following the introduction of the SMP. Evidence from the postal and Eurostat surveys indicates that competition intensified in all EU banking and credit markets in the post-SMP period, but only relatively small price adjustments were made in response to these increasingly competitive conditions. For corporate loans, price decreases were reported in the majority of countries but only about one in six respondents suggested that the SMP had been largely responsible for these reported price reductions, although over 50% attributed some slight role to the SMP. Time series analysis of the price of loans to the corporate sector revealed no conclusive evidence of price reductions due to SMP. Similar conclusions were reached in other market segments, including mortgages, personal loans and savings accounts, although the estimated impacts do vary from country to country, with perhaps the largest SMP impacts being experienced in Greece, Italy and Spain. Moreover, although there has been a general tendency for financial product prices to converge over the past two decades, there is no strong evidence that the SMP has been a major contributing factor.

The ERE (1997) study also revealed that for products identical to those reported in the Cecchini Report, significant price differences across countries remain, although credit card prices have fallen (by comparison with Cecchini) across the board and the range of prices has narrowed by about 30%. The range of mortgage prices between member states was also found to have narrowed, although as the price of mortgages has not decreased across the board it is not possible to say whether this convergence is towards a lower average price. For commercial loans, current cheque accounts and personal equity transaction costs, substantial price differences across countries persist. The most common strategic responses by banks in the retail segment were product diversification and innovation, domestic merger activity, and a generally greater market orientation.

More recent research on international price comparisons by Gardener *et al.* (2000) for the Cruickshank Report also identified significant price differences between the UK, France and Germany for 'standardised products' in selected retail financial markets. (The UK is, of course, not a member of EMU but is party to the SMP). This research examined prices for six personal sector financial products and seven SME financial products. The comparisons were made for 'standardised' products and prices, incorporated both interest (rate charged minus inter-bank rate) and charges, and the information was assembled through survey and desk research. Cross-country differences in average prices for the personal sector between France and Germany were quite small for current accounts, credit cards and mortgages, and slightly greater differences existed for consumer loans and savings accounts. However, with the exception of consumer loans and credit cards, somewhat greater differences were noted between average prices in the UK and prices in France and Germany, the two EMU members. For SMEs, current account charges were substantially higher in France than in Germany, but prices of secured loans, unsecured loans and factoring were very similar, and small but significant differences existed for hire purchase and leasing products. The comparisons for the UK present a mixed picture and there is no systematic relationship between prices in the UK and prices in France and Germany. Thus, prices for SME loans are similar to those in France and Germany in the secured market but somewhat higher in the unsecured market. Current account charges are much higher than in France and about equal to those in Germany. Factoring and invoice discounting prices are typically lower in the UK than in the two EMU countries. No general conclusions on the tendency of prices in the EU to converge can be drawn from this research. There is evidence of quite similar prices in some markets and quite big cross-country differences in others.

It is clear, therefore, that the price benefits from the SMP and other factors supporting greater market integration of retail banking are likely to have been modest compared with those anticipated in the Cecchini Report and to exhibit considerable variability across different market segments. What does this tell us about the potential price impacts of EMU? At a general level, insofar as foreign exchange risk has been a major obstacle to cross-border transactions in financial products and to cross-border mergers/joint ventures, EMU may be perceived as a necessary but not sufficient condition for further market integration of retail banking in

Europe and for releasing the benefits of price reductions and price convergence. Moreover, the extent to which EMU will significantly enhance the scope for further integration of European retail financial markets and exert significant downward pressure on prices will depend on a number of factors, some of which are specific to selected market segments (and are likely to exist in a number of countries) and some of which are country-specific and influence contestability across different countries. Factors in the former category include the need to have local knowledge, the extent of deterrents and costs of switching between providers, barriers to market entry such as a local branch network, responsiveness of product demand to removal of currency risk, degree of product standardisation, extent of economies of scale to be realised in cross-border market penetration, scope for direct selling, and the ease and costs of making price comparisons. Country-specific factors include the structure and operation of fiscal policy, anti-trust and competition policy, the extent of state banking, legal hindrances, and constraints on the marketing and selling of certain financial products.

Table 1.1 presents some of the key factors influencing market integration and prices across the EU and speculates on their relative importance for accelerated price convergence for a selected range of financial products as a result of EMU. For example, for SMEs the importance of the local bank branch and the sunk costs associated with developing a long-term relationship with the local bank branch are very important in constraining the scope for market integration in this market segment. By contrast, the removal of foreign exchange risk is potentially an important factor integrating the consumer loan market, as is the opportunity for direct selling through the use of new communications technologies. Equally, markets where there are opportunities for centralising costs and spreading them over a large number of customers offer scope for EMU to catalyse market integration.

4 CONCLUDING REMARKS AND POLICY IMPLICATIONS

A central theme of this chapter has been that EMU will reinforce many of the forces for change currently impinging on the EU retail banking market and intensify competitive pressures across a range of retail markets. In particular, whilst it is agreed that the impact of the SMP has to date been limited and that many of the concerns highlighted in the Cecchini Report remain, in a number of respects EMU may be an important catalyst for releasing the full potential and benefits from the SMP and technological change. With the removal of currency risk and other advantages derived from separate currencies, banks will expand their market horizons and consolidate to secure economies of scale and scope and to diversify credit risk across a wider geographic area. Like the US financial services industry before its phase of restructuring, the EU financial services sector is suffering from excess capacity and EMU will give an added impetus to consolidation. At the same time national and regional banks will seek to protect those markets where they enjoy the benefits of strong historical links with their customer base and their local knowledge of customers' financial needs and risk profiles. Nevertheless, the ability to exploit local monopoly power will be undermined by increasing price transparency, technologically supported market penetration, and the removal of currency-based market segmentation, and local and regional banks will have to compete with national and foreign banks and other service providers. Inevitably there will be a coexistence of mergers/joint ventures and alliances with specialist niche players in selected market segments.

It is difficult to disagree with Vives (1998) that 'the opening of the banking sector to competition is good but supervision has to be very vigilant with institutions that develop problems'. This message is all the more pertinent in the context of the introduction of EMU following in the wake of the SMP and further opening the banking market to competition. For policymakers there are several other policy tensions. There is a need to provide a framework which both encourages restructuring and effective rivalry whilst avoiding excessive risk-taking as competition intensifies. At the same time it is important that the financial needs of the personal and SME sectors are met, and that economic and social distress associated with consolidation takes place at an acceptable pace. Moreover, as in other sectors, although concentration and exploitation of monopoly power at a national level is becoming a less relevant anti-trust issue, in many retail financial market segments it remains an important consideration (Cruickshank, 2000). For example, the Cruickshank Inquiry concluded that there was a substantial case for reference to the Competition Commission under Section 51 on the grounds of monopoly provision of current account and other banking services to SMEs. Cruickshank also identified high concentration in the supply of current accounts to the personal sector and switching constraints. It argued for policy initiatives to improve consumer representation and redress, and greater transparency. These policy concerns are reflected in the 1999 EC Financial Services Action Plan which drew attention to a number of obstacles currently preventing consumers and providers from benefiting from enhanced competition.

Table 1.1 The relative importance of different factors influencing market integration and price convergence in the medium term following the introduction of EMU (1 = not important; 5 = very important)

Financial product	Removal of foreign exchange risk	Improved market access from new IT/telecom. distribution	Opportunity for direct selling	Realisable economies of scale from larger market	Switching cost/'sunk cost' by customer	Importance of local presence and other tax/legal entry barriers
Personal current account	2	2	2	3	4	4
Savings account	3	3	3	2	2	2
Consumer loan	4	3	3	2	2	2
Credit card	3	3	2	3	2	2
Mortgages	3	3	3	3	2	3
SME current account	2	2	2	3	4	4
SME loan	2	3	3	3	4	4
Leasing/HP	2	3	3	3	3	2

References

Cecchini, P. (1988) *The European Challenge in 1992; the Benefits of a Single Market* (Gower, Aldershot).

'Cruickshank Report' (March 2000), *Competition in UK Banking: A Report to the Chancellor of the Exchequer* (Stationery Office, London).

DataMonitor (1999), *IT in US Retail Banking and IT in European Retail Banking.*

Dermine, J., *European Banking with a Single Currency,* mimeo (INSEAD, Fontainbleau, France).

Economic Research Europe Ltd (1997), *The Single Market Review: Impact on Credit Institutions and Banking,* (Kogan Page, London)

European Central Bank (1999), *Effects of Technology on EU Banking Systems* (ECB, Frankfurt).

European Central Bank (1999), *Possible Effects of EMU on the EU Banking Systems in the Medium to Long Term* (ECB, Frankfurt).

Gandy, T. (1999), *The Network Bank* (CIB Publishing, London).

Gardener E.P.M., P. Molyneux and J. Williams (1999), *EMU and European Banking,* mimeo (Institute of European Finance, University of Wales, Bangor).

Gardener E.P.M., P. Molyneux and B. Moore (2000), *International Price Comparisons and the Competitiveness of UK Banking,* unpublished PACEC Ltd/IEF 1998 research summarised in Appendix E of the Cruickshank Report (*see above*)

Hughes, J.P., W.P. Lang, L. Mester and G. Moon (1996), 'Efficient banking under interstate branching', *Journal of Money, Credit and Banking,* 28 (4).

Hughes, J.P., W.P. Lang, L. Mester and G. Moon. (1998), *The Dollars and Sense of Bank Consolidation,* Federal Reserve Bank of Philadelphia, WP no. 98-10.

Monti, M. (1996), *The Single Market and Tomorrow's Europe: A Progress Report from the European Commission* (EC, Brussels).

Moody's Investor Service (February, 2000), *Online Winds of Change: European Banks Enter the Age of the Internet.*

Morgan Stanley Dean Witter (1999), *The Internet Credit Card Report: A Primer on the Industry and its Role in E-Commerce.*

TCA (1999), unpublished paper on international comparisons of the use of technology and banking (TCA Consulting, New City Court, 20 St. Thomas Street, London, SE1 95D).

Vives, X. (1998), *Competition and Regulation in European Banking,* mimeo, (Institut d'Analist Economica, CSIC, Barcelona).

Walter, I. (1999), *Financial Services Strategies in the Eurozone,* Cahiers BEI/EIB Papers, Vol. 4 (1), pp. 145-66.

White, W.R. (1998), *The Coming Transformation of Continental European Banking,* Bank for International Settlements Working Paper no. 54, Monetary and Economic Department (BIS, Basle).

2   Belgium

Rudi Vander Vennet

1   MARKET STRUCTURE AND PERFORMANCE

1.1 The Belgian banking sector

The Belgian financial sector accounts for 9.5% of the total value added
and 5.5% of total employment generated by the service sector. Belgium
remains a country where banks are at the centre of financial flows and
where economic agents rely predominantly on intermediated funding. The
ratio of total bank assets to GNP amounted to 295% in 1997. In Europe,
only Luxembourg and Switzerland exhibit higher ratios.

Table 2.1 shows the number of institutions active on the Belgian
banking market. These numbers refer to credit institutions as defined in
the Second Banking Coordination Directive and comprise commercial
banks, savings banks and (former) public credit institutions. In 1997 the
banking sector consisted of 134 institutions, of which 94 were
domestically incorporated and 40 reside under foreign law. Of the former,
63 operate with a Belgian majority ownership while 31 have a dominant
foreign shareholder. Table 2.1 clearly illustrates a number of trends. The
overall number of credit institutions has declined substantially, from 176
in 1980 to 134 in 1997. Since outright failures are uncommon in Belgian
banking, the main mode of exit is through merger or acquisition. This
trend is, however, restricted to domestic banks. Over the past decade the
number of subsidiaries of foreign banks has grown by a third. The same
observation holds for the number of representative offices. A remarkable
feature is the number of banks that are active on the Belgian market under
the EU rules of free servicing. The number of demands for cross-border
servicing evolved from 39 in 1993 (the first year this option was available)
to 241 in 1997. The vast majority of the initiating banks are from
neighbouring countries, such as the UK (92) and Luxembourg (38). It
stresses both the openness and the apparent attractiveness of the Belgian
banking market.

Table 2.2 illustrates the relative importance of the largest Belgian
banks. Major changes occurred in 1998 and 1999 when some of the big
banks merged.

Table 2.1 Structure of the Belgian banking sector, 1980-1997

| | Number of credit institutions | | | | Share of assets |
	1980	1985	1990	1997	
Credit institutions under Belgian law	149	137	122	94	87%
with Belgian majority ownership	112	100	85	63	69%
with foreign majority ownership	37	37	37	31	18%
Credit institutions under foreign law	27	28	35	40	13%
Total	176	165	157	134	100%
Representative offices	18	28	41	40	
EU free servicing[1]	-	-	-	241	

[1]Credit institutions active on the Belgian market under the EU rules on free servicing.

Source: Belgian Banking Association *and* Finance Commission Reports

Before that date the biggest seven credit institutions constituted a core group of diversified banks which were substantially larger than the next group of medium-sized institutions. It is clear that even the largest Belgian banks are relatively small by international standards, although some are now part of Benelux-wide financial services firms.

Table 2.2 The largest Belgian banks

	Total assets[1] 1995	World ranking[2] 1995	Situation 1999
Generale Bank (GB)	4739	89	Fortis Bank[3]
Gemeentekrediet (GKB)	3503	135	Dexia[4]
Bank Brussels Lambert (BBL)	3225	146	ING-BBL[5]
Kredietbank (KB)	3076	119	KBC[6]
ASLK-Bank	2572	192	
CERA Bank	1210	311	
BACOB Bank	1188	177	Artesia[7]

[1]Consolidated assets in BEF billion: 1euro = BEF40.3399. (*Source*: Belgian Banking Association and annual reports)
[2]Ranking based on tier 1 capital. (*Source*: The Banker)
[3]Merger of Generale Bank, ASLK-Bank and the Dutch banking subsidiaries of the Fortis Group
[4]Merger of GKB and Crédit Local de France
[5]Since 1998 BBL is part of the ING Group
[6]Merger of Kredietbank, CERA and a number of Belgian insurance companies
[7]Merger of BACOB and Paribas Belgium

A series of relevant bank characteristics are listed in Table 2.3. The Belgian credit institutions have a combined network of 7,358 branches, which makes Belgium one of the most densely branched countries. The expansion of local branches occurred primarily in the 1970s and 1980s, and it provides banks with a privileged access to a stable pool of local savings funds. The major disadvantage is the increasing burden of the high sunk costs associated with brick-and-mortar investments, especially in a period of increasing reliance on electronic banking channels. As a result, banks are gradually reducing the number of branches, usually by merging the small ones into larger entities. The shift to electronic servicing and distribution is apparent from the number of ATM and POS terminals, and the number of bank cards in circulation. From Table 2.3 it is clear that the payment habits of Belgian bank clients are rapidly shifting from cheques to electronic fund transfer devices. Total employment in the banking sector remains relatively stable, yet it exhibits a slow but persistent decline since its 1990 peak year.

Table 2.3 Resources in Belgian banks, 1993 and 1997

	1993	1997
Number of banks	151	134
Number of branches	7890	7358
Employment	76281	76931
ATMs	2636	4991
POS	34010	50020
Number of accounts (000)	30392	31222
Processed cheques (million)	78.8	52.3
Debit cards (000)	6071	7432

Source: Belgian Banking Association (1996)

1.2 Ownership structure and privatisation

Until the early 1990s, the Belgian banking sector could be subdivided into three broad subgroups: commercial banks, savings banks and public credit institutions. Although the major functional restrictions between these types of institutions were gradually abolished in the 1970s and 1980s, the degree of despecialisation and diversification remained limited. In particular the activities of the six government-owned banks were more or less restricted to the specialised purpose for which they were once established: mortgage lending (Central Bureau of Mortgage Lending, CBHK), household saving and residential mortgages (General Savings Bank, ASLK), industrial loans (National Institute for Industrial Credit, NMKN), loans to communities (Belgian Community Bank, GKB), small business financing (National Institute for Professional Credit, NKBK), and agricultural loans (National Institute for Agricultural Credit, NILK). This picture changed dramatically in the 1990s due to the full or partial privatisation of the public banks.

The reasons invoked by the Belgian government at the initiation of this vast privatisation programme were straightforward. Most importantly, with an eye on the Maastricht criteria, the proceeds from the asset sales had to be used to support the budget consolidation efforts and the reduction of the public debt ratio. Moreover, the specialised nature of most public banks was becoming a threat to their competitive viability. Most institutions exhibited low profitability and relatively poor operational efficiency levels.

Finally, enhanced domestic and foreign competition in almost all banking market segments had gradually reduced the need for the Government to influence market behaviour through direct ownership.

Within this general environment of deregulation and increased competition the Government decided to make the management of the public banks more autonomous and to expand their scope of activities. Most of the privatisations were and are handled through a Privatisation Commission and the Federal Holding Corporation (FPM).

The first public bank to be privatised was ASLK. In 1993 the government sold 49.9% of the bank's equity to the Fortis group, a Belgian-Dutch financial conglomerate with its core activities in banking and insurance. At the end of 1998 Fortis acquired full ownership of ASLK-Bank and ASLK-Insurance. The acquisition of Generale Bank in 1999 led to the creation of Fortis Bank, a merger of the Belgian and Dutch banking subsidiaries of the Fortis Group. In 1995 ASLK acquired the full ownership of the long-term credit bank NMKN, after a fierce takeover battle with BACOB Bank involving multiple competing tender offers. By 1997 NMKN had been fully integrated, both operationally and financially, into ASLK-Bank, now Fortis Bank. In 1996 the community bank GKB formed an alliance with Crédit Local de France, a French bank active in the same type of activities, that is the financing of local authorities. The alliance goes by the name of Dexia. Belgian local authorities remain the majority owner of GKB-Holding, but a substantial part of the equity of the bank is listed on the Brussels Stock Exchange. The agricultural bank NILK has been fully privatised; a majority of shares was sold to Suisse Life, a Swiss insurance company, in 1995 and to the Belgian co-operative bank BACOB in 1996. Currently the Federal Holding Corporation is in the process of privatising the two remaining public financial institutions, NKBK and CBHK.

As a result of the privatisations, a series of bank mergers among private banks (see Section 3.2 below), and the regulatory changes aimed at harmonising the market conditions for all credit institutions, most Belgian banks are now privately owned and operate in a harmonised and deregulated environment. Nevertheless, the ownership structure of some banks remains relatively closed, primarily due to the presence of holding companies, such as KBC/Almanij, or to the use of the co-operative or mutual form of incorporation, such as BACOB/Artesia.

1.3 Market structure and performance

The Belgian banking sector is usually characterised as relatively concentrated. Table 2.4 gives the evolution of concentration measured as the share in total assets (deposits) of the top three, top five and top ten banks over the last two decades. The numbers indicate that concentration may have fallen somewhat from 1975 to 1985, but it has remained fairly

constant thereafter. In 1994 the five largest banks accounted for
approximately 55% of the assets and 60% of bank deposits. While
competition has undoubtedly become more intense, empirical evidence
suggests that this market structure may have enabled banks to earn
oligopoly rents, especially when entry barriers such as the high branch
density are taken into account (see Vander Vennet, 1994). The
consequence of the recent mergers involving the largest banks is that
measured bank market concentration has risen substantially; the small
group of remaining large banks (see Table 2.2) controls more than 70% of
both total assets and deposits.

Table 2.4 Concentration in Belgian banking[1]

	Year	*Top 3*	*Top 5*	*Top 10*
Total assets	1975	40.8	59.5	74.6
	1985	33.0	48.1	66.6
	1990	30.4	47.2	65.1
	1996	37.0	55.0	71.4
Deposits	1975	49.2	67.3	85.6
	1985	46.9	63.8	81.0
	1990	44.1	63.9	81.1
	1996	39.1	60.8	78.2

[1]Share in total assets (deposits) of the top 3, top 5, and top 10 banks.
Source: Belgian Banking Association (1998).

Table 2.5 gives a number of key indicators of bank performance over
the last decade. The interest margin (calculated as net interest income over
earning assets) has narrowed considerably, from 2.22% in 1985 to a mere
1.18% in 1997. This evolution reflects the intensification of competition in
the market for bank intermediation. Cost/income ratios as a measure of
operational efficiency are relatively high compared to international
standards and exhibit only a modest decline in the 1990s. As a result, the
return on assets of Belgian banks has remained fairly constant and the
resulting return on equity has been below 10% during the 1990s.
Moreover, the ROE of a considerable number of small and medium-sized
banks has persistently been below the yield on government bonds (BBA,
1998). Part of the explanation for the modest average profitability of the
Belgian banking sector can be found in the structure of revenues and costs
(see also Bonte and Holvoet, 1996).

Table 2.5 Performance of Belgian commercial banks in %, 1985-1997

	1985	1990	1993	1994	1995	1997
Interest margin	2.22	2.07	1.63	1.68	1.51	1.18
Return on assets	0.28	0.22	0.28	0.26	0.24	0.26
Return on equity	11.60	8.51	8.72	7.83	8.34	9.54
Risk asset ratio	-	-	11.0	12.1	11.9	11.5
Cost/income ratio	-	69.60	62.4	65.1	67.8	66.6

Source: Belgian Banking Association *and* BFC

Table 2.6 shows the balance sheet structure of Belgian banks. On the liability side, approximately half of the funding consists of customer deposits and some 40% are interbank deposits. The funds are invested in nearly equal proportion (approximately one third each) in commercial loans, securities (primarily government bonds) and interbank loans. As deposit markets become more competitive, due to the availability of investment alternatives such as mutual funds, as credit markets become more contestable, especially in the area of housing and consumer loans, but also in the segment of credit to small enterprises, and as the government steadily reduces its borrowing needs, bank profits are becoming increasingly vulnerable. In Belgian banks, a further disadvantage is the dominant reliance on interest-related revenues.

Table 2.6 Balance sheet structure of the Belgian banking sector in BEF billions, 1993 and 1997 (ECU 1=BEF 39)[1]

	1993	1997	% of total assets
Total assets	22709	29205	100.0
Loans	7785	9529	32.6
Securities	6475	8432	28.9
Interbank assets	7382	9333	32.0
Deposits	11448	13565	46.4
Interbank liabilities	9025	11919	40.8
Total capital funds	858	1388	4.8
Off-balance sheet	110575	206225	706.1

Source: Belgian Banking Association (1998) *and* BFC (1998)

Table 2.7 indicates that the interest margin is still the primary component of total revenues, while fee business represents less than 20%. Yet in 1997 the notional amount of off-balance sheet activities exceeded the on-balance sheet volume by a factor of seven. Risk asset ratios are only available for recent years. They indicate a solid capital coverage, well above the required minimum level.

Table 2.7 Components of bank profits in BEF billions, 1993 and 1997

	Large credit institutions		All credit institutions		
	1993	1997	1993	1997	%
Interest margin	193.9	224.7	278.2	321.5	60.4
Non-interest investment income[1]	51.0	74.8	81.6	97.2	18.3
Other revenues	48.1	73.8	77.0	113.7	21.4
Banking product	293.2	372.8	436.8	532.4	100.0
Expenses[2]	211.7	257.9	308.9	367.9	69.1
(of which personnel)	(129.0)	(141.7)	(171.2)	(187.3)	35.2
Provisions	37.5	45.5	52.2	69.4	13.0
Taxes	13.2	26.4	24.0	39.4	7.4
Net profit	31.1	55.9	52.5	75.2	14.1

[1]Income from dividends, securities trading and currency operations
[2]Including depreciation

Source: Banking and Finance Commission Annual Report, 1997/1998

2 REGULATORY FRAMEWORK

2.1 Regulatory framework prior to the SMP

Before the mid-80s the bulk of the banking and financial legislation in Belgium dated back to the 1930s. The core regulations for banks, holding companies and financial markets were enacted after the financial crisis of the Great Depression years. Also in those years, the Banking Commission, now the Banking and Finance Commission (BFC), was established to supervise the sector. Modernisation of banking and financial legislation occurred in the late 1980s and early 1990s. The legislative initiatives at the EU level have undoubtedly provided a major impetus for these changes. This is especially true for the new banking legislation, which is essentially aimed at transposing the relevant EU Directives. For some laws, such as the takeover regulation or the disclosure rules for shareholdings in listed companies, specific events have accelerated the modernisation effort, for example the failed hostile takeover of Société Générale de Belgique. In general, the Belgian legislator has been rather slow to implement the SMP-related changes (see Gardener *et al.*, 2000).

2.2 Main SMP legislation

2.2.1 Banking legislation

After the stock market crash of the early 1930s, Belgium introduced a strict legal separation between holding companies and commercial banks similar to the US but unlike, for example, that in Germany. The main bank regulation was laid down in Royal Decree No. 185 of 9 July 1935. From then onwards, the prudential supervision of banks was confined to the Banking Commission, an autonomous supervisory authority, separate from the central bank. In the course of time the legislation was adapted to institutionalise the trend towards despecialisation of various types of credit institutions. Examples are the Mammoth Law of 1975 (which expanded the scope of activities of both commercial and savings banks) and the transformation of ASLK into a public bank with the possibility to offer the full range of bank services. In 1990, a Royal Decree allowed Belgian banks to hold equity participations in non-financial companies, but only for investment purposes and subject to strict limits.

The 1989 Second Banking Directive provided the major impetus to modernise Belgian banking legislation. Implementation was accomplished with the law of 22 March 1993 on the legal status and control of credit institutions (hereafter the 1993 Banking Law), which has fundamentally reformed the country's banking legislation and consolidated the previous scattered jurisprudence. The major objective of the law was to transpose the 1989 Second Banking Directive, the 1992 Consolidated Supervision Directive and the 1993 Capital Adequacy Directives. At the same time the legislator seized the opportunity to modernise and streamline the operational conditions and supervision of the banking sector. The 1993 Banking Law introduced the principles of the single passport and home country control into Belgian legislation. Authorised credit institutions are exempt from any further authorisation when they want to set up branches in another member state or when they perform cross-border services from the home state. Consistent with the legislator's intention, the 1993 Banking Law is a faithful transposition of the Second Banking Directive. However, the Belgian law is more restrictive on two important issues: the transparency of credit institutions' shareholders and the possibility for credit institutions to hold equity participations in non-financial companies. The main features of the Law are now described.

In accordance with the Second Banking Directive, the Law defines a credit institution as an undertaking whose business it is to receive deposits from the general public and to grant loans on its own account. Both activities have to be present simultaneously to be a credit institution. The law also lists the other activities credit institutions can undertake and which are subject to mutual recognition. This list of activities, including securities transactions, for example, is reproduced in the annex to the Second Banking Directive. Credit institutions may engage in a number of other activities for which the mutual recognition is not automatic, provided there is a close relationship with the traditional banking business. When applying for authorisation, a credit institution has to indicate the category in which it wishes to be authorised (bank, savings bank, public credit institution, communal savings bank). This choice has no consequences on the status or the supervision of the institution but it does confer the right to use protected names such as 'bank' or 'savings bank'. This allows specialised institutions to tailor their brand image for marketing purposes. The so-called Merchant Bank Law of 20 March 1996 introduced merchant banks as a specific type of credit institution. The legal status of these institutions is identical to that of other credit institutions. The only difference is that merchant banks can use the name and specialise in activities related to the securities business. A number of Belgian stockbroking firms have used this avenue to diversify their activities (for example, it allows them to take deposits).

The Law regulates the establishment, activity and supervision of credit institutions in order to protect savings and ensure the smooth operation of the credit system. Before a credit institution can operate under Belgian law it must be duly authorised by the BFC. Any application must contain a detailed programme of operations and must specify the structure of the organisation to support the activities. The BFC takes a decision within three months of receipt of a complete application. If rejected, the applicant can lodge an appeal with the Minister of Finance. The following conditions are necessary requirements for authorisation:

- the credit institution must have initial paid-up capital of at least 250 million BEF (about 6 million euro). During the existence of the bank, its capital may not fall below this threshold
- at least two persons with the necessary professional ability and appropriate experience have to be responsible for the daily management of the bank (the four-eyes principle)
- the bank's management structure, administration, accounting procedures and internal control systems must be appropriate to the proposed activities. In view of the increasingly complex nature of bank products and risks, the internal audit capacity of banks has been the subject of closer scrutiny by the BFC in recent times

- the applicant must participate in a collective deposit guarantee system.
- the BFC has to judge the fit and proper character of any shareholders having a direct or indirect stake of at least 5% in the credit institution's capital . This requirement is stricter than prescribed by the Directive. Moreover, a change in the credit institution's shareholdings must be notified in advance to the credit institution and the BFC if it affects a proportion of the capital or the voting rights by 5% or any multiple of 5%. The rationale for these thresholds is that they correspond to those applied in the 1989 law on the disclosure of significant shareholdings in publicly listed companies. The BFC also has the power to intervene directly if any physical person or corporation holding 5% or more of the capital is judged to damage the sound and prudent management of the credit institution. By way of sanction, the BFC may suspend the voting rights attached to those shares or force the shareholder concerned to sell its shares.

In order to safeguard the independence of the operational management of the bank, the BFC can conclude a Protocol on the autonomy of bank management with credit institutions. Basically, it states that the management of the bank has to be composed of two levels, the management committee and the board of directors. The management committee is responsible for daily management, in accordance with the broad strategic guidelines set out by the board of directors. It is composed of people having full-time employment with the bank. The board of directors supervises the management committee and defines the general policy orientations of the institution. The board is composed of the members of the management committee, representatives of the shareholders and, preferably, independent directors. This setup is designed to prevent conflicts of interest and to limit the power of large shareholders in the daily business of the bank. Reference shareholders are requested to sign the Protocol and commit themselves to maintaining the stability of the credit institution and the independence of its management. And, indeed, a large number of institutions have signed the agreement, which was first introduced in 1991. Yet, despite this corporate governance structure, recent events have illustrated that the interests of the bank and its large shareholders may diverge (for example, BBL).

In operation, a credit institution must comply with the capital requirements imposed by the BFC in a decree of December 1995. The Belgian rules are exact copies of the guidelines laid down in the EU Directives on capital requirements and in the BIS guidelines. Essentially, credit institutions have to obey a risk-assets ratio in the sense that total own funds (tier 1 plus tier 2 capital) must always be greater than 8% of the weighted risk volume. Moreover, the total risk concentration on one counterparty may not exceed 25% of the bank's own funds. In adherence to the Capital Adequacy Directive, Belgian credit institutions have to maintain additional capital funds against their market risk exposure. For this purpose banks may use internal value-at-risk models, provided they are approved by the BFC. The BFC also calculates a gearing ratio, relating external funds to the credit institution's capital base.

In the 1993 Banking Law, the power of Belgian credit institutions to hold shares in other companies has been further liberalised towards the universal banking model contained in the Second Banking Directive. However, the Belgian rules on this matter are more restrictive than those of the Directive. The most important rules can be summarised as follows:

- credit institutions may hold unlimited participations in Belgian or foreign credit institutions, stockbroking firms, insurance companies or other corporations, provided their principal activity is situated in the field of financial services
- credit institutions may hold shareholdings in their trading portfolio when these shares were acquired with the intention of resale, for example in the course of a corporate equity offering
- banks may hold shares in settlement of doubtful or unpaid debts, but only for a maximum period of two years
- credit institutions may invest in non-financial companies insofar as no single qualified shareholding (that is a stake of at least 10% of the share capital) exceeds 15% of the bank's own funds. Moreover, the total amount of non-financial shareholdings may not exceed 45% of the credit institution's own funds. Initially these thresholds were set at 10% and 35%, but a Royal Decree of June 1996 has increased the limits to 15% and 45%. The limit for a single qualifying shareholding (15%) is now equal to the one set by the Second Banking Directive but the overall limit is still lower (45% as opposed to 60%).

The 1993 Banking Law also realised a full harmonisation of supervision. All credit institutions incorporated under Belgian law are subject to the prudential control of the BFC. The BFC disposes of broad administrative and investigative powers to assess compliance with laws and regulations and to verify the appropriate character of an institution's management, internal procedures and the soundness of its bank policies. In line with the principle of home country control, the activities of Belgian credit institutions in other EU member states, either through cross-border servicing or through the establishment of a branch, are supervised by the BFC. An important change introduced by the Law is the consolidated supervision. The major principle is that a Belgian parent bank and its domestic and foreign subsidiaries are subject to supervision on a consolidated basis. Also, when a Belgian credit institution forms a consortium with other financial companies, all corporations in the conglomerate and their subsidiaries will be supervised on a consolidated basis. In order make this control effective, the BFC has to cooperate with other Belgian supervisors such as the Control Office for Insurance Companies and, until recently, the Intervention Fund for Stockbrokers (whose supervisory powers have been transferred to the BFC in 1997), and conclude bilateral information agreements with other EU supervisors. When the parent company of a Belgian credit institution is a financial holding company, the consolidated supervision must be conducted at the holding company level, without implying, however, that the financial holding itself is submitted to an individual supervision. The BFC's main supervisory tools are an examination of monthly, quarterly and annual accounts supplemented with special reports, on-site inspections and collaboration with accredited statutory auditors. When the BFC judges the operation of a credit institution to be wanting, it has broad powers to rectify the situation and impose deadlines. These measures include the appointment of special inspectors, the temporary suspension of certain activities, the replacement of directors or, as an ultimate sanction, the withdrawal of a credit institution's authorisation. In practice, when serious difficulties arise, the BFC will persuade the shareholders of the bank to transfer their holdings to third parties with the necessary capital.

If a worst-case scenario should occur, the interests of the depositors are protected by a deposit insurance scheme organised by the Law of 23 December 1994, which implements the 1994 Council Directive on deposit guarantee mechanisms. All credit institutions must participate in the deposit guarantee fund administered by the Institute for Rediscount and Guarantees. When a credit institution defaults, the Institute will reimburse the deposits expressed in BEF or any other EU currency up to 15,000 euro until 31 December 1999 and up to 20,000 euro thereafter. Branches of credit institutions incorporated in other EU states may voluntarily join the Belgian deposit guarantee scheme.

The regulation of cross-border banking activities in the 1993 Banking Law closely follows the provisions laid down in the Directive. A Belgian credit institution wishing to establish a branch in another EU member state is required to notify its intention to the BFC. When the BFC has no objection it will communicate all relevant information to the host country's supervisory authorities. The same rules apply for the provision of cross-border banking services. Conversely, a credit institution governed by the law of another EU country may carry out banking activities in Belgium via a branch without having to obtain prior authorisation from the

BFC and without having to maintain endowment capital. The BFC will register the branch as soon as it has received the information from the home country supervisor. According to the principle of home country control, the supervision of registered branches of EU credit institutions is conducted by the supervisory authorities of the home country. Nevertheless, Belgian bank branches are still subject to a degree of control by the BFC and the National Bank of Belgium on matters concerning liquidity, monetary policy, issues related to the general good, and the supply of statistical information. The establishment of a Belgian branch by a non-EU credit institution is subject to the same requirements as those applicable to the establishment of a Belgian credit institution.

Credit institutions established in Belgium must comply with the Law of 11 January 1993 aimed at preventing the use of the financial system for purposes of money laundering. The principal obligation is that banks have to identify customers properly. For habitual customers, identification is required at the moment the financial relationship is initiated; for occasional customers the requirement applies for any transaction above 10,000 euro. For transactions deemed suspicious, the obligation holds regardless of the amount involved. The BFC has issued guidelines to aid banks in detecting possibly improper financial operations. Secondly, credit institutions have to notify suspicious transactions to a specialised Unit for Financial Information composed of magistrates and financial experts. After examination, the Unit will communicate any evidence of involvement in money laundering to the judicial authorities. The BFC aims to ensure that all credit institutions develop internal policies, procedures and control systems to prevent this type of abuse. In a number of cases, the BFC has imposed administrative sanctions upon credit institutions that failed to comply with these obligations.

2.2.2   Other financial legislation

The new banking legislation is only part of a vast programme of regulatory reform initiated in the late 1980s and aimed at modernising the Brussels financial centre. Apart from the banking legislation, the most important reforms targeted the markets for government debt instruments and the organisation of the Brussels Stock Exchange. In 1989 a major reform of the markets for government debt was accomplished by introducing a tender system for the issuance of both long-term bonds (called OLOs) and short-term Treasury bills. This ended the bilateral monopoly between the Treasury and a consortium of banks, whereby the banks received fixed commissions for the underwriting and distribution of government bonds. As a result, the reform has affected both bank income and the ease with which the Treasury bills, that were previously issued on tap, can be used in bank liquidity management. An even more dramatic decision was the reduction of the withholding tax on revenues from fixed-income securities from 25% to 10% in March 1990. Following this, bank customers massively shifted their savings from the relatively cheap common savings accounts and short-term deposits to longer-term and higher yielding savings instruments. Again this has put increased pressure on bank interest margins (see Dermine, 1996). Meanwhile the withholding tax has been gradually increased to 15% and, in the current environment of low interest rates, the ordinary savings accounts have regained their popularity.

Major reform of the Brussels Stock Exchange was accomplished with the Law of 4 December 1990 on financial transactions and financial markets. Its main innovation was that the profession of stockbroker had to be exercised in the legal form of a corporation instead of a private partnership. Moreover, banks were allowed to acquire shares in (and later, set up autonomously) stockbroking firms. Among other things, the Law regulated the establishment of mutual investment corporations with either fixed or variable capital, SICAF (Société d'Investissement à Capital Fixe) or SICAV (Société d'Investissement à Capital Variable). These types of instruments have gained a considerable market share, partly because of their favourable tax treatment (circumventing the withholding tax by capitalising the revenues). The Law also introduced strict rules to combat insider trading. However, the only case that has been the subject of judicial pursuit has resulted in an acquittal before the Court of Appeals. Based on the rules for the establishment of other financial markets, the Belgian Futures and Options Exchange (Belfox) began operations in 1991. The futures contract on a Belgian government bond is the most actively traded product. A few years after the Law's enactment, the regulation of Belgian financial markets had to be adapted to the provisions of the Investment Services Directive. The ISD was implemented with the Law of 6 April 1995 which introduced the single passport and home country control for investment firms, similar to the rules for banks. Among other things, the Law has also modernised the governance structure of the Brussels Stock Exchange through a management committee and a board of directors, it established a code of conduct for financial intermediaries, and it regulated the direct access of banks to the stock market. Following an international trend the stock exchange, the derivatives market and the clearing institution have merged into a new entity called BEX (Brussels Exchanges), which is actively pursuing alliances with other European exchanges.

2.3 Remaining barriers to the SMP

The legislation of the SMP is now largely implemented. Nevertheless, a number of barriers continue to exist. They mostly consist of specific legal provisions related to consumer protection and to the tax treatment of financial revenues. One example is a series of obligations surrounding the structuring and marketing of consumer and mortgage loans. For example, the variability of mortgage interest rates is linked to the behaviour of a benchmark rate based on the evolution of government bond yields. In the tax area, revenues from financial investments are subject to a withholding tax which now stands at 15% for interest income and 25% on dividends. However, the interest income on so-called common savings accounts, the only remaining savings instrument for which a maximum interest rate is set by the Minister of Finance, is exempt from this tax up to a maximum interest income of BEF 55,000. Foreign residents are eligible for reimbursement of the withholding tax. While some of these remaining rules may impose administrative and regulatory costs on banks, their influence is probably negligible. In fact, the pronounced presence of EU banks on the Belgian market illustrates that these potential obstacles do not deter effective competition from foreign financial service suppliers.

3   IMPACT OF THE SMP

3.1 Bank strategies

In general it can be stated that deregulation, internationalisation and increased competition have rendered the Belgian banking markets more contestable. Although the exact impact of the SMP is difficult to assess, it is clear that the major forces in reshaping the banking environment have been the regulation-induced intensification of functional diversification and the focus on operational efficiency. Faced with this changing environment, small and large banks have adapted their strategies. It has to be noted that the starting position of the Belgian banking sector was generally unfavourable. A strong reliance on interest-related income sources and the large proportion of government bonds in total assets are disadvantages in view of the growth of investment alternatives, such as mutual funds, and the gradually decreasing government borrowing requirements. These trends are putting increased stress on the sustainability of bank profit margins. As has been already noted, a number of less diversified, mostly small and medium-sized banks have persistently earned ROEs below the yield on government bonds during the 1990s (BBA, 1998).

Among the strategic options with respect to diversification and universality, low cost versus high value banking, and the important issue of scale (see Canals, 1993), Belgian banks have chosen diverging paths. The move towards bancassurance seems to be a general trend. A number of banks pursue this avenue through the combination of banking and insurance activities within a financial services group (Fortis), others have opted to establish specialised insurance subsidiaries. A number of small savings banks are also actively engaged in insurance (Argenta). All major banks have gained access to the stock exchange and are developing securities trading and underwriting activities. Some have done so by acquiring existing stockbrokers (BBL's acquisition of Raemdonck); others develop in-house expertise (KBC Securities). A number of former stockbroking firms have adopted a bank charter (Bank De Martelaere). As mentioned in Section 2, Belgian banks are allowed to become full universal banks by holding equity stakes in non-financial corporations. In practice, most banks hold only limited amounts of equity participations in their balance sheets. The most important reason is that banks are the major managers of mutual funds through which the bulk of equity investments are actually held.

3.2 Mergers and acquisitions

The EU has witnessed a takeover wave in banking in the years preceding the Single Market (see Vander Vennet, 1996). Belgian banks, however, have been notably absent from the takeover scene during this period. Only a small number of minor transactions were recorded. Part of the explanation is that the largest Belgian banks are themselves the result of multiple mergers in the 1960s and 1970s. However, considering the relatively modest size of even the largest institutions coupled with the overbanked nature of the Belgian market, especially in terms of brick-and-mortar branches, one could have expected a further consolidation. After the completion of the Single Market, the number and value of bank takeovers has increased somewhat. Examples are the acquisition, after a fierce tender offer contest, of the partly state-owned NMKN in 1995, which gave ASLK-Bank the opportunity to expand its activities into corporate lending, and the acquisition of Paribas Bank Belgium, a bank focused on private banking, by BACOB in 1997. Clearly, both post-SMP and pre-EMU considerations have driven these transactions.

A number of other deals were characterised by the acquisition of smaller competitors by a large bank in order to strengthen its market position. Examples include the takeover by Kredietbank of Bank van Roeselare and Spaarkrediet, and the acquisition by BBL of BCL and SEFB. These transactions can be described as defensive takeovers, aimed at consolidating established positions in the retail deposit market or gaining access to previously unserved local regions. A noteworthy merger between two smaller banks was the combination of Bank Nagelmaeckers, which specialised in private banking, and Codep, a small savings bank. Another innovative alliance was the agreement in 1995 between Generale Bank and the Postal Bank, whereby Generale obtained the possibility to market its products through the extensive postal branch network. Among cross-border transactions, the acquisition by Generale Bank of Credit Lyonnais Netherlands (part of the troubled French Crédit Lyonnais Group and later converted into Generale Bank Netherlands, now part of Fortis) and the alliance of GKB with Crédit Local de France, forming the Dexia group, stand out.

The big shake-up of the banking sector occurred in 1998 and 1999 (see Table 2.2). The Dutch ING Group acquired BBL, a deal which can be counted as one of the first large cross-border bank acquisitions in the EU. ING had already launched an unsuccessful bid for BBL in 1992, but in 1998 it succeeded in establishing a second home market. In a similar fashion the new Fortis bank was created after the takeover of Generale Bank by the Fortis group and the merger with ASLK-Bank and the smaller Belgian and Dutch banking entities of the group (except Mees Pierson) in 1999. The Generale acquisition occurred after a fierce takeover battle between Fortis and ABN-AMRO in an attempt to create the largest Benelux-based commercial bank. Domestically, the friendly merger of Kredietbank, CERA and the insurance company ABB created KBC Bank. It is obvious that EMU has been the major driver behind these operations. Mergers between the large institutions should also make it possible to downsize and rationalise the branch networks. All three new big banks are integrated financial services firms combining commercial (retail and corporate) banking, insurance and securities-related activities.

3.3 Internationalisation

The Belgian banking sector has always been characterised by a relatively high degree of internationalisation, but there is a clear asymmetry between the presence of foreign banks in Belgium and the foreign presence of Belgian banks. The major reason for the pronounced presence of foreign financial services providers is the long-standing tradition of openness of the Belgian market, both in terms of access by institutions and in terms of cross-border and foreign currency-denominated activity. As a result, Belgium is host to a considerable number of US, Japanese and EU bank branches and subsidiaries. Table 2.1 shows that 71 of the 134 credit institutions active on the Belgian market are either owned by a foreign parent bank or operate under foreign law. A marked evolution is also the very rapid increase in the number of foreign banks targeting the Belgian market through the system of free servicing: their number increased from 39 in 1993 to 241 in 1997 (see Table 2.1). Apart from this phenomenon, the SMP has brought no significant changes.

On the other hand, Belgian banks have gradually expanded their modest foreign presence. By the end of 1996, Belgian banks were present or represented in 63 countries through a combined network of 40 branches, 37 subsidiaries and 47 representative offices. Their major focus remains the financial servicing of Belgian exporting companies. The major commercial banks have established a physical presence in the most important financial centres such as London, New York and Tokyo. Belgian banks also hold a total of 44 participations in foreign local banks and own 37 foreign financial service companies other than banks (BBA, 1997). Cross-border bank takeovers, although few in number, have targeted neighbouring countries, especially France and the Netherlands (for example, Generale Bank acquired Crédit Lyonnais Netherlands and Banque Parisienne de Crédit in France). Finally, a number of banks entered into cross-border joint ventures and strategic alliances, but again the numbers are small.

3.4 Prices and margins

One clear consequence of the SMP has been a change in the focus of bank strategy from collusion and regulatory capture towards a more market-compatible pricing of products and services. The most visible aspect of this evolution was the abolition not only of outright interest rate controls but also of a series of explicit and tacit cartel agreements, whereby large banks acted as the price leader in various product segments. As a result, price competition in the Belgian banking and credit markets has arguably intensified in the post-SMP period. Although it would be difficult to argue that the SMP constitutes the single major cause for this trend, it is clear that ongoing interest rate deregulation, an acceleration in the pace of despecialisation, and competition from foreign entrants are closely related to various SMP events. The results of the PACEC survey (1996, p. 43) indicate that prices for corporate and retail customer loans have experienced small decreases since the implementation of the SMP, although the respondents attribute these reductions only to a minor extent to the SMP. The predominance of small and medium-sized enterprises in Belgium, and the large number of banks active in this segment, probably explain this finding. Most Belgian banks active in corporate lending have tried to compensate for the squeeze of interest margins by cross-selling fee-related corporate services such as risk management.

In the area of retail mortgages, the reported price falls due to the SMP are rather modest. However, over recent years most banks increasingly tend to consider residential mortgage loans as captive products, to which other products and services, such as savings accounts or insurance, are linked. As a result, competition in the mortgage segment has increased substantially. Specific events such as the yearly building fair 'Batibouw' are often the occasion for a fierce battle for market share. As a result, the mortgage rates offered by a number of banks are only a few basis points higher than the yield on government bonds. Again, the SMP has been instrumental in creating this environment.

The impact of the SMP on deposit rates is generally considered to be minor (PACEC, 1996, p. 48). The overall evolution of interest rates, the relative attractiveness of alternative investments, and specific events such as changes in the withholding tax on fixed-rate investment revenues are probably of greater importance. Some of the observed price rigidity may also be due to the rather conservative investment behaviour of Belgian savers and the high degree of bank loyalty. It also has to be noted that the price of the common savings account, which is still a very popular product, has, until recently, not been characterised by price competition among the leading banks. On the other hand, smaller savings banks (Argenta) and foreign subsidiaries (Crédit Lyonnais, now part of Deutsche Bank) have introduced high-yielding savings accounts, subject to the withholding tax, as a competitive instrument.

3.5 Costs and revenues

Although it is problematic to disentangle SMP effects from other structural and cyclical developments, the evidence on the evolution of the cost and revenue structure of the Belgian banking market reinforces the notion of a more diversified and competitive banking sector. As already shown in Table 2.5, the interest margin has narrowed considerably over the period 1990-1997 as a reflection of more intense competition in both the deposit and loan markets. In fact, the interest margin of Belgian banks has become one of the lowest in the EU. Most of the decline can be attributed to the increase of funding costs due to the deregulation of interest rates and the abolition of interest rate cartels. Also, the loan markets have become more competitive as a result of disintermediation, despecialisation and foreign entry. Whereas granting loans to small and medium-sized enterprises used to be the prerogative of a few large banks and specialised institutions, most banks have by now developed credit-screening skills and are actively soliciting market share. Moreover, subsidiaries of large foreign banks (ABN-AMRO, ING, Deutsche Bank and others) are very competitive participants in the corporate banking market.

Belgian banks have tried to compensate for this profit squeeze by increasing their reliance on fees, commissions and other non-interest income sources. However, the ratio of non-interest revenues to total gross income has only evolved from 25.5% in 1990 to 26.7% in 1994 (PACEC, 1996, p. 120), which still leaves Belgian banks well below the EU average. There is, however, a marked difference in terms of relative diversification among the various types of financial institutions. Commercial banks rely much more heavily on non-interest revenues than savings banks (31.2% versus 8.4% in 1994). This suggests that savings institutions remain predominantly focused on the transformation of retail deposits into loans and securities, whereas commercial banks are becoming more diversified. In fact, the move towards increased universality is far more pronounced for the large commercial banks.

3.6 Efficiency, scale and scope economies

On the supply side of bank services, a number of studies have documented the presence of scale economies in EU banking (Altunbas, Gardener and Molyneux, 1996; Vander Vennet, 1994). Although a number of methodological caveats have to be taken into account, cost function estimations indicate that the smaller banks especially should be able to realise relative cost reductions through an expansion of their scale of operations. In addition, the evidence indicates that moderate economies of scope are present for a broad range of products and output levels. These conclusions also apply to the Belgian banking market (see also Gathon and Grosjean, 1991). By decreasing cross-border barriers to entry, the SMP may have extended the potential relevant market size for banks, especially in wholesale markets and investment services. Since banks are able to expand their scale in terms of the number of customers served, be it through trade, cross-border establishment, alliance or by straightforward acquisitions, economies of scale should be realisable. Moreover, since banks are allowed to expand their range of activities and diversify into insurance and securities business, there should be an increased potential to realise economies of scope from the joint production of these various services.

In order to test this hypothesis, PACEC (1996) looks at the evolution of non-staff operating costs as a proportion of total assets and cost income ratios for a broad sample of banks. For the Belgian banking sector, both indicators suggest a moderate improvement of cost efficiency in the years following the implementation of the SMP. Yet Belgian banks remain at the lower end of the efficiency ranking in an EU perspective. The same conclusion can be drawn from the estimates of X-inefficiency, a measure capturing the difference between actual and minimum costs. The degree of operational inefficiency declined somewhat over the 1990-94 period, but it remained around 20% and the X-efficiencies appear to exhibit cyclical movements associated with the business cycle. Moreover, the moderate improvement of operational efficiency in Belgian banking occurred for all size classes. As a result, it would be hazardous to attribute this effect to scale economies. In view of the more pronounced evolution towards bancassurance (see Section 3.1), one might expect that scope economies could become more important drivers of improved cost efficiency. However, it is clear that the current distribution arrangements between bankers and insurance companies do not permit the full realisation of the benefits of bancassurance, yet. It is thus safer to attribute the modest improvement of cost efficiency in Belgian banking to the rise in cost awareness on the part of bank managers facing enhanced competition.

4　BANK PREPARATIONS FOR EMU

Following the decision of the Council on 2 May 1998, Belgium was able to participate in EMU from 1 January 1999 onwards. The irrevocable exchange rate of the euro was fixed at 40.3399 Belgian francs for one euro. Fulfilling the requirements to enter EMU has been one of the explicit goals of Belgian governments since the Treaty of Maastricht. As a result, Belgium passed the Maastricht criteria, although the public debt criterion had to be interpreted with sufficient discretion. In accordance with the official timetable, the euro was introduced from 1 January 1999 onwards and will become the sole legal tender in 2002. As a result, Belgian banks had, and still have, a clear incentive to prepare their operations for the full transition to the single currency. In fact, in terms of preparedness for the euro, international surveys have consistently indicated that Belgian banks are among the most advanced in the EU (*Economist*, 1997).

4.1　The changeover plan during the transition to EMU

Belgium was one of the first EU countries to prepare a so-called 'national changeover plan' for the introduction of the euro. The plan deals with the monetary relations in the first stage of EMU (from 1 January 1999 to the end of 2001) between five groups of economic agents: households, companies, public administrations, banks and financial markets. Two principles have guided the recommendations:

- no compulsion, no prohibition; that is economic agents should be able to use the euro when they want, but no actor can be forced to do so during the transition stage

- only the professional actors must be ready to perform transactions in euro, while the customer still has the choice to use the national currency.

As a result, the banking sector will have to handle payment transactions and money transfers in both BEF and euro. The euro/BEF conversion of the payments and the customer accounts has to be performed by the banks at zero cost to the customer.

The ability to use the euro during the first stage requires adequate flows of information between the economic agents such as invoices, tax files, accounting statements, and so on. Two additional rules should enable a smooth functioning: firstly, the rule of neutrality of the public sector (all actors may use the euro in all the documents required by official bodies, especially in relations with tax and other regulatory authorities); and, secondly, the rule of monetary homogeneity (economic actors may opt to conduct their full administration in euro). The changeover to the euro implies that the following transactions will be conducted in euro: transactions in the framework of monetary policy; the issuance of government securities; listing and settlement of financial market operations; interbank payments. For example, early in 1999 the Belgian government launched a relatively large euro-denominated security issue for which the underwriting and distribution was undertaken by an international syndicate of investment banks. Full conversion to the euro, including all retail transactions, is scheduled for 2002.

4.2 EMU challenges for Belgian banks

Revenues from trading the currencies of EMU member states will disappear. The compensation from euro trading will be very partial for most Belgian banks. In view of the size of the eurocurrency market and the increased competition, it can be predicted that a few large, presumably non-Belgian, banks will specialise in euro trading.

The introduction of the euro will eliminate one of the few remaining barriers to entry in the retail banking market. As a result, the Belgian market, with its very high household savings ratio, will become more contestable and banking competition more transparent. Increased foreign entry to the Belgian market is to be expected, especially in view of the large number of free servicing demands (see Table 2.1). The likely shift of customers to new suppliers will probably be gradual for most banking products, the main reasons for this being the existence of switching costs, reputation effects, customer knowledge and the high branch density. In fact, foreign entrants would find it hard to expand profitably by increasing the number of branches. Alternatively, they would have to acquire an existing branch network or target the Belgian market through non-brick distribution channels. The early entrance of specialised financial service suppliers is more likely and can sometimes be accomplished at relatively low cost due to the possibilities offered by new technologies such as direct banking or cyberbanking.

In the segment of corporate banking, competition is already intense, partly spurred by the strong presence of foreign suppliers. Profit margins are narrow and fee-generating capacity is relatively low. The introduction of the euro will only increase the pressure. Traditionally, Belgian banks have close ties with small and medium-sized enterprises, but the single currency will undoubtedly enhance the accessibility of these companies to the services of banks of other EMU member countries. From January 1999 onwards money and capital markets are denominated in euro. In the markets for government securities, the entry barriers will also diminish. This especially applies to government bond markets. Moreover, the Belgian Treasury has decided to convert all outstanding debt instruments into euro. Furthermore, due to the decreasing borrowing needs of the Belgian Government, the expansion of the public debt market will be modest. In such a scenario the future role of so-called primary dealers remains unclear (Van den Spiegel, 1996). One can also expect a further concentration of bond trading and related activities in derivatives. Smaller banks will have to rely on their placing capacity and established customer relations in order to distribute the government savings bonds (government bonds targeted to the general public).

Stock market quotations are also in euro. Since monetary policy is now conducted by the ECB for the EMU as a whole, it is expected that interest rates and the timing of business cycle movements will further converge so that stock market integration will increase further (see Hardouvelis *et al.*, 1999). This will induce investment managers to shift their asset allocation focus from geographical to sectoral diversification (see also Tilmant, 1997). Being a player in the euro capital markets will thus require sufficient scale, capital and expertise. Moreover, there will be increased competition from internationally diversified non-bank asset managers such as insurance companies and pension funds. In order to survive in this market segment, locally operating banks will have to try to maintain a comparative advantage vis-à-vis local companies based on information advantages and established customer relations. In this field, the Belgian banks clearly face a major challenge. The increased depth and liquidity of euro capital markets should also accelerate the pace of financial disintermediation. Since Belgian corporations use relatively little non-bank funding, banks may try to compensate for the loss of loan revenues by advisory and placement fees. In corporate eurobond markets one can still observe a fairly close correlation between the nationality of the issuer and the lead manager, although traditional ties will probably loosen further.

4.3 Banking sector responses

For the Belgian banking sector, the introduction of the euro constitutes the most important challenge of the decade. Not only do banks face substantial transition expenses and revenue losses, they will undoubtedly be faced with increased competition from foreign financial services providers. The most important direct cost is the upgrade of computer systems and staff training which will cost Belgian banks an estimated BEF 21 billion over the period 1996-2000. In addition, banks will lose revenues as monetary union reduces the number of currencies they trade. Belgian banks are known to trade a disproportionately large amount of foreign exchange, amounting to a daily volume of about $50 billion. Consequently, the total cost of the transition has been estimated by the Belgian Bankers Association at BEF 42 billion (a little less than 1 billion euro) over five years, or approximately 8% of gross profits yearly. The sum may even be higher since the loss of revenues in areas such as international payments, correspondent banking or yield curve arbitrage are very difficult to assess.

More worrying still is the threat from new competitors. Foreign banks, especially from Germany, France and the Netherlands, are lining up to enter the market, while UK insurers such as Royal & SunAlliance and Commercial Union are already undercutting domestic rivals' prices. The Belgian banks are countering the threats with a mixture of innovations in terms of product differentiation and a targeted geographical expansion, focused on the major trading partners and Eastern Europe. Based on their expertise in international trade finance, the large Belgian banks offer a wide range of services in euro. This has at least allowed them to retain most of the domestic exporters as customers. Moreover, banks are using the necessary updating and re-engineering of their technological infrastructure to improve their operational efficiency and to enhance their capabilities in the field of non-brick distribution channels. Arguably, small banks may be disadvantaged because of the inherent scale effects associated with technological investments. Entering into domestic or cross-border alliances and exploiting network effects may be a possible alternative. The competitive viability of retail banks will depend on the efficiency of their distribution channels, the flexibility of their technological infrastructure, their capital basis, and the degree of success in product differentiation (low cost for standardised products versus high value-added for tailored services).

The single currency will fundamentally alter the profession of asset management on the euro capital markets. The changes occur within a framework of structural growth of mutual investment and institutional asset management, primarily related to demographic developments. A number of Belgian banks are diversifying actively in securities activities and most of them are already offering mutual funds focused on specific sectors or regions. An adequate diversification based on risk characteristics and liquidity may give a distinct advantage to these instruments in the eurozone. A number of mostly large banks are also upgrading their investment banking skills. Over the last couple of years, the number of initial public offerings on the Brussels Stock Exchange and the volume of corporate security issues has increased substantially. In most cases, Belgian banks have actively participated in these fee-generating transactions. Finally, a few banks are seeking to expand their investment banking scope though a number of relatively small takeovers in neighbouring countries. In recent times, Generale Bank has acquired Fimagest and Kredietbank bought Transbourse, both French stockbrokers. Clearly, Belgian banks are restricted to maintaining a regional focus, compared to the pan-European strategy of the big banks which have underlined their ambitions by acquiring a number of London-based investment houses. Yet a presence in the major financial centres of the EMU zone will require a minimum scale, sufficient capital strength and access to highly skilled personnel.

5   CONCLUSIONS

From this contribution it should be clear that the Belgian banking sector has undergone significant changes but still faces a period of substantial restructuring. It is equally clear that the SMP and EMU are dominant and mutually dependent causes of this trend. However, it remains difficult to isolate the specific impact of SMP because its implementation coincided with a number of other important structural developments, especially in the technological field. Nevertheless, the SMP has certainly intensified bank competition and further increased foreign entry. It has induced a shift from regulatory capture and collusive behaviour towards a more market-based pricing of products and services. These trends have caused a substantial narrowing of the traditional interest margin. In terms of bank strategy, the SMP has provoked a shift from a predominant supply-side approach to a post-deregulation demand-based strategy. One of the effects of the SMP has certainly been to increase the operational productivity and the overall risk return efficiency. Yet, the bottom line profitability of Belgian banking remains relatively modest. A closer inspection reveals that these general conclusions may sometimes hide significant differences between certain groups of financial institutions. Whereas most large banks, and a number of smaller ones, have carefully examined their options, a considerable number seem to operate in a strategic vacuum. In these institutions, the pace of the restructuring is slow and the approach purely defensive.

Undoubtedly, EMU presents an even bigger challenge to Belgian banks than did the SMP. In terms of the practical implementation of the single currency, Belgian banks are among the leaders in the EU. However, the transition will entail substantial direct costs, primarily linked to the upgrade of the technological infrastructure, and revenue losses, especially in the field of currency trading. Moreover, the Belgian banking market will experience a further surge of foreign entry which will have an additional impact on the already vulnerable interest margin and the profitability of the intermediation business. Yet EMU should induce well-positioned banks to use their comparative advantages to increase the efficiency of their operations and to adopt a sustainable euro-compatible strategy. Achieving a balanced mix of income sources, increasing the operational efficiency of the traditional banking activities, maintaining a solid capital coverage, and building on information advantages should allow some of the existing banks to perform well. However, a substantial number of the small and medium-sized banks and savings institutions will probably not be able to maintain a strategy of autonomy. Finally, the creation of Benelux-based integrated financial services firms, such as Fortis and ING-BBL, shows that some of the large institutions take an even more pro-active attitude. The next logical step for them is to enter into pan-euroland alliances or mergers (see also Danthine *et al.*, 1999).

References

Banking and Finance Commission (1995/1996), *Annual Report* (BFC, Brussels)
Banking and Finance Commission (June 1998), *Statistics* (BFC, Brussels)
Belgian Banking Association (March 1997), *Het Belgische Bankwezen* (BBA, Brussels)
Belgian Banking Association (June 1998), *Statistical Compendium of the Banking Sector* (BBA, Brussels)
Bonte, R. and L. Holvoet (1996), 'Rendabiliteit van het Belgisch bankwezen', *Bank- en Financiewezen*, February, pp. 58-64.
Canals, J., (1993), *Competitive Strategies in European Banking* (Clarendon Press, Oxford)
'Cruickshank Report' (March 2000), *Competition in UK Banking: A Report to the Chancellor of the Exchequer* (Stationery Office, London).
Danthine, J.P., F. Giavazzi, X. Vives and E.L. von Thadden (1999), *The Future of European Banking* (Centre for Economic Policy Research, London)

Dermine, J., (1996), 'European banking integration: ten years after', *European Financial Management*, November, pp. 331-51.

Economist (1997), 'Survival tactics', August 9th, pp. 69-70.

Gardener E.P.M., P. Molyneux and B. Moore (2000), *International Price Comparisons and the Competitiveness of UK Banking*, unpublished PACEC Ltd/IEF 1998 research summarised in Appendix E of the Cruickshank Report (*see above*)

Gathon, H. J. and F. Grosjean (1991), 'Efficacité productive et rendements d'échelle dans les banques belges', *Cahiers Economiques de Bruxelles*, 2, pp. 145-60.

Hardouvelis, G.A., D. Malliaropulos and R. Priestley (1999), *EMU and European Stock Market Integration*, CEPR Discussion papers, no. 2124, April (Centre for Economic Policy Research, London)

Molyneux, Philip, Yener Altunbas and Edward Gardener (1996), *Efficiency in European Banking* (John Wiley, Chichester)

Tilmant, M. (1996), 'Le paysage bancaire après l'euro: quelle stratégie de développement adopter?', *Revue de la Banque*, November, pp. 535-41.

Van den Spiegel, F. (1996), 'De gevolgen van de euro voor de beleggingsproducten', *Bank- en Financiewezen*, November, pp. 551-56.

Vander Vennet, Rudi (1994), 'Concentration, efficiency, and entry barriers as determinants of EC bank profitability', *Journal of International Financial Markets, Institutions and Money*, 4 (3/4), pp. 21-46.

Vander Vennet, Rudi (1994), 'Economies of scale and scope in EC credit institutions', *Cahiers Economiques de Bruxelles*, 4 (114), pp. 507-48.

Vander Vennet, Rudi (1996), 'The effect of mergers and acquisitions on the efficiency and profitability of EC credit institutions', *Journal of Banking and Finance*, November, pp. 1531-58.

3   Denmark

Morten Balling and Anders Grosen

1   MARKET STRUCTURE AND PERFORMANCE

1.1   Size of the banking market 1985-1998

As indicated in Table 3.1, the number of banks and savings banks in Denmark has been declining since 1985. The decline is primarily the result of a wave of mergers and acquisitions.

Table 3.1   Banks and bank branches in Denmark

At year's end	1985	1990	1995	1998
Number of banks and savings banks	217	220	198	191
Number of branches	3331	3079	2215	2178*
Number of employees	51879	54930	46563	42483*
Total assets[1]	765.0	1145.0	1014.8	1450.3
Capital and reserves[1]	52.7	70.8	70.0	90.8

Notes: [1]DKK billion; *1997 figures.
Sources: Danish Financial Supervisory Authority, Statistical Ten-Year Review and Statistical Yearbook; Danish Bankers' Association, Annual Report 1998.

The number of branches has also declined. Mergers in the banking sector have in many cases been motivated by the need for cost reductions and branches near to each other have been closed wherever possible. Another important factor has been technology. The use of electronic payments has expanded from a level of 106,000 transactions in 1985 to a level of 289,888,000 transactions in 1997. The increasing use of telephone orders and home banking, the strong decline in the use of cheques and bank notes, and the extensive use of the universal 'Dankort-system' in which all Danish banks participate, all imply that Danish bank customers have to visit their bank branch less and less. If they want cash, they can obtain it in the supermarket, where it is almost always accepted that customers can make transactions at a higher amount than the value of the goods bought.

The degree of market concentration in the banking sector can be measured roughly by the so-called five firm concentration ratio (C5 ratio). The basis for the calculation is the 'total assets' item from the balance sheet of all banks. For Denmark, the average C5 ratio for the period 1979-92 has been calculated at 59.6, which is one of the highest ratios in Europe in that period. Due to two very big mergers between the largest Danish banks in 1989-90, the average C5 ratio increased to 87.0 when balance sheet figures from 1993-94 are used. At the end of 1996, the total assets of Den Danske Bank A/S represented 35% of total assets in the banking sector, while total assets of Unidanmark A/S represented 25%. Measured in terms of C5 ratios, the Netherlands and Denmark have the highest market concentration in the banking sector in Europe.

According to Table 3.1, the total capital and reserves of Danish banks declined slightly between 1990 and 1995. The decline reflects big losses in the period 1990 to 1992. As with banks in the other Scandinavian countries, Danish banks during the 1980s involved themselves strongly in the financing of building projects and real estate development, and they were accordingly hit hard when these markets collapsed at the end of the 1980s. In several cases, bank restructurings and mergers in this difficult period were brought into being with help from the Danish Financial Supervisory Authority because it feared that bankruptcies would undermine public confidence in the financial system as a whole. The central bank, Danmarks Nationalbank, supported some of the bank restructurings by temporary guarantees, and the tax authorities approved deductions in taxable income to buyers in connection with purchases of banks in trouble. Compared to the other Scandinavian countries, however, the Danish banking system performed better during this crisis period. In Denmark, government support was given primarily in the form of guarantees and the use of public funds was very limited.

During this period, most of the biggest Danish savings banks were transformed into commercial banks. An amendment to the Danish banking law facilitated such transformations, and the boards and managements of the savings banks wanted incorporation in order to obtain the opportunity to increase their capital base by selling their shares in the stock market. The new legal basis also gradually removed the remaining barriers which impeded the access of savings banks to provide all types of banking services: they could now operate under the universal banking system and engage in international financial activity under the same rules as the 'old' commercial banks.

The Danish economy is open. Foreign trade represents approximately one third of the GDP, and Danish banks have therefore been strongly involved in the financing of exports and imports for many years. During the 1970s and the beginning of the 1980s, the Danish monetary authorities used a series of monetary policy measures to stimulate capital import in order to finance the current account deficit. During that period the Danish level of interest rates was consistently kept higher than the interest level for instance in Germany, and it was therefore profitable for Danish companies to seek financing abroad. By doing so they exposed themselves to exchange risk, but the existence of the intervention limits under the European Monetary System (EMS) contributed to a reduction of that risk. In order to meet the needs of their corporate customers, many Danish banks established branches or subsidiaries in London, Luxembourg, Frankfurt and the Cayman Islands. Only to a limited extent did these units provide financial services to non-Danish customers.

1.2 Ownership structure and privatisation

Danish bank shares are, to a very considerable extent, owned by institutional investors. That is also the case for shares issued by other companies which are listed on the Copenhagen Stock Exchange. The extent of institutional stock ownership is primarily the result of tax legislation. Danish taxpayers have the right to deduct in their income tax forms their contributions to pension funds and insurance companies, and, due to the very high level of income tax, there is a strong incentive to choose to save through institutions. On top of that, dividends and capital gains on shares are, in contrast to interest income from bonds, exempted from the so-called 'Realrenteafgift', which is a tax on the real returns on pension fund assets. With effect from 1 January 2000, the real return taxation has been replaced by a flat 26% taxation on nominal returns. Under the old tax rules, Danish pension fund portfolio managers were thus induced to invest a considerable share of the institutional portfolios in stocks. Information from the Danish Financial Supervisory Authority shows that 30.2% of the shares of the biggest Danish bank, Den Danske Bank, was owned by institutional investors at the end of 1996. Institutional share ownership is even higher for some of the smaller Danish banks.

The role of institutional investors in the Danish stock market has also been stimulated by political decisions to create special pension institutions. Arbejdsmarkedets Tillægspension (ATP-Fonden) and Lønmodtagernes Dyrtidsfond (LD-Fonden) have, since their establishment in the 1960s, grown to become two of the biggest shareholders in Denmark. When they cooperate with insurance companies and pension funds, the two institutions can play a decisive role when transfer of ownership in big Danish companies takes place.

Privatisation of banks has not been an important issue in Denmark. Bank share ownership by the central government or by local government has been very limited. There is, however, one example of privatisation. In 1991, the payment system Postgiro was separated from the Government-owned mail services, transformed into a joint stock company GiroBank A/S, and the shares were sold to the public. In 1995, Girobank A/S merged with Sparekassen Bikuben A/S into BG Bank A/S. The transaction created the third biggest bank in Denmark.

1.3 Competition

The Danish banking system has been a universal banking system for many years. The biggest commercial banks have traditionally offered a very broad menu of banking services. Corporate customers have, in the same institution, access to cash management services, short-term financing, portfolio management, derivatives, guarantees, investment banking, and services related to foreign exchange markets. Small banks and savings banks do not have the expertise and capacity to offer all these financial services, but in several cases they have cooperation agreements with big competitors for services which they do not offer themselves.

The market for banking services to corporate customers indicates that there is strong competition among the big financial institutions in Denmark. It is common for big Danish industrial companies to use more than one bank, and they compare prices, interest rates and other conditions before they decide where to place a transaction. In many cases big Danish companies also have regular business relations with foreign banks. Transactions in foreign exchange markets and cash management within multinational companies are often offered at very competitive rates and prices by banks outside Denmark, and the presence of this competition is, of course, reflected in the prices of such services in the Danish corporate market.

In the Danish retail market for banking services, the pattern of competition is somewhat different. Some of the smaller Danish banks and savings banks are very active in this market and the application of rather aggressive marketing methods is not uncommon. Foreign banks play, however, only a very modest role in the retail market. The retail market can be characterised as oligopoly, combined with a few aggressive small banks.

As mentioned in Section 2 below, recent amendments to the Danish banking legislation allow banks to acquire or establish insurance companies and real estate mortgage institutions. Conversely, such institutions have also been allowed to acquire or establish banks. There are, accordingly, almost no legal restrictions left which create barriers among different types of financial markets. Financial conglomerates controlled by the biggest banks, real estate mortgage institutions and insurance companies play a very important role in the Danish financial system.

1.4 Banking performance

Since 1985 the earnings of Danish banks have been very volatile. The accounting regulations prescribe that realised as well as unrealised gains and losses on the portfolio of bonds and shares shall be reflected in current accounting income. The same principle applies to gains and losses on foreign exchange exposures. In view of the considerable interest rate and share price fluctuations, combined with the observation that the bond portfolio often represents approximately 25% of total assets in the banking sector, bank earnings volatility is not surprising. As has been mentioned, the biggest deficits in the Danish bank accounts were observed from 1990 to 1992. Depreciations and provisions for losses on bad debts reached record levels in those years. The level of bank earnings has improved considerably since 1993. This improved earnings performance is the result of better profitability and, therefore, creditworthiness of the banks' business customers as well as cost reductions in the banking sector related to mergers, fewer branches, investment in automation and information technology, and reduction of personnel.

There is no clear pattern with respect to economies of scale in the Danish banking system. The ratio between earnings before taxes and total assets decreases slightly with bank size in some years, while it increases in other years. The same remark applies to the ratio between earnings before taxes and total equity capital. Return on equity is a very volatile measure of profitability, partly due to the high degree of mark-to-market accounting mentioned above.

2 REGULATORY FRAMEWORK

2.1 Regulatory framework prior to the SMP

Prior to 1986, Danish banking law contained provisions implementing the First Banking Directive (73/183/EEC) on the removal of barriers to the right to establishment and the free exchange of financial services, and the First Banking Coordination Directive (77/780/EEC) on the coordination of laws, regulations and administrative provisions relating to the taking up and pursuit of the business of credit institutions. Danish law regulated both the establishment and the activity of commercial banks and savings banks. The provisions in the law limited the scope of operations of the two types of institutions to what was called 'bank and savings bank activity', that is operations and functions in connection with monetary and credit transactions, securities, and related services. Thus the institutions were, for instance, not allowed to offer insurance services. The law contained separate chapters on the establishment of banks, the contents of statutes, the management structure, the minimum level of own funds, liquidity, accounting, disclosure, auditing, application of surplus, merger procedures, supervision and penalty clauses. According to the law, the Danish Financial Supervisory Authority should monitor the activity of banks and savings banks in order to safeguard the stability of the system and act in cases where violations of minimum requirements concerning disclosure, liquidity or equity capital were observed.

Danish foreign exchange regulations were liberalised gradually during the 1970s and the first half of the 1980s. Prior to 1986, there were some restrictions on Danish residents holding positions in foreign currencies and some reporting obligations with respect to the holding of foreign securities. These provisions were maintained for tax reasons.

2.2 Main SMP legislation

Every year, the European Commission publishes a report in which the degree of implementation of Community law in the individual member countries is analysed. The latest report at the time of writing is the Fifteenth Report on Control of the Implementation of Community Law (1997, COM (1998) 317 final, EU Commission, Brussels, May 1998). Item 2.2.4.6. of the report gives a survey of the implementation measures concerning Directives on financial services. Of the 48 Directives in this area which were in force at the end of December 1997, Denmark had informed the Commission of the implementation of 48, in other words 100%. It is not possible to draw a sharp line between the Directives which are part of the SMP and those that are only related to the SMP. A small sample of the most important SMP and SMP-related Directives has been selected and the implementation of main rules from those Directives into Danish legislation is described below.

In May 1990, the Danish Parliament passed a new law (No. 306) which amended Danish banking legislation in a number of important ways. The aim of the law was primarily to adjust Danish legislation to the principles and requirements in Directives that had recently been adopted by the EU Council in order to implement the internal market for financial services in Europe before the end of 1992. The four most important Directives concerned were: the Directive on a Solvency Ratio for Credit Institutions (89/647/EEC); the Directive on the Own Funds of Credit Institutions (89/299/EEC); the Directive on the Annual Account and Consolidated Accounts of Banks and other Financial Institutions (86/635/EEC); and the Second Banking Coordination Directive (89/646/EEC) on the coordination of laws relating to the taking up and pursuit of the business of credit institutions and amending Council Directive (77/780/EEC). The law came into force in Denmark on 1 January 1991.

In accordance with the Second Banking Coordination Directive, Law 306 established the single banking licence. When an EU bank is allowed to operate by the supervisory authorities in its home country, it is automatically entitled to establish branches and to offer cross-border financial services in the other EU countries. According to article 6.a.1, a bank with its headquarters in another EU country can establish a branch in Denmark and start operations two months after the date on which the Danish Financial Supervisory Authority has received notification from the supervisory authority in the bank's home country. The article contains a specification of the information which shall be included in such notifications. Article 6.a.5 determines that a bank in another EU country is entitled to provide cross-border financial services in Denmark when the Danish Financial Supervisory Authority has been notified by the authorities in the bank's home country that the required conditions for operations are met. Thus, by passing Law 306, the Danish Parliament endorsed the two main principles in the Second Banking Directive: the principle of mutual recognition of supervisory systems in other member countries and the principle of homeland control. One year earlier, the same two principles had been extended by the Danish Parliament to apply to real estate mortgage institutions and credit institutions other than banks in the European Community. Law no. 841 of 20 December 1989 implemented these principles for real estate mortgage institutions.

Paragraph 1 of Law 306 extended the range of financial services and transactions banks are allowed to carry out. This extension was partly derived from the list of activities submitted to mutual recognition, which was appended to the Second Banking Directive. The law introduced the concept of 'accessory activity' without giving a precise definition. According to the minutes of the debate in the Danish Parliament, it was expected, however, that many banks would utilise the more liberal rules to expand their activity into functions related to sale of computer services, real estate brokering, and different kinds of advisory services. The law also allowed banks to own subsidiaries engaged in insurance business and real estate financing.

The Directive on a Solvency Ratio for Credit Institutions and the Directive on the Own Funds of Credit Institutions are both based on capital adequacy considerations. The implementation of the Solvency Ratio Directive meant that the focus in Danish banking law with respect to the calculation of the minimum capital requirements was moved from the liability side of the balance sheet of the bank to the asset side. In addition, a long list of off-balance sheet items was included in the solvency calculation. According to the law, it is the duty of the board of directors in each bank and of the supervisory authorities to ensure that at all times the own funds exceed a minimum level, which is calculated as 8% of the risk-weighted assets (some off-balance items included). The Danish Financial Supervisory Authority issued an order in which all items on the asset side of the bank balance sheet and on the off-balance sheet were classified according to credit risk. For most Danish financial institutions, the capital requirements following from the solvency rules in the EC Directive were considerably lower than the rather strict requirements that applied before. The 1990 banking law therefore contained a transition period from 1991 to 1995 during which the minimum solvency ratio was gradually reduced from a level of 10% to 8%.

The implementation of the Own Funds Directive redefined the concept of liable capital in the banking law as the sum of core capital and supplementary capital. Core capital consists of share capital, retained earnings and surplus on emissions. Supplementary capital consists of obligations of the bank with a long or undetermined maturity where the rights of the creditors are subordinated to all other claims on the bank.

Directives 91/633/EEC and 92/16/EEC amended the Directive on the Own Funds of Credit Institutions (89/299/EEC). The new Directives implied some minor changes in the calculation of the core capital in relation to general credit risks and introduced common principles of capital adequacy for banks and investment service companies. With effect from 1996, all relevant financial institutions and companies in Denmark had to submit to capital adequacy requirements that supplemented the credit risk provisions that applied before and included cover of price risks on the institutions' bond and stock portfolios and foreign exchange exposures.

In Chapter 7 of Law 306, Directive 86/635/EEC on the annual account and consolidated accounts of banks and other financial institutions was implemented in Danish legislation. In the same chapter, a number of provisions in the Fourth Company Law Directive (78/660/EEC) concerning minimum standards of financial reporting and the Seventh Company Law Directive (83/349/EEC) on consolidated accounts were extended to apply not only to incorporated firms in general but also to financial institutions covered by Danish banking law. Disclosure requirements concerning firms in the financial sector contained, however, a number of exceptions due to the special character of those firms.

Directives 83/350/EEC and 92/30/EEC on the supervision of credit institutions on a consolidated basis should, of course, be seen in the context of the Directives on consolidated accounts. The idea of supervision on a consolidated basis is that the authorities supervising a parent credit institution can make a more soundly based prudential judgment about the financial situation of that credit institution by including activities of other credit institutions or financial companies in which the parent has a major participation. The provisions of the 1992 Directive which extended the obligations of the Danish Financial Supervisory Authority to look at the exposures of financial parent companies and their subsidiaries as a whole, were implemented by an amendment of the Danish banking Law 17 in December 1992. The amendment was also inspired by Commission Recommendation 87/62/EEC of 22 December 1986 concerning the monitoring and control of large exposures of credit institutions.

Commission Recommendation 87/63/EEC concerning deposit insurance schemes in the Community did not oblige the member states to implement such schemes, but the Recommendation was taken into consideration by the Danish Parliament in the autumn of 1987. On 23 December 1987, Parliament passed Law 850 on a Deposit Guarantee Fund. The establishment of the fund implied that all retail deposits in Danish banks up to a limit of DKK250,000 were protected against default of the bank. Recently, the limit has been increased to DKK300,000. Deposits relating to pension arrangements were protected without any limit.

2.3 Other domestic regulatory landmarks

Efforts to liberalise international capital movements in Europe go back at least to the ratification of the Treaty of Rome in 1957. The early capital liberalisation Directives in the EEC predate, of course, the Single Market Programme. The adoption of Directive 88/361/EEC on the implementation of article 67 of the EEC Treaty took place simultaneously with the adoption of several Directives related to the SMP, and it also deals with capital liberalisation. It can hardly be said to belong to the SMP but it is certainly important in connection with the efforts to create integrated European financial markets. In the autumn of 1988, the Danish monetary authorities decided to lift all remaining foreign exchange regulations with effect from 1 October 1988.

The Danish legislation on the Stock Exchange was revised in 1979. The primary object of the Copenhagen Stock Exchange Act of December 1979 was to bring about a legal basis for the Minister of Industry to issue administrative Government notices concerning the implementation of EEC Directives. The first of these EEC Directives concerning stock exchange matters was 79/279/EEC. It aimed at coordinating the conditions for the admission of securities to official stock exchange listing. It was implemented in Denmark in March 1980, prior to the required date. The next Directive was 80/390/EEC, the Listing Particulars Directive, which prescribes a number of detailed disclosure requirements that must be fulfilled prior to approval of the listing. The third Directive was 82/121/EEC which stated the information to be published on a regular basis by companies whose shares have been admitted to official stock exchange listing. In a later Directive the time allowed to member states for implementing the three Directives was extended to 30 June 1983. After further postponements of the implementation procedure initiated at the Community level, in November 1983 the Danish Minister of Industry issued four new orders relating to the Copenhagen Stock Exchange:

- Order No. 525 of 10 November 1983 relating to the Copenhagen Stock Exchange: it regulates the structure of the Stock Exchange, the rules for quotation, monitoring, and so on
- Order No. 526 of 10 November 1983 on the conditions to be fulfilled in order to be included on the official list of securities quoted on the Copenhagen Stock Exchange
- Order No. 527 of 10 November 1983 on the requirements to be met by the prospectus published before securities can be admitted for official quotation on the Copenhagen Stock Exchange, and
- Order No.528 of 10 November 1983 on the requirements to be fulfilled for small and medium-sized companies to be admitted to Share Market III. The order took effect from 1 April 1984.

In May 1986 a major reform of Danish Stock Exchange legislation was passed in the Parliament, later called 'Exchange Reform I'. This package of Laws included Law 316 on the Copenhagen Stock Exchange, Law 317 on Certain Credit Institutions, and Law 318 on amendment of Danish Company Law. Major features of Exchange Reform I were:

- the old monopoly of the stockbrokers was repealed and incorporated broker companies were given the right to make transactions by means of the electronic systems of the Stock Exchange
- oral quotation on the stock exchange floor was replaced by an electronic stock exchange trading system
- reporting obligations applying to broker companies, banks, and credit institutions with accounts in the Danish Securities Centre (VP) were introduced.

In the 1970s the supervisory board of the Copenhagen Stock Exchange adopted a set of ethical rules concerning securities trading. The rules contained some recommendations on disclosure of information and on insider dealing. With effect from 1 January 1987, enforceable rules were included in the Law on the Copenhagen Stock Exchange. In 1989, the EU Council adopted Directive (89/592/EEC) on Insider Trading. In December 1991, the board of the Copenhagen Stock Exchange used its authority according to the law and adopted new rules on the disclosure of information by market participants and new ethical rules. The provisions came into force on 1 January 1992.

In 1993, the EU Council adopted two Directives of great importance to the further integration of organised markets in Europe for bonds, shares, and other financial instruments. According to introductory remarks in the two Directives (Directive 93/22/EEC of 10 May 1993 on investment service in the securities field and Directive 93/6/EEC of 15 March 1993 on capital adequacy of investment firms and credit institutions), the EU Council considered the documents to be very important instruments in the implementation of the internal market. The provisions of the two EU Directives were implemented in Denmark by the passing of four laws:

- Law 358 of 14 June 1995 amending the banking law
- Law 353 of 6 June 1995 amending the law on real estate mortgage institutions
- Law 1071 of 20 December 1995 on stockbroking companies, and
- Law 1072 of 20 December 1995, the Securities Trading Bill.

This package of laws was referred to as 'Exchange Reform II'. When the Minister of Business Affairs in May 1995 presented the proposed Securities Trading Bill to the Parliament, she indicated that the Government wanted to increase competition in the financial market because this would contribute to a strengthening of the international competitiveness of Danish financial institutions and markets. The majority of the rules in the new laws came into force on 1 January 1996, but the Minister was given some discretion with respect to the dates when some of the new provisions should have effect in Denmark.

The new legislation meant the implementation of rules in Denmark taken from Directives concerning a 'European' passport for banks and investment companies entitled to offer investment service in all EU countries, provided they have a licence granted by the home country authority. These institutions can offer services on a cross-border basis but they have also the right to become members of stock exchanges and other regulated markets in other EU countries on equal terms with local institutions should they find local presence to be attractive. In addition, the new laws also implied 'European rules' concerning transparency, disclosure of price and turnover information, and disclosure obligations in connection with takeover bids. According to article 35 of the Securities Trading Bill, a person or an institution who has inside information is prohibited from buying or selling securities. The rules in chapter 10 of Law 1072 implemented Directive 89/592/EEC on Insider Trading into Danish legislation.

An important institutional consequence of the passing of the Securities Trading Bill was that the Copenhagen Stock Exchange was privatised and converted into a limited liability company in the spring of 1996. The equity capital of the new company, Københavns Fondsbørs A/S, was initially distributed to the securities dealers (60%), the bond issuers (20%), and the listed companies (20%).

The Second Council Directive (88/357/EEC) on the coordination of laws and administrative provisions concerning direct insurance, apart from life insurance, and amending Directive (73/239/EEC), was implemented in Denmark by Law 304 of 16 May 1990 on the exchange of insurance services. The accompanying Law of 16 May 1990 contains provisions concerning insurance company and pension fund ownership of subsidiaries with activities that are outside the licence of the parent, but still subject to supervision from the Danish Financial Supervisory Authority. According to the provisions, Danish insurance companies and pension funds can own shares in banks but normally only on a portfolio basis. In practice, insurance companies and pension funds are often amongst the biggest shareholders of Danish banks, and they therefore have the opportunity to use their voting power in bank stockholder meetings if they want to do so.

2.4 Remaining barriers to the SMP

As has been explained above, the Danish regulatory framework concerning financial markets and institutions has been continually adjusted to EU Directives and regulations ever since Denmark joined the Community in 1973. After 26 years of amendments created with a clear European integration perspective, there are very few barriers left.

One area in which EU harmonisation efforts have had relatively limited success is that of income tax. Some of Denmark's tax rules contain elements of formal or informal discrimination which can exert an influence on international capital flows and the competitiveness of financial institutions. The most important example was probably Realrenteafgiftsloven. This was a law which, up to 1999, contained the rules according to which the return on pension fund portfolios and other income derived from savings for retirement should be taxed. The law was passed by the Danish Parliament in June 1983 as Law 222. In 1997 the tax raised DKK13 billion. The calculation of the tax was very complicated. It followed that insurance companies and pension funds outside Denmark found it difficult to enter into pension arrangements with Danish taxpayers. In a way, the law could be characterised as a technical barrier to the integration of the market for pension services. The decision of the Danish Parliament to abolish the real return taxation law with effect from 1 January 2000 may reflect a desire to remove a barrier to integration in this area.

Another area in which some regulatory barriers can still be found is the portfolio composition rules for institutional investors. Insurance companies and pension funds are allowed to invest in both Danish and foreign bonds, shares, real estate, bank deposits and other financial instruments. The EU Directives on Insurance, (92/49/EEC, 92/96/EEC, and 90/619/EEC), contain investment rules concerning those insurance company assets which correspond to their obligations regarding the customers. The Directives do not have provisions concerning the composition of other assets, and the adopted EU rules are minimum rules. Partly due to these rules, partly due to the preferences of the Danish portfolio managers, domestic securities and financial instruments play a much larger role in the balance sheets of institutional investors than comparable foreign assets.

3 IMPACT OF THE SMP

By way of introduction, the impact of the SMP on the Danish banking and credit sector is discussed in terms of the Merton classification of financial institutions. In Table 3.2, financial intermediation is classified according to transparency with direct lending at one end of the spectrum and organised markets with listed securities at the other end. In Denmark the organised markets are dominated by real estate mortgage bonds. Together with the market for government bonds, the real estate mortgage market constitutes the largest EU bond market in relative terms and the third largest bond market in absolute terms. In comparison with this, the Danish equity market is much less developed. It should also be mentioned that life insurance companies and pension funds manage a large part of the Danish long-term savings, partly due to the right of taxpayers to deduct contributions to pension funds and insurance companies on the income tax form.

Table 3.2 Classification of financial institutions

Degree of Transparency							
Opaque		*Translucent*					*Transparent*
Direct lending	Commercial banks	Insurance companies and Pension funds	Mutual funds	Futures and Options markets	Equity market	Real estate mortgage market	Government bond market

Note: idea from Robert Merton ('A functional perspective of financial intermediation', *Financial Management*, Vol. 24, No. 2, Summer 1995)

Competition and financial innovation are driving the banking and credit sectors towards more economic efficiency. In terms of the classification in Table 3.2, a secular pattern away from opaque institutions towards transparent institutions appears. However, financial innovation in intermediation does not, of course, proceed in a vacuum. The process and the specific form it takes is significantly influenced by the surrounding institutional and regulatory environment. In this section we will examine the impact of the SMP on financial intermediation in Denmark.

The deregulatory aspects of the SMP have contributed to an intensified competition by opening up the financial system to new players. Institutions from other countries can access the Danish financial market just as Danish companies can access markets abroad.

What may be more important, however, is that the SMP has broken down lines of demarcation between different business areas and different kinds of financial institutions. This means that an increasing number of institutions are providing financial services and products. The regulatory part of the SMP programme has also initiated legislation that supports development towards more transparency in the financial markets, such as the pricing of products and services. Until now the global trend towards securitisation by non-financial companies is not seen as an opportunity or a threat to the Danish banks, mainly because the majority of Danish companies is relatively small.

At the same time consumers in Denmark have become far more price- and cost-conscious. Today consumers often require an explicit price on services, a tendency that slowly erodes traditional bank cross-subsidisation practice so that prices of specific products and services reflect the actual costs. In short, there is a tendency to replace non-price competition with price competition, which implies a more transparent pricing on bank products and services.

3.1 Bank strategies

In practice the SMP is one of a collection of strategic drivers shaping bankers' strategies and the banking and credit sector structure. The relative importance of the strategic drivers is shown in Table 3.3, which presents the results of a postal survey carried out for this study in early 1996 and covering the EU countries. The Danish figures are compared with the figures from the responses from all the EU countries.

Table 3.3 Importance of factors influencing bank strategies, 1993-1995

Factor	Denmark	EU
Technological change	73	76
Competition from domestic firms	66	72
Domestic regulatory developments	42	66
Competition between banks and non-banks	55	65
Competition from firms in other EU countries	33	49
EU SMP programme	37	50
Competition from firms in non EU countries	30	42
0 = not important; 25 = little importance; 50 = quite important; 75 = very important; 100 = critically important		

Source: Postal survey 1996

Table 3.3 shows that over the three years in question (1993-95) technological change and competition from domestic firms have very much influenced the development of banking strategy in Denmark as well as in the other EU countries. The Danish respondents suggest that the SMP has merely been of minor importance to the development of their corporate strategy. This result reflects the fact that before the SMP, the Danish financial market was one of the less regulated markets. This is consistent with the findings in Table 3.4 where a very low level of change in strategy due to SMP is reported from Denmark. Table 3.5 reports the relative importance of various legislative changes. From interviews with bankers we have received the impression that both tables understate the relative importance of regulatory and legislative change in banking strategy in Denmark.

Table 3.4 Extent to which strategy has been revised in response to the SMP for various broad product areas

Product area	Denmark	EU
Investment area	21	55
Off balance sheet activities	22	52
Corporate customer loans	28	51
Other retail saving products	2	49
Corporate customer deposits	22	48
Retail deposits (sight and time)	2	43
Retail customer mortgages	20	43
Retail customer loans	4	42
Retail insurance products	14	41
0 = not at all; 25 = slightly; 50 = to some extent; 75 = to a large extent; 100 = totally		

Source: Postal survey 1996

Table 3.5 Relative importance of various legislative changes

Legislation	Denmark	EU
Own funds & solvency ratio Directives	65	77
Second banking Directive	58	66
Liberalisation of capital flows	76	63
Deregulation of interest rates	59	55
0 = not at all; 25 = slightly; 50 = to some extent; 75 = to a large extent; 100 = totally		

Source: Postal survey 1996

Firstly, all persons interviewed stressed that deregulation and integration were processes that have had a decisive impact on the management's whole way of thinking and reasoning. An example of this tendency is the large impact on risk management techniques. The Basle Accord and the Capital Adequacy Directive (93/6/EEC) have influenced and inspired new management techniques for market risk. The bankers interviewed also stressed that the influence had a dual effect in that developments within banking influenced the regulatory environment and vice versa. Many of the bankers expressed the opinion that forthcoming EU Directive drafts influenced strategy decisions that were taken long before the Directives were implemented in Danish legislation. The Investment Services Directive (93/22/EC), among others, was mentioned as an example. It was not implemented until 1 January 1996 but it had already had a significant impact on the banks' actions before then.

Secondly, we think that the high degree of concentration within the Danish banking system is partly a result of the internal market integration. As mentioned above, the two largest Danish banks, Den Danske Bank A/S and Unibank A/S, represented 60% of the total assets in the Danish banking sector at the end of 1996.

There is also an increasing strategic priority to utilise bank distribution capacity to sell other financial products in addition to the traditional ones. In particular, this strategy is followed by the two largest Danish banks which manage life insurance companies, real estate mortgage institutions, leasing and factoring companies, and so on. This development has been possible as a consequence of deregulation.

For at least the last four years the two largest Danish banks have followed a regional (Nordic) strategy rather than a European strategy. This means that, internationally, both banks concentrate their resources on developing the Scandinavian market. Within the market for traditional banking products, their efforts are mainly directed towards the big companies, while stockbrokers and investment banking activities are oriented towards selling Scandinavian securities to the rest of the world.

The largest Danish banks wish to be bridgeheads to the Scandinavian market for securities. Recently the largest Danish bank, Den Danske Bank, has also engaged in ordinary retail banking in Sweden and Norway. Den Danske Bank has bought the sixth largest Swedish bank and a minor Norwegian bank, and thereby initiated what the Danish newspapers call 'the Nordic banking war'. In mid-1999 Den Danske Bank also bought a minor real estate finance institution in Sweden. At the same time one of the largest Danish insurance companies, Codan, bought the second largest Swedish insurance company, Trygg-Hansa, with a share of nearly 20% of the Swedish insurance market. The largest cross-border merger in the Nordic banking sector so far took place at the beginning of 2000 when MeritaNordbanken (Finnish-Swedish) and Unibank (Danish) merged. These events can probably be interpreted as the first real signs of regional competition in retail banking, real estate financing and insurance business in Scandinavia.

All in all, we think that the broader market orientation has had an important impact on the strategic thinking of Danish banks. The increasing need for banks to adapt to the pressures of the external markets is now more recognised than before. Combined with the heavy losses in the period 1990-1992, the external pressures inspire an increasing strategic focus within the banks on productivity (cost management) and on overall internal risk/return (internal capital allocation) efficiency.

3.2 Internationalisation

The primary aim of this section is to examine the hypothesis that the implementation of the SMP has stimulated increased internationalisation of the banking and credit market in Denmark. Evidence about this can be derived from the postal survey in which respondents were asked whether they had increased cross-border trade post-SMP. The responses from Denmark and the EU are shown in Table 3.6.

Table 3.6 Changes in cross-border trade in Denmark and other EU countries since the full implementation of the SMP for main product areas

Product area	Denmark	EU
Off balance sheet activities	45	54
Investment management	25	49
Other retail saving products	3	42
Corporate customer loans	39	36
Corporate customer deposits	41	35
Retail deposits (sight and time)	5	30
Retail customer mortgages	18	28
Retail insurance products	0	28
Retail customer loans	4	26

Note: 0 = not at all; 25 = slightly; 50 = to some extent; 75 = to a large extent;
        100 = totally
Source: Postal survey

All in all, Table 3.6 shows that the level of trade undertaken by the banking institutions in other EU countries has increased slightly. For all

EU countries, the largest increase in cross-border trade has been in off-balance sheet activities and investment management. It is further seen that, except for corporate loans and deposits, the Danish respondents report smaller increases for the main product areas than is the case for the other EU countries. The limited activity increase in the retail sector partly reflects the fact that the costs of establishing networks, as well as social barriers, remain relatively important obstacles to cross-border trade and these barriers are likely to be of particular significance where retail markets are concerned.

Table 3.7 shows that Danish respondents are of the opinion that the SMP has been a relatively unimportant factor when it comes to increasing trade.

Table 3.7 Extent to which the SMP has been responsible for any reported changes in trade of domestic institutions in other EU countries

Extent	Denmark	EU
Totally	0	1
To a large extent	0	36
Slightly	51	54
Not at all	44	7

Note: figures are % of respondents
Source: Postal survey

The postal survey reflects the fact that Danish banks have not directly been exposed to competition from other banks with regard to retail customers and small companies. The direct competition concerns loans and special services to big internationally-oriented Danish companies, and stockbroking and investment banking activities. By the end of 1998 about 15 international banks had established branch offices in Copenhagen. Due to statistical problems it is difficult to measure their activities but, measured by manpower, their activities are increasing.

The competitive reaction to the threats from these entrants has primarily been an intense price competition. Until recently no merger, acquisition or new alliance has been formed in response. As mentioned above, the Scandinavian strategy chosen recently by the two largest banks can be seen as an offensive strategy after withdrawing some of their activities from other places in Europe and overseas. For a brief description of the representation of the Danish banks abroad see Section 1.1, where it is mentioned that Danish bank branches or subsidiaries previously established in London, Luxembourg, or Frankfurt were primarily motivated by the needs of their Danish corporate customers.

3.3 Prices and margins

The impact of the SMP on prices and margins has apparently been quite small for the EU as a whole. See Tables 3.8 and 3.9 for the reported price changes for different types of loans and deposits over the period investigated.

Table 3.8 Price changes for different types of loans since full implementation of the SMP

Product Area	Denmark	EU
Corporate customer loans (large firms)	-36	-29
Corporate customer loans (small firms)	-21	-24
Retail customer loans	-25	-21
Retail customer mortgages	-31	-16

-50 = large decrease; -25 = small decrease; 0 = no change; 25 = small increase; 50 = large increase

Note: price is defined as the margin between the rate charged to customer and money market rate; changes in the margin due to business cycle effect are excluded.
Source: Postal survey

Table 3.9 Price changes per corporate and retail customer deposits since full implementation of the SMP

Product area	Denmark	EU
Corporate customer deposits (large firms)	-18	-25
Corporate customer deposits (small firms)	-13	-24
Retail customer deposits	-31	-23

- 50 = large decrease; - 25 = small decrease; 0 = no change; 25 = small increase; 50 = large increase

Note: price is defined as the margin between the rate charged to customer and money market rate; changes in the margin due to business cycle effect are excluded.
Source: Postal survey

The extent to which the SMP has been responsible for any changes in deposit pricing and loans is reported in Tables 3.10 and 3.11.

Table 3.10 Extent to which the SMP has been responsible for any reported changes in deposit prices

Extent	Denmark	EU
Totally	0	0
To a large extent	0	13
Slightly	53	68
Not at all	46	19

Note: Figures are % of respondents; price is defined as the margin between rate charged to customer and money market rate
Source: Postal survey

Table 3.11 Extent to which the SMP has been responsible for any reported changes in loan prices

Extent	Denmark	EU
Totally	0	0
To a large extent	5	16
Slightly	5	54
Not at all	90	30

Note: Figures are % of respondents; price is defined as the margin between rate charged to customer and money market rate
Source: Postal survey

From the postal survey it is seen that Danish respondents attribute very little of the margin reduction to the SMP. This is consistent with the relatively deregulated Danish markets prior to the introduction of the SMP programme compared to several other EU countries with a relatively regulated status prior to the SMP.

Besides deregulation there could be several other reasons to support the conclusion of the postal survey that the impact on prices had been quite small during the three years before 1996. It should be remembered that the Danish banking and credit sector has reached a high degree of concentration with oligopolistic pricing tendencies. Moreover, the increased focus of the banks on cost-income ratios and ROE as key objectives, following their heavy losses in 1990-92, has also discouraged price cuts in response to intensified competition. After recovering from the losses, it is the authors' impression that price competition has intensified in recent years. It should also be mentioned that the reregulation process has increased incentives for banks to ensure full risk coverage on all their products and therefore it has also placed an upward pressure on bank margins.

3.4 Bank economies

Firstly, we will address the problem of scale economies. We must initially stress that this kind of investigation is subject to some uncertainty. It is especially difficult to investigate the impact of the SMP in connection with realisation of scale economies in the EU banking sector.

No doubt scale economies do exist at the micro level. There is evidence from the postal survey that the SMP has extended the relevant market size, particularly at the wholesale end of the market. However, the number of different products, especially those offered by the large banks, has increased in many countries. In turn this raises the overall management cost disproportionally thereby pulling in the direction of diseconomies. Consequently, the existence of scale economies is an empirical question. Unfortunately it is likely that scale economies will be influenced both by the business cycle and by the different composition of bank input and output. Given these factors it is difficult to identify a clear SMP impact.

However, the main result of the postal survey and other analyses of scale effects is that it is not bank size and synergies of joint production that are most important but the cost efficiency of the specific bank. An impression of the performance of Danish banks in this respect is given in Table 3.12, which shows recent trends in cost-income ratios for Danish and EU commercial banks between 1990 and 1994.

Table 3.12 Cost-income ratio

	1990	*1991*	*1992*	*1993*	*1994*
EU					
Commercial	70.11	70.25	68.62.	65.86	71.11
Savings banks	68.48	69.50	69.70	65.60	66.87
Denmark					
Commercial	68.44	71.28	68.76	65.17	64.93
Savings banks	69.66	69.14	66.83	61.98	63.54

4   BANK PREPARATIONS FOR EMU

4.1 The impact of EMU on the Danish banking sector

In the spring of 1997, a postal survey was carried out in which a sample of Danish financial institutions was asked to answer 14 questions in a questionnaire. The aim of the survey was to collect evidence concerning the expectations of the institutions with respect to the effects of EMU on opportunities in financial markets and the possible strategic reactions by Danish decision-makers. The main results of the postal survey are summarised and evaluated in this section. The results should be studied in the light of the 1993 Danish referendum on ratifying the Maastricht Treaty, which included a reservation concerning EMU participation. At the time when the respondents answered the questions, it was accordingly most likely that Denmark would not participate completely in EMU from the beginning. Policy statements from the Danish central bank and the Government gave the impression in the market that the authorities would maintain a stability-oriented economic policy in order to continue to meet the Maastricht convergence criteria, and that the Danish krone would participate in a close intervention arrangement with the euro from the beginning of EMU Stage 3. In fact, ERM 2 was established with effect from 1 January 1999.

Table 3.13 Extent to which the introduction of EMU is expected to increase or decrease market opportunities

	No effect	Increase		Decrease	
		Major	Minor	Minor	Major
Retail customer deposits	58		25	17	
Other retail savings products (pensions, unit trusts, etc.)	68		25	8	
Retail customer mortgages	50		50		
Retail insurance products	92		8		
Corporate customer deposits	50		33	18	
Corporate customer loans	50		42	8	
Government bond market	42	17	33	8	
Corporate bond & equity markets	33	25	42		
Fund management	42		58		
Foreign exchange	17		17	42	25
Corporate advisory such as M&A	58	8	24	8	

Note: figures are % of respondents
Source: Postal survey 1997

Danish financial institutions are used to being exposed to international competition. For decades they have operated in liberal and deregulated markets and it is therefore not surprising that the answers to Question 2 show that most of them expect EMU to have no effect, or only a minor effect, on their market opportunities (see Table 3.13). The only important

Table 3.14 Importance of certain sources of competitive advantage within the domestic market

	Long-term historical access to customer[1]	Credit risk evaluation	Customer home currency asset preference	National currency denomination[2]	Economies of Scale and Scope[3]	Product innovation and differentiation
Retail customer deposits	46	32	35	30	27	26
Other retail savings products (pensions etc.)	43	23	34	30	27	25
Retail mortgages	40	37	34	33	35	30
Retail insurance products	33	18	18	24	29	25
Corporate deposits	22	23	21	20	23	30
Corporate loans	26	30	22	23	28	35
Govt. bond market	18	14	18	16	15	25
Corporate bond & equity markets	22	29	18	20	21	29
Fund management	26	24	23	24	26	33
Foreign exchange	22	22	16	19	23	24
Corp. advisory M&A	19	26	9	13	16	24

1. Including control of branch plant and other distribution networks
2. National currency denomination which facilitates understanding of national monetary policy, etc.
3. Joint production synergies
The figures within the table are ranks given by respondents (from 1 to 5) multiplied by the number of answers for each rank.

Source: Postal survey 1997

exception to this concerns the banks' opportunities in the foreign exchange market. The majority of the Danish respondents expect a decrease of their activity in the foreign exchange market with the introduction of the euro.

Answers concerning the level to which the introduction of EMU threatens their share of the domestic market also give a fairly non-dramatic picture (Q3). Market shares for retail products are not considered, or only slightly considered, threatened by the introduction of EMU. The expected threat is somewhat greater with respect to corporate products and markets for bonds and equities.

Only a few Danish financial institutions feel that their market shares in other EU countries will be threatened by the introduction of EMU (Q4). Possible effects are expected in the markets for corporate customer deposits and loans, and in markets for bonds, equities and foreign exchange.

With respect to the effects of EMU on the respondents' markets outside the EU (Q5), an overwhelming majority answers 'no effect'.

In response to the question of where increasing competition might come from as a result of EMU, most Danish financial institutions do not expect to be exposed to increasing competition in retail banking markets (Q6). Some expect increasing competition in corporate banking, and they expect foreign banks in the EU and outside the EU to be the most important competitors. Finance companies, niche players, specialist savings and mortgage institutions, domestic and foreign insurers are not expected to become tougher competitors either in the corporate banking market or in capital markets and investment banking. In the market for foreign exchange, it is again mutual competition among banks, domestic as well as foreign, which is expected to increase as a result of EMU.

The majority of respondents do not expect to increase their merger and acquisition activity in other EU countries as a result of the introduction of EMU (Q7). Some of them, however, expect to be more active in opening subsidiaries or as partners in alliances or joint ventures. A few of them expect that EMU will stimulate their sourcing of funds in other EU countries.

The competitiveness of a financial institution in domestic markets for different products depends on a number of factors. Table 3.14 shows that Danish respondents think that long-term historical access to the customer is particularly important in markets for retail customer deposits, pension products, retail mortgages and retail insurance products (Q9). Danish retail customers can be expected to have a strong preference for using Danish financial institutions which are familiar and where several members of the staff have been known to the customers for years. Long-term experience is not nearly as important in markets for corporate financial products. In these market segments, economies of scale and scope, and product innovation and differentiation are considered to be more important to competitiveness. The respondents do not seem to consider customer home currency asset preference as particularly important in connection with competition. Retail customers are expected to prefer to have assets and liabilities denominated in domestic currency, but corporate customers are expected to be ready to have other currencies in their portfolio. Many of them have several years of experience in managing multicurrency portfolios.

The threat to the sources of competitive advantage in the domestic market by the introduction of EMU is considered to be most serious in the markets for corporate deposits and loans, and government and corporate bonds and equity (Q10). The answers give the impression that Danish financial institutions are somewhat concerned about increasing competition from big foreign institutions which can benefit from a high credit standing and economies of scale and scope.

There is a clear geographical pattern among those countries which are expected to be more aggressive following the introduction of EMU (Q11). Danish financial institutions, particularly, expect to be exposed to tougher competition from institutions with headquarters in Sweden, the UK, Germany and the Netherlands. It is from its closest neighbours that the toughest competition is expected. UK banks are expected to be the most serious competitors in markets for corporate financial products, bonds and equities, while banks in Sweden are feared the most in retail markets. New examples of cross-border collaboration among financial institutions as a consequence of EMU are expected with colleagues in the UK, Sweden and Germany in particular.

Table 3.15 shows that when the Danish respondents were asked if they would change their strategy because of the introduction of EMU, the answers with regard to retail products show that there will be no or only a slight change of strategy (Q12). In the markets for corporate products, bond and equity markets, and the foreign exchange market, strategy changes are contemplated. This pattern seems to conform with the institutions' expectations on how EMU is going to change the competitive situation in the financial system.

The Danish respondents seem to focus on improvements of service quality, product diversification, innovation and rationalisation as strategic responses to the EMU-related changes in the product areas identified in Table 3.15 (Q13). Innovations in information technology affect the channels through which different bank services are distributed. The introduction of a single currency is expected to have only a minor effect on the choice of distribution channels, in particular in internet banking, TV-screen banking, postal banking and ATM banking (Q14).

Table 3.15 Change in strategy as a result of the introduction of EMU

	No change	*Slight change*	*Significant change*
Retail customer deposits	80%	20%	
Other retail savings products (pensions, unit trusts, etc.)	73%	27%	
Retail customer mortgages	67%	33%	
Retail insurance products	91%	9%	
Corporate customer deposits	40%	20%	40%
Corporate customer loans	37%	37%	26%
Government bond market	50%	30%	20%
Corporate bond & equity markets	30%	40%	30%
Fund management	40%	30%	30%
Foreign Exchange	27%	45%	28%
Corporate advisory such as M&A	60%	10%	10%

Note: figures are % of respondents
Source: Postal survey 1997.

4.2 Scenarios for Danish participation in EMU

Denmark is one of the EU countries which, in the late 1990s, met the EMU convergence requirements but, as mentioned above, the Danish 1993 referendum includes a reservation concerning EMU participation. The Amsterdam Treaty was approved by a Danish referendum in the spring of 1998.

In the spring of 2000 the Danish Government decided to carry out a referendum on Danish participation in EMU in September 2000. If the referendum gives a majority in favour of participation, the date for the participation could very well be as late as year 2002, at the time when euro notes and coins are to be introduced into the euro countries.

4.3 Perceived barriers to EMU

The postal survey indicates that the financial institutions do not expect that the introduction of EMU will affect their activities and strategies to any appreciable extent.

We think that this evaluation is based on the assumption that EMU does not set up important barriers between the 'in' and 'out' members of EMU. According to the most expected scenario, Denmark will be among the 'outs' for at least some years and therefore it is important that the Danish financial infrastructure is prepared. For that reason, the Danish Bankers' Association has formed groups to prepare for EMU. The work in these groups is coordinated with the Danish Financial Supervisory Authority (Finanstilsynet), the central bank, and the electronic-based Danish Securities Centre (Værdipapircentralen).

The Danish economy is very open. It is expected that demand for the euro in Denmark will be substantial even in the 'out' situation, especially in the corporate sector. Therefore, the financial sector in Denmark must be prepared to operate parallel payment systems for Danish krone (DKK) and euro.

For an 'out' country it was necessary to negotiate separately the conditions for inter-country payments and securities trading. Conditions for joining both the TARGET system for international payments and the international securities trading system for 'out' countries were fixed in 1998. The Danish Bankers' Association had feared that the successful Danish Security Centre would lose a considerable part of the international transactions if the conditions for the 'out' countries were not known well before the start of EMU. Since 1 January 1999 the arrangement seems, however, to have worked satisfactorily.

4.4 Banking sector scenarios in the run-up to EMU and beyond

The answers given in the EMU postal survey of spring 1997 seem to correspond well to the SMP postal survey of 1996. Danish financial institutions have been used to being exposed to international competition for decades therefore they do not expect major revisions in their business activities and strategic reactions due to EMU. Besides, we believe that the majority of the respondents expect that the prospects of the euro will accelerate the reality of a single European banking market. Consequently, the competitive pressure on the banks is enhancing. In time this could squeeze margins further, which is why it is crucial for banks to strengthen their competitive position.

As mentioned in Section 3.1, the two largest Danish banks have followed a Nordic strategy as a response to the SMP and EMU. They see the Nordic region as their home market as do their competitors in the other Nordic countries. All the major Nordic banks are either already represented in each other's markets or are about to establish such presence.

This development has recently been supported by close cooperation between the Copenhagen and the Stockholm stock exchanges. The two exchanges have signed a contract which establishes Europe's first cross-border securities trading system (SAX 2000). The exchanges see this agreement as the first step towards the creation of an integrated Nordic securities market, therefore the other Nordic exchanges are invited to participate. The goal is to make the Nordic securities market significantly more interesting from a global point of view. It should be mentioned that the Nordic exchanges are relatively small on their own, but together they represent Europe's fifth largest market. Together they should have the opportunity to attract international investors, intermediaries and listed companies.

4 France

Dominique Plihon

The structure and operating conditions of the French banking system have undergone far-reaching changes since the mid-1980s. One of the most significant of these developments has been a transformation of shareholder structures and a gradual return of banks to the private sector. The banking industry has also been marked by liberalisation, which has been boosted by the SMP, and booming capital markets, which have contributed to greater competition against a background of slower economic growth in the early 1990s.

This new context led to a sharp decline in traditional intermediation business, which has been offset by accelerated growth of trading activities through the rapid growth of banks' securities portfolios and off-balance-sheet transactions. Another effect of liberalisation has been a steadily growing volume of international activity, both on capital markets and through the development of foreign investment.

The new environment has given rise to an unprecedented wave of financial restructuring in the world economy, an area in which continental Europe seems to have lagged behind. There is a great probability that EMU will accelerate banking restructuring, as is suggested by the aborted giant merger of three large French banks (BNP, Société Générale and Paribas) launched in March 1999, which was aimed at creating the world's largest bank in terms of balance-sheet size.

1 MARKET STRUCTURE AND PERFORMANCE

1.1 Size of the banking market

The French banking system is comprised of six groups of credit institutions:

- 359 commercial banks organised under the Companies Act 1984, including 56 branches of foreign banks
- 124 cooperative and mutual banks which belong to three major networks: Banques Populaires, Caisses Régionales de Crédit Agricole, and Caisses Fédérales de Crédit Mutuel

- 34 savings banks
- 21 municipal credit banks
- 645 financial holding companies
- 26 specialised financial institutions which are governed by special statutes and undertake operations on behalf of the State.

The total number of reporting credit institutions has sharply declined in recent years, from 2001 in 1984 to 1209 in 1998, as can be seen in Table 4.1. A large part of this reduction in the number of institutions is due either to the discontinuation of business which, in a climate of fierce competition, offered no further growth prospects, or to consolidation of institutions with similar characteristics, particularly among the savings banks network. Altogether, 688 new institutions were created since 1984, representing 57% of the total number of credit institutions at December 1998.

Table 4.1 Evolution of the number of reporting credit institutions, 1984-1998

Reporting credit institutions	*End of 1984*	*End of 1989*	*End of 1995*	*End of 1998*
Commercial banks	349	404	360	306
Subsidiaries of banks from the European Economic Area			46	53
Cooperative banks	195	176	132	124
Savings banks	468	224	35	34
Municipal credit banks	21	21	20	21
Financial holding companies	940	1 206	821	645
Specialised financial institutions	28	32	31	26
Total	2 001	2 063	1 445	1 209

Source: Banque de France: Comité des Etablissements de Crédit et des Entreprises d'Investissement

The French banking system is fairly concentrated. The largest institutions have grown bigger in recent years. The five largest institutions collected 70.1% of total deposits and supplied 46.4% of bank loans in 1998. However, the size of the largest French banks remains fairly small. There are few French banks sufficiently well capitalised to confront the major international players: in 1999, the stock market value of BNP-Paribas, the largest French bank, was smaller than that of the largest banks in other European countries. Had it been successful, the 1999 merger between BNP, Société Générale and Paribas would have created a new SBP group among the largest European players, with a stock market value of about $60 billions.

Table 4.3 Stock market value of the largest banks in European countries, July 1999 *(euro billions)*

France	*Germany*	*Netherlands*	*UK*	*Switzerland*
BNP-Paribas	Deutsche Bank	ING Group	Hongkong and Shanghai Bank	United Bank of Switzerland
34	35	50	107	66

Source: Fitch IBCA

Table 4.4 Ranking of the 12 largest European banks in own capitals, end 1998 *(euro millions)*

Banking institutions	*Nationality*	*Own capitals*	*European rank*
ING Group	Netherlands	29 077	1
Hongkong and Shanghai Bank	UK	28 488	2
BNP-Paribas	France	23 468	3
Groupe Crédit Agricole	France	22 649	4
United Bank of Switzerland	Switzerland	18 705	5
Deutsche Bank	Germany	17 922	6
Crédit Suisse Group	Switzerland	16 664	7
ABN-AMRO	Netherlands	15 393	8
BSCH	Spain	14 239	9
Bayerische Hypo und Vereinsbank	Germany	12 941	10
Rabobank Nederland	Netherlands	12 520	11
National Westminster Bank	UK	12 331	12

Source: Fitch IBCA

The ranking of European banks in 1998, according to the criterion of own capitals, shows that BNP-Paribas Group and Crédit Agricole, a mutual group, were the third and fourth largest banks.

Table 4.2 Concentration of banking operations

Percentages of total operations	Deposits					Loans				
	1992	1993	1994	1995	1998	1992	1993	1994	1995	1998
5 largest institutions	59.3	67.2	67.8	68.1	70.1	45.6	45.8	45.8	46.8	46.4
10 largest institutions	74.2	82.5	83.3	84.1	85.1	61.8	62.7	63.0	64.6	67.5
20 largest institutions	81.3	87.8	88.3	88.6	89.5	74.7	75.3	75.0	75.9	77.1

Source: Commission Bancaire

1.2 Ownership structure and privatisation

The ownership structure of the French banking system has been deeply transformed in recent years, following the three waves of privatisation which took place between 1986 and 1999, as shown by Table 4.5.

Table 4.5 Major privatisation operations in the banking sector

First wave, 1986 – 1987
Compagnie Financière de Suez
Compagnie Financière de Paribas
Crédit Commercial de France
Société Générale
Banque Industrielle et Mobilière Privée
Banque du Bâtiment et des Travaux Publics
Second wave, 1993 – 1994
Banque Nationale de Paris
Banque Worms
Third wave, 1997- 1999
Crédit Industriel et Commercial (CIC)
Banque pour l'Industrie Française (Groupe GAN)[1]
Comptoir des Entrepreneurs (Groupe AGF)[1]
AGF Banque (Groupe AGF)[1]
UAP Banque (Groupe UAP)[1]
Crédit Lyonnais

Note:[1] Indirect privatisations caused by the privatisation of the three insurance groups (GAN, AGF and UAP) to which these banks belong.
Source: Banque de France: Comité des Etablissements de Crédit et des Entreprises d'Investissement

In 1985, before the privatisation operations began, nationalised banks controlled 87% of total sight deposits. In 1998, only 25% of deposits were collected by public banking institutions. The number of banking groups under the control of French groups has reduced slightly from 208 in 1984 to 172 in 1998; and the number of banking groups belonging to the public sector dropped sharply from 124 to 9 during the same period, as indicated by Table 4.6. At the same time, the number of family-owned institutions also declined from 34 in 1984 to 13 in 1998. This highlights another major change in the French banking system, which is now dominated by large groups at the expense of small banks whose family shareholders do not have the resources to ensure a durable presence and a robust growth.

Table 4.6 Evolution of the ownership of French banking groups

Type of banking group	No. of banks 1984	No. of banks 1998	Evolution 1984-1998
Public banking groups	112	8	-104
Private banking groups	0	53	+53
Mutual banking groups	5	48	+43
Subsidiaries of specialised financial institutions	2	2	0
Insurance groups	10	9	-1
Banks belonging to industrial groups	18	25	+7
Diversified financial groups	9	3	-6
Independent ownership	34	13	-21
Other	18	11	-7
Total	208	172	-36
(of which public sector)	124	9	-115

Source: Banque de France: Comité des Etablissements de Crédit et des Entreprises d'Investissement

The growing influence of large banks has gone hand in hand with the strengthening of mutual and cooperative groups: the number of banks belonging to mutual groups has risen from 5 in 1984 to 48 in 1998. In addition to growing, mutual groups have also taken an active part in the reshaping of the French banking system in recent years. Crédit Agricole acquired Indosuez in 1997 and Crédit Mutuel took over the CIC group when the latter was privatised in 1998. The banques populaires have also taken successive stakes in Natexis (as seen in Table 4.9).

Another major feature of the transformation in the French banking system is greater openness. The number of foreign-owned banks rose from 140 in 1984 to 187 in 1998. This openness is a direct result of the liberalisation of a long protected system which is now subject to competition and is attracting a growing number of foreign operators. Lastly, the principles of freedom of establishment and the free provision of services within the EU, set out in the Second Banking Coordination Directive of December 1989, have established a legal foundation for the single banking market which officially came into existence on 1 January 1993.

1.3 Competition

The modernisation and liberalisation of financial markets since the mid-1980s have fostered competition from non-banks (investment funds and insurance companies) and the markets. Many administrative barriers that compartmentalised banking business in Europe have been lifted or eased since transposition of the European Directive of 24 June 1988 on the liberalisation of capital movements (88/361/EEC).

The effects on traditional banking intermediation have been keenly felt, leading to disintermediation of credit and capital and the 'marketisation' of bank financing. French banks have experienced increasing competition from two sides: first, direct finance supplied by the markets to firms has reduced the financing share of banks; second, non-bank financial institutions are playing a greater role in financing the economy. The intermediation role of banks has declined strongly since the beginning of the 1990s, as shown by Table 4.7. This decline in the intermediation share of banks has been compensated by the development of financial intermediation by mutual funds and insurance companies, maintaining the global intermediation ratio in the French economy around 60%.

Table 4.7 Evolution of the financial intermediation ratio, 1986-1997 *(percentage rates of total financing flows)*

	1986	1990	1992	1994	1995	1996	1997
Total intermediation ratio[1]	58.5	66.9	53.1	34.8	54.9	39.8	56.3
Banks	45.1	58.4	36.6	5.7	33.6	9.6	37.0
Mutual funds	7.7	5.1	9.4	15.2	9.8	11.9	8.2
Insurance companies	5.7	3.4	7.1	13.9	11.5	11.1	11.1

Note: [1] financing by the three groups of institutions/total financing.
Source: Banque de France: Conseil National du Crédit

2 REGULATORY FRAMEWORK

2.1 The French Banking Act 1984

The French banking system is regulated by the French Banking Act of 1984. Under this Act, authorisation as a credit institution is required for a broad range of operations: deposit-taking, loans, guarantees, or payment services. In order to ensure fair competition among the providers of these various services, the French Banking Act gives an extensive definition of banking operations and of credit institutions. It also lays down a common set of requirements for their organisation and operation.

As in all the countries of the EU, and in accordance with the principles of the first two Directives on Banking Coordination, credit institutions need an authorisation from the French banking authorities before starting operations in France, unless they are incorporated and authorised in another Member State. Authorisation is granted by the Credit Institutions and Investment Firms Commission (CECEI) after examination of the quality of the shareholders, the fitness and properness of the managers, the quality of the proposed organisation and business plan, and is conditional upon the institution having sufficient paid-up capital and being in an appropriate legal form.

Authorised credit institutions may carry out in France any banking and financial operations which are permitted within the category to which the institution belongs. They are subject to special requirements regarding their accounts and the operational standards to which they must adhere. They must also comply with the compulsory reserve requirements laid down by the Monetary Policy Council of the Banque de France. Credit institutions are subject to ongoing supervision and, for that purpose, have to submit periodic reports. They are also subject, from time to time, to on-site supervision by Banque de France inspectors acting on behalf of the Commission Bancaire, which is in charge of the supervision of credit institutions.

2.2 The Financial Activity Modernisation Act 1996

This Act is the transposition into French law of EC Investment Services Directive 93/22 relating to investment services in the securities field. The Act defines the activities linked to securities transactions, creates a single status for financial intermediaries, changes the organisation of the markets, and reforms the authorities in charge of supervision of financial activities.

According to the Act, investment services may only be provided by particular intermediaries (investment service providers) which may be either investment firms or credit institutions that have an authorisation to provide investment services. Whatever the applicant, the granting of authorisation is subject to conditions concerning minimum capital, the fitness and properness of the senior managers, legal identity, and the quality of the shareholders. These players are under the supervision of the Financial Markets Council and the Commission des Opérations de Bourse (COB or Stock Exchange Committee).

The first list published in December 1996 contained 964 investment service providers, including 140 investment firms and 637 credit institutions providing investment services out of a total of 1273 authorised credit institutions (see Table 4.1).

3   IMPACT OF THE SMP

3.1 Mergers, acquisitions and alliances

The SMP had a stimulating effect on the restructuring of European banking sectors. It induced cross-border operations of two types. First, agreements and alliances have taken place between European banking groups. Second, mergers and acquisitions have also taken place at an increasing rate: such operations amounted to 52 in 1985 and to 238 in 1990. If one takes into account both types of operations, 803 operations took place between 1991 and 1995 for a total amount of about $25 billions, as indicated in Table 4.8. Four countries have been particularly active in these cross-border banking operations: the UK, Germany, France and the Netherlands.

Table 4.8 Cross-border banking mergers, acquisitions and alliances in the European single market, 1991-1995

	Buying operations		Selling operations	
	Number of operations	*Millions of dollars*	*Number of operations*	*Millions of dollars*
France	162	4 379	91	1 371
Belgium	22	1 161	23	1 580
Germany	117	5 326	40	1 718
Italy	81	2 247	91	1 193
Netherlands	100	4 337	18	748
Portugal	9	470	27	602
Spain	48	2 033	69	3 451
UK	181	4 177	132	16 327
Other	83	1 542	61	2 943
Total	803	25 392	552	29 933

Source: KPMG, European Countries Investing Abroad, Banking & Finance, 1991-1995

In France, as in most European countries, the major restructuring operations took place at the domestic level (see Table 4.9)

Table 4.9 Major restructuring operations in the French banking sector, 1992-1999

Type of operations	Year	Institutions concerned
M&As between French institutions	1995	Creation of Natexis following a merger between Crédit National and BFCE
	1996	Acquisition of Indosuez bank by Crédit Agricole
		Creation of the Banque de Développement des PME (BDPME) following a merger between CGPME and SOFARIS
	1997	60% takeover of Société Générale by Crédit du Nord
		Acquisition of Compagnie Bancaire by Paribas
		LMBO of banques populaires by Natexis
	1998	Acquisition of CIC (privatised by Crédit Mutuel)
		Acquisition of Sofinco from the Suez-Lyonnaise des Eaux group by Crédit Agricole
	1999	Merger between BNP and Paribas
Cross-border operations	1996	Merger of Crédit Local de France and Crédit Communal de Belgique to constitute the Dexia group
		Alliance BNP/ Dresdner bank
Takeover by foreign banks	1992	Européenne de Banque by Barclays
	1993	Caisse Centrale de Réescompte by Commerzbank
	1995	Sovac by General Electric
	1996	Banque Veuve Morin-Pons by San Paolo
Operations between insurance companies	1996	Acquisition of UAP by Axa
	1997	LMBO of Allianz by AGF

Source: D. Plihon, 1998, 'Les banques: nouveaux enjeux, nouvelles stratégies', Documentation Française

3.2 Internationalisation

Traditionally, the international activity of French banks is very important. In recent years the three main components of international banking grew markedly:

• the share of bank operations with non-resident players tripled since 1988 due to the liberalisation of exchange rate controls in the late 1980s as a result of the SMP

• the share of foreign currency operations/total balance-sheet is now well above 20% on average for all reporting banking institutions

• subsidiaries of French banks located abroad increased strongly during the last decade.

The internationalisation rate of banking activity, which takes into account the evolution of the three components just mentioned, rose sharply from 32.5% in 1988 to 48% to 1997, as shown in Table 4.10.

Table 4.10 Internationalisation rate of reporting banking institutions, 1988-1997 *(% average share in international activity/total activity)*

Percentage rates	1988	1990	1992	1994	1996	1997
Metropolitan activity: (a) in francs with non-residents[1]	2.2	3.4	5.0	5.5	6.0	6.4
(b) in foreign currencies[2]	17.7	18.1	18.8	19.8	20.0	23.4
Activity of subsidiaries abroad[3]	12.6	12.9	16.1	14.3	16.2	18.2
Internationalisation rate: [1] + [2] + [3]	32.5	34.4	39.9	38.6	42.2	48.0

Source: Commission Bancaire, annual reports

At the end of 1997, French banks controlled 464 subsidiaries abroad, about half of which were located in the European Economic Area (EEA). Their number increased strongly thanks to the SMP. As a result, French banks made important foreign direct investment in the 1990s, a large part of which is going to the EEA, as can be seen in Table 4.11.

Table 4.11   Foreign direct investments by French banks, 1992 and 1997
(*assets in FFR billions*)

	1992	*1997*
Germany	7 717	15 749
UK	7 687	8 688
Italy	4 094	3 165
Spain	5 613	7 391
Netherlands	7 717	2 445
Belgium	n.d.	809
Other EU countries	5 982	17 443
Total EU countries	38 810	55 670
US	6 218	28 141
Japan	819	1 773
Other countries	26 930	44 161
Total	72 777	129 745

Source: Comité des Etablissements de Crédit et des Entreprises d'Investissements
   (CECEI), 1997 annual report

The French banking system plays a very active role in the
international banking system. This can be seen in Table 4.12, which shows
the importance of the portfolio of international assets held by French
banks, which was fourth in the world at the end of 1998 after Japan,
Germany and the US.

Table 4.12   International assets held by banks of major industrial
countries, end-1998

Country	*$billions*	*Percentage share*
Japan	1 823.2	18.7
Germany	1 792.1	18.4
US	1 025.9	10.5
France	*1 017.5*	*10.5*
Switzerland	887.6	9.1
UK	548.0	5.6
Italy	475.4	4.1
Other banks	2 166.9	22.3
Total	9 736.7	100.0

Source: Banque de France, annual report on the balance of payments

Table 4.15 Evolution of the number of employees, 1986-1998

	Number of employees		Structure in %	Evolution 1986-1998	
	1986	1998	1998	Number of employees	%
Commercial banks	254 409	224 000	54.4	-30 409	-11.9
Mutuals and cooperative banks	118 111	121 985	31.0	+3 874	+3.3
Savings banks	27 162	36 336	8.8	+9 174	+33.8
Municipal credit banks	1 035	1 200	0.3	+165	+15.9
Specialised financial institutions	11 422	6 200	1.5	-5 222	-45.7
Financial companies	19 500	21 800	5.3	+2 300	+11.8
Total	431 639	411 521	100.0	-20 118	-4.7

Source: Comité des Etablissements de Crédit et des Entreprises d'Investissement (CECEI)

Table 4.16 Productivity indicators: all reporting credit institutions, 1990-1997

Millions of francs	1990	1991	1992	1993	1994	1995	1996	1997	1990/97 (%)
Deposits/employee	10.4	9.7	10.0	9.6	10.0	11.3	12.1	13.2	+ 26.9
Loans/employee	12.9	15.0	14.8	15.0	14.8	15.6	15.8	16.5	+ 27.9
Total balance sheet/employee	33.8	39.2	39.6	40.8	42.0	46.0	49.8	54.0	+ 59.8
Gross income/employee	0.73	0.84	0.86	0.94	0.88	0.90	0.94	1.0	+ 41.0

Source: Commission Bancaire: Analyses Comparatives, Tome 2

3.3 Costs and revenues

French commercial banks exhibit the highest cost-income ratios among the major industrial countries. Furthermore, the cost-income ratio has been increasing from 1988 to 1997, as is shown in Table 4.13. Staff costs are largely responsible for this bad result. It is noticeable, however, that the ratio of operating expenses to total assets is lower in France than in the US, the UK and Germany.

Table 4.13 Evolution of commercial banks' operating expenses in major industrial countries, 1988-1997

	% of gross income			*% of average balance sheet total*		
	1988	*1992*	*1997*	*1988*	*1992*	*1997*
US						
Operating expenses	65.7	64.8	60.8	3.4	3.9	3.6
(of which staff costs)	30.5	27.1	25.7	1.6	1.6	1.5
Japan						
Operating expenses	56.0	70.1	71.2	0.9	0.9	1.0
(of which staff costs)	31.3	36.6	35.8	0.5	0.5	0.5
Germany						
Operating expenses	69.2	63.7	66.6	2.2	2.0	1.6
(of which staff costs)	45.0	39.6	37.6	1.4	1.3	0.9
UK						
Operating expenses	65.2	66.1	60.3	3.3	3.0	2.1
(of which staff costs)	38.3	36.1	32.5	2.0	1.7	1.1
France						
Operating expenses	73.0	72.5	74.8	1.8	1.6	1.1
(of which staff costs)	44.1	41.6	43.2	1.1	0.9	0.7

Source: OECD

The cost-income structure is different in the three major bank networks in France. Table 4.14 shows that the best results are obtained by the mutuals and cooperative banks which have the lowest cost-income ratio. The number of employees in the banking sector, which amounts to 2% of the active population, has shown a 4.7% decrease from 1986 to 1998. This decline in the level of employment concerned commercial banks and specialised financial institutions, while the number of employees increased in other networks, as shown in Table 4.15. Since

1990, the French banking sector has experienced a significant increase in apparent labour productivity measured by ratios using different definitions of bank output, as seen in Table 4.16.

Table 4.14 Structure of cost and income in the three main French bank networks, 1988-1997 (*% of gross income*)

	1988	*1990*	*1992*	*1994*	*1997*
Commercial banks					
Interest income	79.5	74.8	53.8	52.0	37.2
Non interest income	20.5	25.2	46.2	48.0	62.8
Operating expenses	73.0	77.9	72.5	79.9	74.8
Provisions (net)	12.2	11.9	24.6	26.4	17.6
Mutual and cooperative banks					
Interest income	90.8	88.5	85.8	71.5	55.5
Non interest income	9.2	11.5	14.4	28.5	44.5
Operating expenses	76.0	73.8	68.8	67.7	66.1
Provisions (net)	10.6	13.9	16.3	18.7	12.6
Savings banks					
Interest income	76.7	86.0	84.7	80.2	71.6
Non interest income	23.3	14.0	15.3	19.8	28.4
Operating expenses	79.2	82.2	77.1	88.5	82.7
Provisions (net)	6.1	3.9	8.9	4.9	6.0

Source: OECD

3.4 Prices, margins and returns

French banks have been characterised by low returns on equity (ROE) during the 1990s, compared to returns obtained by banks in other industrial countries, as is shown by data in Table 4.17. From 1992 to 1997, the average ROE of large French international banks has been as low as 4.9%, while the average ROE of US and UK banks exceeded 16%. There are two main causes for the low ROE ratios of French banks. First, as we have seen, French banks experienced high cost-income ratios relative to banks in other industrial countries. Second, as is indicated in Table 4.18, the operating margins of French banks have declined sharply since the mid-1980s.

Unlike their foreign competitors, particularly the Anglo-Saxon banks, French institutions suffer from inadequate profitability on their domestic lending activities. This is due to fierce competition among French banks which leads to excessively low lending rates charged by banks to their customers. This situation is worsened by the fact that French banks do not charge as much for banking services, in the form of commissions, as their foreign counterparts.

Table 4.17 Return on equity (%) of large international banks[1] in industrial countries, 1992-1997

	1992	*1993*	*1994*	*1995*	*1996*	*1997*	*Average 1992–97*
US	20.2	15.6	14.9	15.6	15.7	15.6	16.3
UK	8.7	13.9	21.3	9.6	20.2	19.5	17.2
Germany	8.4	8.8	7.2	8.4	9.3	7.6	8.3
France	4.6	2.4	1.4	4.0	7.6	9.6	4.9
Japan	3.2	2.2	-1.3	-2.0	0.6	-13.5	-1.8
Spain	12.4	12.5	11.6	11.4	11.7	14.2	12.3
Italy	3.7	4.1	1.8	2.7	2.4	-1.7	2.1
Switzerland	8.4	11.9	7.3	6.6	-2.3	2.8	5.8

Note: [1]Five largest banking groups in each country
Source: Bankscope: Commission Bancaire

Table 4.19 Global operating margins of commercial banks: an international comparison, 1988-1997 (*% of total balance sheet*)

	France	*Japan*	*US*	*UK*	*Germany*
1988	2.0	1.17	3.54	3.25	2.19
1989	1.67	1.00	3.51	3.14	2.04
1990	1.57	0.90	3.46	2.95	2.04
1991	1.43	1.11	3.62	2.97	2.16
1992	1.16	1.26	3.89	2.62	2.21
1993	0.93	1.25	3.90	2.45	2.18
1994	0.89	1.33	3.78	2.34	2.18
1995	0.80	1.45	3.72	2.32	1.98
1996	0.70	1.50	3.73	2.20	1.83
1997	0.56	1.31	3.67	2.20	1.83

Source: OECD

As a result of these unfavourable factors, the global operating margin of French commercial banks has been the lowest among major industrial countries since 1992, as illustrated in Table 4.19.

Table 4.18 Evolution of commercial banks' operating margins, 1984-1997 (average apparent interest rates in %)

	1984	1986	1988	1990	1992	1994	1996	1997
Customer operations								
Average return on customer lending	12.8	10.8	10.0	10.6	10.5	8.2	7.5	7.3
Average cost of customer funds	6.2	4.1	3.8	4.5	4.5	4.9	4.2	3.7
Margin	6.6	6.7	6.2	6.1	6.0	3.3	3.3	3.9
Interbank operations								
Average return on loans	10.5	7.4	7.5	9.4	7.8	6.8	6.1	6.0
Average cost of borrowed funds	10.0	7.2	7.4	9.6	8.3	6.5	5.9	5.8
Margin	0.5	0.2	0.1	-0.2	-0.5	0.3	0.2	0.2
Operations on financial market								
Average return on portfolio	n.d.	n.d.	12.2	9.8	8.3	3.5	6.8	6.1
Average cost of financial funds	12.6	7.9	7.8	8.2	9.3	6.7	6.5	7.2
Margin	n.d.	n.d.	4.4	1.6	-1.0	-3.2	0.3	-1.1
All operations								
(a) Average return on assets	11.6	8.8	9.8	10.0	9.2	6.7	6.7	n.d.
(b) Average cost of liabilities	9.0	6.3	7.4	8.2	7.7	5.9	5.4	n.d.
(a)-(b) Global operating margin	2.6	2.5	2.4	1.8	1.5	0.8	1.3	n.d.

Source: Average rates computed from Commission Bancaire data

However, the decline in the interest margin of French banks has been accompanied by a change in the structure of bank income due to a sharp increase in non-interest income, the share of which went from 20.5% in 1988 to 62.8 % in 1997 for commercial banks, as is shown in Table 4.14. In particular, income from international operations and from trading (off-balance sheet transactions and securities transactions) has risen strongly in recent years.

4 BANK PREPARATIONS FOR EMU

4.1 Individual banks' preparations

Banks prepared themselves actively for the single currency. Most institutions created committees in charge of coordinating euro programmes. The changeover to the euro has a high cost for banks. First, banks will forego income derived from intra-European currency foreign exchange transactions: this decrease in income is estimated at about 3% of gross income. Second, banks will incur extra expenses directly linked to the preparation for the euro, estimated at FRF20 billions, which represent about 2% of operating expenses. The principal sources of these extra costs are in information systems (55%), marketing and public relations (16%), and employee training (9%).

Table 4.20 Euro preparation costs for major French banks (*FFR billions*)

BNP	1.5
Crédit Lyonnais	1-1.5
Société Générale	1
Banques Populaires	1.8
CCF	0.25
Européenne de CIC	0.2
Banque Française de Crédit Coopératif	0.03-0.04

Source: A.F.B.

4.2 The Paris financial centre

A Banking and Financial Working Group on the Changeover to the Euro was created at the beginning of 1995 under the aegis of the Banque de France to coordinate and monitor the preparations of the banking and financial community. It comprised representatives from the main French financial institutions, their trade associations, the French Treasury and market executive bodies such as MATIF SA, the futures and options exchange, and the market's business arm, la Société des Bourses Françaises (SBF).

Discussions conducted with representatives of the banking and financial community within the Working Group resulted in the publication of a plan for the banking and financial community on 3 March 1997. This plan defined the general principles regarding the transition to the euro for the institutions in the financial centre and identified the key strategic issues and the main tasks that the banking and financial community had to deal with before introducing the single currency. It was based on the legal framework for the euro as defined by the two draft community regulations presented at the European Council meeting in Dublin in December 1996. It also adopted the European Monetary Institute's conclusions on the organisation of the single monetary policy. The report analysed the impact the changeover would have on relations between the central bank, the Treasury, credit institutions and their customers with respect to each type of market, whether foreign exchange, futures or equity markets.

The Working Group also published the technical terms of reference for the operational aspects of the investment programmes that are necessary for the Paris financial centre in order to make a successful transition to the euro. These documents give a detailed definition of the practical terms and conditions for setting up this programme.

The Paris financial centre has made the following decisions:

- all financial markets (foreign exchange, futures, interest rate and equity markets) will switch to the euro when the Monetary Union is implemented on 1 January 1999
- all inter-bank large value payment and settlement systems (TBF, SNP) will also make the changeover on 1 January 1999, as will the delivery/payment systems (RELIT, RGV) and the clearing houses of the SBF and of MATIF SA.
- the operating principles of the other payment systems during the transition period preceding the introduction of euro-denominated banknotes and coins, and the overall changeover of the public to the euro have been established. These principles will allow credit institutions in the Paris financial centre to meet the demand for means of payment in euro, mainly from business.

4.3 Continuation of the work of the banking and financial community

After the plan for the banking and financial community was published in March 1997, work continued on three main issues:

- the follow-up of the planning and technical constraints related to the implementation of TBF, which is France's access to the TARGET system
- the definition of a very detailed plan for the changeover weekend at the end of 1998
- preliminary reflections on the end of the transition period and the widespread introduction of the euro among the general public in the course of the overall changeover of accounts and banknotes and coins into euro.

Important decisions were taken by the various bodies involved, in particular in the following fields :

- credit institutions decided to create specific euro cheques
- the stock of existing public debt denominated in French francs will be converted into euro.

5   CONCLUSIONS

Like many of its European counterparts, the French banking system is currently in a transition phase affecting both its business conditions and its structures. Over the last few years, French credit institutions have sought to compensate for deteriorating margins on domestic intermediation business by diversifying their sources of revenues. They have looked to two main sources of new growth: trading transactions on financial markets and international business. Recent difficulties, such as the financial crisis in emerging countries and roller-coaster stock markets, have induced banks to develop and refine their risk-management methods, especially by tightening up internal controls.

The pace of concentration and restructuring in the French banking sector has accelerated since the mid-1990s. However, the French banking system has been lagging behind banking systems of the major industrial countries for two main reasons. First, French banks are less profitable and have lower stock market capitalisation than their European counterparts. Not only is their capacity to acquire other institutions limited as a result, but they also become potential takeover targets themselves. Second, the present degree of concentration, which puts the French banking system in the middle of the range, limits the scope for major concentrations. One of the distinctive features of the French banking system is the number of medium-sized banks.

Despite these forces of inertia, however, French banks have embarked on a genuine restructuring process, in particular with a view to the introduction of a European single currency. The attempt to merge three large French banks, BNP, Société Générale and Paribas in March 1999, with a view to create the largest bank in the world by the size of its balance sheet, is an illustration of this deep transformation.

5 Germany

Günter Lang

1 MARKET STRUCTURE AND PERFORMANCE

1.1 Size and concentration

When analysing the German banking industry, the first striking feature is its more than proportional weight within the EU banking market. This can be illustrated by the following figures: 22% of the EU population currently live in Germany but have an income share of about 25%; the total assets of the credit institutions add up to more than 27% of EU value. The greatest difference lies in the number of banks, with 39% of all EU institutions being German banks. One of the most important properties of the German market, its fragmentation, can be seen from the last mentioned figure.

Table 5.1 Size of the German banking market, 1985-1998 (*figures since 1990 include Eastern Germany*)

	1985	*1990*	*1995*	*1998*
Number of banks	4740	4720	3785	3403
Commercial	245	332	332	327
Savings	590	769	624	594
Cooperative	3655	3042	2591	2249
Number of branches	39925	44345	48224	45227
Number of branches per 1000 capita	0.61	0.63	0.59	0.55
Assets as percentage of GDP	*185%*	*220%*	*223%*	*256%**

Note: *Figure for 1997
Source: Deutsche Bundesbank

Table 5.1 gives some details of the size and structural changes in the German market. Obviously, a significant decline in the number of independent institutions has occurred since 1990, which was mainly driven by cooperative banks and savings banks mergers. More than 1500 mergers could be observed between cooperative banks alone since 1985.

Surprisingly, bankruptcies of credit institutions are totally irrelevant to this concentration process. Because the reduction in the number of banks was partly offset by an increase in the branching network, the total number of banking offices in 1998 is about the same as in 1990. Compared to other EC member countries, the network of bank branches is relatively intense and often cited as the main reason for an 'overbanked' Germany.

In spite of the impressive merger wave, the German banking market is showing the lowest concentration level within the EU. In particular, the three largest credit institutions represent just 16% of total assets, slightly up from 12% in 1990. By comparison, the mean value of the five-firm ratio (CR-5) within the EU stands at 53%, with a negative correlation between country size and concentration (ECB 1999, pp. 23 f.). Interestingly, although the commission business does not find its expression in the value of assets, there is no significant difference in calculating market shares by total assets and revenues respectively. Details about the latest market shares are given in Figure 5.1.

Figure 5.1 Market shares by revenues and assets, 1998

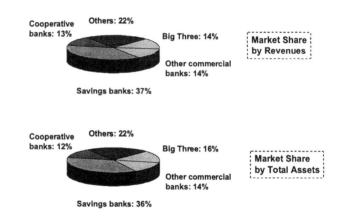

Note: Savings banks and cooperative banks include head organisations. Revenues calculated as interest plus commission revenues
Source: Deutsche Bundesbank

As far as the ownership structure of banking firms is concerned, commercial banks as well as cooperative banks are privately owned, while savings banks and some of the 'other banks' are state owned. Traditionally, savings banks play a dominant role in urban areas, whereas cooperative banks are strong in rural regions. In contrast to Italy and France, there is no serious discussion about privatising savings banks.

Another important feature of the German banking system is the widespread principle of universal banking. With the exception of 'other banks' in Figure 5.1, the market consists of universal banks. Even small cooperative banks are offering a broad spectrum of products, ranging from retail and wholesale banking to commission business like brokerage or the supplying of insurance contracts. Many commercial banks, as well as the head organisations of savings banks and cooperative banks are furthermore engaged in investment banking. These head organisations consist of banks at the state or at the federal level ('Landesbanken' or cooperative central banks) as well associations of member firms. The associations are entrusted with tasks in the field of supervision, deposit insurance and representation of interests.

Finally, when considering the market share of foreign banks, their role seems to be marginal one. There are about 150 branches and subsidiaries of foreign institutions in Germany and these cover a market share of just 4.4%. This figure clearly underestimates the competitive pressure from abroad, however. For example, foreign banks in London and Luxembourg play an important, if not dominant, role in some fields of off-balance sheet activities. Furthermore, because of relatively high income tax rates, considerable amounts of privately owned fortune may be hidden in foreign bank accounts outside Germany.

1.2 Economies of scale and scope

When discussing the structure of the banking sector, the technological characteristics of this sector play an important role. Optimal firm size is particularly at the core of interest. For example, if a main impact of the SMP is an increase of competitive pressure, and if there are economies of scale, then mergers and acquisitions are a suitable strategy to reduce costs by exploiting size advantages. However, if the optimal size of a credit institution is relatively small, the conclusion would be that no cost incentive for external growth exists.

Unlike in the US and in some other European countries, however, there are only a few empirical papers dealing with this question in Germany (see Berger and Humphrey (1997) for an overview). Important exceptions are Economic Research Europe's *Single Market Review* (1997), where some estimations can be found, and the papers of Altunbas and Molyneux (1996), Lang and Welzel (1998), or Schure and Wagenvoort (1999). As a general result of these studies, the existence of scale economies finds strong support, with some differences about the threshold from which diseconomies can be expected.

To be more specific: the concept of ray scale elasticity (RSCE) can be used for evaluating the relationship between size and costs. This popular measure tells us by which percentage total costs of a bank are increasing if all output quantities are growing by one per cent. Figure 5.2 provides condensed information on the measure RSCE from the estimations of Lang and Welzel (1998), which are based on a representative sample from about 1500 German banks.

Figure 5.2 Ray scale elasticity (RSCE) by bank size

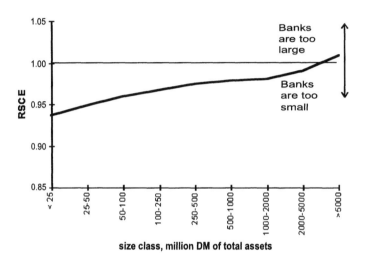

size class, million DM of total assets

Note: Scale economies calculated at mean size for each size class: scale economies
        are evident if RSCE takes a value of less then one
Source: Lang and Welzel (1998)

The number of observed outputs per firm is five. From this figure we see that economies of scale diminish with increasing size and that banks in the largest class already face moderate diseconomies. These results, therefore, indicate an average cost curve with an optimal size of a German bank somewhere in the range of DM2 to DM5 billion of total assets. This is considerably higher than the threshold usually identified with US data, which is probably mainly due to differences in the regulatory environment. At the same time this optimal size is lower than other studies using European data tend to find (Altunbas and Molyneux, 1996; ERE, 1997).

The recent paper of Schure and Wagenvoort (1999) confirms the results from Lang and Welzel, however. Furthermore, there is strong evidence in favour of an L-shaped average cost curve: being too large is not as costly as being too small.

Apart from economies of scale, the question of economies of scope also arises. This is of special interest for the German market because its domestic banks traditionally are universal banks with a broad output spectrum. It is not immediately clear, however, if there is a cost advantage in comparison to specialised institutions. In many other countries brokerage business as well as investment banking business is separated from retail and wholesale banking. Therefore, the cost relationship between the (core) intermediation business and the commission business has to be evaluated.

To measure existence and intensity of economies of scope, the Kolari and Zardkoohi (1987) indicator (MSCOPE) can be employed. This compares a large bank with a small bank. MSCOPE then compares the cost effects from two alternative strategies: expansion of all outputs of the small bank according to the proportions suggested by the output structure of the large bank or, secondly, expansion only of the intermediation or the commission business. MSCOPE gives the percentage cost difference between both growth strategies, with positive values indicating a cost advantage from expanding the whole product range. In contrast, negative values point towards diseconomies of scope because in this case a specialised expansion would improve the cost situation.

Interestingly, the empirical estimations do not support the German universal banking system. As can be seen from Figure 5.3, which provides information on whether or not there are economies of joint production between the intermediation and the commission business, only small banks can realise a cost advantage. As for larger banks, they suffer from cost neutrality or even a cost disadvantage. Therefore, by only viewing the cost side, a split into two units (retail and wholesale banking versus a commission unit) should not be hindered. More favourable are the estimations for the cost relationship between the different intermediation outputs, where significant economies of scope have been found (see, for example, ERE, 1997, pp. 88ff.).

Finally, before turning to the competitive conditions within the German banking market, it should be noted that economies of scope might also arise from an output diversification effect, as well as from additional customers who enjoy an advantage from being served with several products at one bank. This allows universal banks to extract some of the additional consumer surplus by charging higher fees (see Berger *et al.*,

1987, pp. 504-5). Traditional cost or production functions are not able to capture these factors, however.

Figure 5.3 Economies of scope by bank size

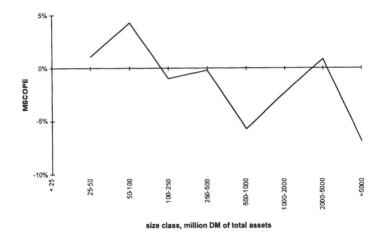

Note: Economies of scope evaluated at mean size for each size class. Positive values indicate a cost advantage of a parallel expansion of the interest and the non-interest business.
Source: Lang and Welzel (1998)

1.3 Competition

Characterising type and intensity of competition is a difficult task, and no general answer to this problem should be expected. Some important landmarks of the competitive situation can be clearly fixed, however. First of all, as will be described in further detail later, the regulatory framework of the German banking sector was never as restrictive as it was in some other member countries of the EU. For example, freedom of establishment and the market mechanism for deposit and loan rates was introduced earlier than in many other member countries (see EC 1997, p. 12, for an overview). Secondly, competition within the savings banks group and within the cooperative banks group is negligible because their head organisations enforce a regional demarcation. A third aspect which should be mentioned is the spatial distribution of the commercial banks, which have concentrated their network of branches in urban areas. As far as the retail banking segment is concerned, competition could therefore be more intense in the cities than in rural regions. And fourthly, as for competition for deposits, life insurance companies are by far the most important non-bank rivals. This can be explained by a discriminating income tax system which gives strong incentives to individuals for signing a capital-based life insurance contract. Actually, about 65% of all German households have signed at least one contract of this kind. More than 30% of all monetary assets are entrusted to insurance companies (Statistisches Bundesamt, 1999).

Taking a more sophisticated point of view, some theory-based work has been done on the German banking industry. Lang (1996), for example, has tested the efficiency hypothesis, which argues that profitability differences between firms can be explained by cost differences. Market prices are assumed as exogenous with this hypothesis. Furthermore, from a dynamic point of view, a market share erosion of the relatively inefficient (high cost) firms can be expected. However, the results indicate only limited support for the efficiency hypothesis, with an exception being the small cooperative banks. For these banks, efficiency differences explain up to 37% of the profitability variance, whereas for credit banks and savings banks R^2-values of less than 10% are measured. The relationship between efficiency and market share tends to be even weaker. On the other hand, the assumption of a monopoly or a perfect collusive behaviour has also been rejected (Lang, 1997; Molyneux *et al.*, 1994).

Putting all these results together, the market imperfection of the finance sector is confirmed. Although far from a monopoly, product differentiation and transaction costs either allow for the existence of inefficiency or (in a few cases) for high profits. However, because of improved information technology, at least for standard products of the banking industry, a move towards intense competition has started. The establishment of low cost direct banks without any branch network is strengthening this trend. As a possible exception, banks may be able to maintain high prices for complex products which have to be explained to the customers.

1.4 Banking performance

As mentioned earlier, German banks were in general not able to translate the existing degree of market imperfection into higher profits. It is, in fact, low profitability which is a main issue in the current strategic debate (*Economist*, 1999a, pp. 14f.). Whereas UK or US banks are achieving a return on equity (ROE) of more than 20%, German banks can realise only a modest 12%. Turning to the return of assets (ROA), the relative position of German banks has only slightly improved. Figure 5.4 indicates that the

German ROA was above the EC average before 1996, but dived below the EC level during the last two years. This trend was even more pronounced for the largest three banks, for which the ROA has halved since 1993.

Figure 5.4 Return on assets, 1993-1998

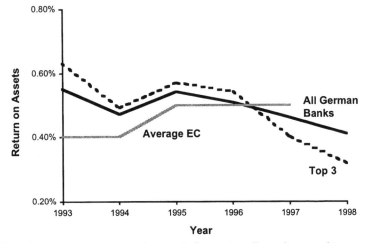

Note: Return on assets = net income before extraordinary items and taxes as percentage of total assets.
Source: Deutsche Bundesbank *and* ECB 1999.

What are the reasons for the low profitability of the German banking sector? Clearly, as will be discussed in more detail later, competitive pressures have increased, resulting in negative consequences especially for interest margins. As the Deutsche Bundesbank additionally stresses, however, income statements are indicating a sharp increase in the cost of data processing. In 1998 only 56% of the overhead (non-interest) costs stemmed from wages, compared to about 70% in 1980. This trend occurred mainly due to high expenditures for information technology. As a result, the overhead costs per unit of total assets could be reduced only slightly, and this reduction was by far overcompensated from the declining interest rate margin.

2   REGULATORY FRAMEWORK

2.1 Regulatory framework prior to SMP

Traditionally, the banking industry differs substantially from other industries with regard to public policy. The main reason for this is the fear of bank runs (systemic risk) as well as a need to protect depositors. From the perspective of the market failure literature, these negative effects are driven by asymmetric information between the management of the firm and the depositors (see Neuberger (1998) for an overview on the microeconomic theory of banking and its empirical verification).

Post-war regulation of the German banking industry can be differentiated into three phases:

- transition from a state-based to a federal regulation system, coupled with important steps towards deregulation
- tightening of the control mechanism and expansion of the deposit insurance as a consequence of the Herstatt bankruptcy in 1974
- and, starting with the implementation of the consolidation surveillance into German law in 1984, a series of reforms towards a single European banking market.

When trying to characterise the regulation framework prior to the SMP, it can be defined as liberal with respect to some important items.

First of all, price regulations like ceiling interest rates on deposits (such as Regulation Q in the US) are nonexistent. This is partly a consequence of free cross-border capital movements which had put the Deutschmark currency area into direct competition with other currency areas. A second important feature is the nonexistent separation of commercial from investment banking and the absence of geographical restrictions. Instead, public policy has focused on regulating bank entry, introducing an internal control mechanism (the 'four eyes principle') and, most importantly, regulating bank portfolios through liquidity rules, capital rules, and so on.

Finally, the important role of private regulation through the head organisations of the three banking groups has to be stressed. These head organisations reduce competition within the cooperative and savings banks groups by regional demarcation as well as by retail price recommendations. Additionally, and more importantly, the federal regulator cooperates closely with the head associations in relationship to tasks which are crucial to the stability of the banking system. For example, the yearly statements of the cooperative banks as well as of the savings banks are controlled by the respective head organisation. Furthermore, even the task of protecting depositors is delegated from the public regulator to the bank associations. There also exist internal deposit insurance systems for the three banking groups which are managed by the groups themselves.

2.2 Main SMP legislation

In the view of German banks, the SMP can be characterised more as a regulatory harmonisation process than as deregulation. The most important changes within the regulatory framework are the realisation of the Basle Capital Accord and the Second Banking Directive. Both were introduced into national law by 1992. The Second Banking Directive especially, which establishes the principle of home country control, was quite important for German banks because of the relatively high degree of outward internationalisation. More details of the legislatory changes can be found in ERE, 1997.

The process of regulatory harmonisation can be considered as ended with the sixth amendment of the Kreditwesengesetz and the passing of a deposit insurance law. Both changes occurred in 1998 and transferred EC directives into national legislation. With regard to the Kreditwesengesetz, the different treatment of securities firms and credit institutions was eliminated. This step was especially important for the German financial system where universal banks and securities firms are direct competitors, but where securities firms were less tightly regulated. With regard to deposit insurance, each non-institutional customer is now guaranteed 90% of a claim against a bankrupt institution, up to a limit of €20,000. For home customers the protection goes beyond this limit, however, because group internal deposit insurance systems also exist and guarantee deposits up to 30% of the firm's equity. German branches and subsidiaries in other EU countries are not allowed to offer this additional insurance to foreign customers.

2.3 Remaining barriers to the SMP

In spite of a broad creation of the single European banking market, there remain some barriers worth mentioning. First of all, and perhaps most important, the market outcome may be disturbed by asymmetric conduct of the regulatory authorities. Especially with regard to multinational banking giants it seems questionable whether national regulators are an appropriate answer. Different interpretations of the legislative framework give incentives to bank managers to choose their home location corresponding to their own preferences. A less stringent regulator in one of the EU member countries may be sufficient to generate extremely high competitive pressures within the single market. The probability of an EU-wide bank run, and of systemic risk, would therefore increase.

Similar problems arise from tax systems, where German banks clearly face a strong disadvantage at the retail level. Because of high income tax rates, many customers decide to open accounts in foreign banks outside German in order to hide their interest incomes. Of course, this kind of competition between member states is important for factor allocation and should not be completely eliminated but it could make sense to avoid a destructive run for tax reduction between states by implementing a (low) EU-wide source tax on interest income.

3 IMPACT OF THE SMP

3.1 Bank strategies

When analysing the impact of the SMP on banking, it is important to differentiate between the process of deregulation and the harmonisation of the regulatory environment. Although both processes are strongly connected, and were taking place at the same time, the consequences for banking firms within the EU are quite different. Two groups can be differentiated at a theoretical level: EU member countries with a relatively free financial market prior to the SMP and those with a tight public supervision. Until the mid-1980s, Germany, the UK and the Netherlands were, generally speaking, the least regulated countries in the EU. The reason was the absence of government controls over interest rates or international capital flows, which were the most important restrictions in other states. In contrast, Spain, Portugal, Greece and Belgium could be classified as the most regulated countries. Because of this disparity, harmonisation can be considered as more important than deregulation for the first group.

Table 5.2 confirms this assumption. The postal survey results indicate that margins are declining in Germany as well as in the EU, with the impact of the SMP being less important for Germany than for other EU countries. However, the extent to which the SMP is claimed to be responsible for these changes is generally small: even at EU level, only one of the six banks judges the contribution of the SMP as being responsible 'to a large extent'.

Table 5.2 Competition and the SMP

	Change in margin for different types of loans			Extent to which the SMP is responsible for these changes			
	Loans to small firms	Retail customer loans	Mortgage loans	not at all	slightly	to a large extent	totally
Germany	-26	-8	-19	5%	95%	0%	0%
EC	-24	-21	-16	30%	54%	16%	0%

Note: -50 = large decrease; -25 = small decrease; 0 = no change
Source: Postal survey

A much more important source for the increasing competition is a trend towards disintermediation. This means that borrowers are borrowing directly from capital markets, while investors are finding attractive alternatives to bank deposits in, for example, money market funds or mutual funds. The spread of information technology is clearly supporting this trend. With the deregulation of the European banking markets, disintermediation maybe somewhat slowed but, as can be seen from the US, the general tendency will not be reversed. Although growing faster than the economy, the relative importance of credit institutions decreased in favour of investment firms (ECB, 1999, p. 16).

The process of regulatory harmonisation, with the introduction of common capital adequacy rules as its core, is supporting this process of disintermediation. Capital adequacy means that, for all loans to non-financial firms, a full 8% equity has to be put aside by banks. However, this is an important disadvantage for the traditional banking system in contrast to non-bank financial institutions which do not face any capital requirements. Furthermore, from the viewpoint of blue-chip borrowers, the incentive for a direct use of the capital market is further increased (*Economist*, 1999a, p. 13).

Turning from these general considerations to the specific challenges for German banks, they could view the SMP more as a challenge than a threat. In contrast to many of their EU rivals, German banks entered the second half of the 1980s with experience in competition. One positive side effect of this history is Germany's relatively low level of bad loans, which is an important problem in some other countries. A second strategic advantage from the competitive environment was the opportunity to adapt gradually to the new market conditions; there was no need for radical changes in management strategy.

A disadvantage is that the German banking market can, up to today, be characterised as a fragmented banking system, in which small cooperative banks and medium size savings banks control significant market shares (see Figure 5.1). Competition between the groups is one reason for the low profitability of German banks relative to banks in most other countries. Furthermore, the relative competitive position between private commercial banks, private (but non-traded) cooperative banks, and state-owned savings banks has changed with the process of regulatory harmonisation. Most importantly, cooperative banks and savings banks do not have access to the equity market but accumulate equity mainly by non-distributed profits. Achieving the Basle Capital Accord, with its emphasis on equity, is a clear disadvantage against listed institutions. The only exceptions are the head organisations of the savings banks, or

Landesbanken, which could raise equity by the transfer of real estate from the state governments to these banks. In contrast to the rest of the banking system, their competitive viability is improving through the process of disintermediation. Only these state-owned banks got a triple A rating from Moody's because of their government guarantee on all liabilities. This rating is an important factor when raising funds on global capital markets.

The strategic responses by the German banking system to the SMP cover three main areas:

- cost reductions
- changes in product range
- changes in market behaviour.

The first strategic response, cost reduction, took various forms, the most important of which was an intense wave of mergers between small banks, a reduction of the branching network, and a substitution for labour by capital. The German bank branch network was cut from 0.61 branches per 1000 capita in 1985 to 0.57 in 1997, which is still well above the numbers for France (0.44), the UK (0.32), or Italy (0.44). Parallel to this reduction a substitution for labour by capital took place. This is best illustrated by the expansion of the ATM network. From 1990 to 1997 the number of ATMs per 1000 capita increased from 0.18 to 0.50, which is significantly above the numbers for Italy (0.44) or the UK (0.38) (see ECB, 1999, for all data).

As a second strategic response, changes in the product range could be observed. That should not be interpreted as an abandoning of the universal banking concept, which is fundamental to the German banking system. However, when facing lower margins in the traditional intermediation business, the expansion of the fee and commission output became one of the main goals, especially for large institutions. This strategy allowed them to participate in the increasing volumes on the securities markets. The very specialised high-margin businesses like initial public offerings (IPOs), M&As, or international refunding are mainly dominated by US investment banks, however (*Economist*, 1999a, p. 18).

In contrast, another field of activity was clearly reduced. The big German banks are prominent for their dual role as lender and owner. Deutsche Bank, for example, is one of the world's biggest industrial holding companies with assets currently worth about DM45 billion. The portfolio of Dresdner Bank represents a market value of DM25 billion. These traditional links are now loosening: since 1994 Deutsche Bank has reduced its stake in 18 of its 20 largest holdings. Similar moves can be observed in other banks. One reason for this retreat is the currently high asset values, allowing large extraordinary gains from these investments. A second reason for banks' concentration on core banking business, aspects of risk diversification, may also be considered. The dual role of lender and owner leads to a double burden if a company is getting into trouble. A reduction in company ownership allows for a broader diversification of the portfolio risk, which is important for credit rating (*Economist*, 1999b).

Changes in market behaviour can be realised by new price strategies or by changes in risk behaviour. It is important to note here that enhanced price transparency, accompanied by increasing competitive pressure, is reducing the possibilities for cross subsidies. An important example of this in the retail business was the subsidisation of payment transactions by the interest business. As Priewasser (1985, pp. 151f.) mentions, a more differentiated, division-orientated price structure has had to be established. Actually, this change in the price schedules has already taken place. The creation of direct banks by the largest commercial banks, which primarily act as brokerage firms, is a further step into product differentiation. A second goal is the strengthening of the commission business.

Finally, the Basle capital accord may have a perverse effect on the risk behaviour of some banks. Currently, for all loans to non-financial firms, the full 8% equity has to be put aside. This reserve requirement is independent of the credit quality of borrower. As a result of this lack of differentiation, the incentive for running risks has increased (*Economist*, 1999a, p. 13; Rode and Moser, 1999). It is questionable if the loan-quality regulation can appropriately deal with this effect.

3.2 Mergers and acquisitions

M&As reduced the number of independent banks from about 4,700 in 1990 to 3,400 at the end of 1998 (see Table 5.1). Two main types of mergers can be differentiated: strategic mergers with at least one large partner and defensive mergers between small banks. Important examples of strategic mergers are the megamergers of Bayerische Hypobank and Bayerische Vereinsbank within Germany, and the acquisition of Bankers Trust in the US by Deutsche Bank. Aside from cost considerations, the increase in market power, international expansion, or a better access to equity markets are the main reasons for strategic mergers. As for defensive mergers, these types of mergers by far dominate merger activity in the German banking market. They are primarily motivated by cost considerations or, in a few cases, by the need to overcome solvency problems arising from bad debt. Economies of scale, which certainly exist for small banks, give theoretical support for defensive mergers.

The relationship between the completion of the Single Market and M&A activity seems to be weak. Obviously, increasing competitive pressure from an integrated European banking market may be interpreted as an incentive to reverse the decline in profitability through mergers. For small banks especially, and hence for the majority of mergers, other reasons than the SMP may be more important, however. For example, the high proportional increase in the costs of data processing or the change in consumer demand towards securities are important sources of economies of scale. External growth by mergers can help to exploit the advantages of being large, but these advantages are not related to the SMP.

Table 5.3 confirms this cautious view on the causality between M&As and the SMP. For most banks in Germany, as well as in the EU, the opening of subsidiaries is considered to be a more important factor than an increase in merger activity.

Shifting the focus to strategic mergers, the completion of the SMP may indeed be a main reason for repositioning national banks. It is important to note here that the German financial sector is one of biggest in absolute terms, but in 1994 only three German banks were among the twenty leading European banks measured by total assets. Because of two megamergers, this number has increased to four, with Deutsche Bank-Bankers Trust becoming one of the largest banks in world. Pan-European megamergers have not yet occurred.

Table 5.3 Company activity and the SMP

| | *Change in activity in other EC countries** | | *Extent to which the SMP is responsible for these changes* | | | |
	Merger activity	Opening of subsidiaries	not at all	slightly	to a large extent	totally
Germany	5.2	29.8	4%	67%	21%	0%
EC	2.9	17.7	15%	58%	23%	0%

Note: 50 = large decrease; 25 = small decrease; 0 = no change
Source: Postal survey

Up to now, a positive effect of M&As on costs and profitability has been assumed as given but Lang and Welzel (1999) show that cost reductions from defensive mergers are far from sure. Based on all 283 mergers between Bavarian cooperative banks which took place between 1989 and 1997, they empirically estimate two potential sources of merger-based cost reductions: size effects from economies of scale and of scope, and X-efficiency gains from post-merger restructuring efforts.

One of their main conclusions is that favourable size effects can only be expected if at least some of branches are closed in the post-merger phase. If the merged unit is not willing to reduce the number of branches, the predicted cost changes lie within a small interval ranging from -4 to 9%, but are zero at average. Aside from the cost-intensive network of branches, a poor mix in the output bundles of the merging banks is the main reason for this pessimistic prediction.

With respect to the post-merger performance, there is no evidence that the merged unit could exhibit X-efficiency levels above those of the separate units. If the merging banks exhibited different levels of X-efficiency, in most cases the more efficient merger partner failed to transfer its management advantages to the weaker partner. Instead, the empirical results point to a levelling off in efficiency differences after mergers took place. Even for mergers which took place five or eight years ago, no X-efficiency gains could be observed.

As for strategic megamergers, the consequences for size efficiency can be expected to be still more negligible. The Hypo-Vereinsbank megamerger may be considered an exception because, in this particular case, the regional density of many branches allowed for a significant reduction of the branching network without a loss in market share. In general, however, the optimal scale of a bank is far below the scale of each individual bank before the merger. More promising for profitability is the output side. As Akhavein *et al.* (1997) point out for the US market, there may be a greatly enhanced profit efficiency because of a shift in the product mix and enhanced possibilities for risk diversification. Vander Vennet (1996) is presuming well exercised managerial efficiency programmes in the case of megamergers among equal partners. Finally, strategic mergers have a clear positive impact on input prices. The absolute size of a bank is important for the conditions under which funds can be raised from the securities market.

3.3 Internationalisation

The degree of internationalisation may be seen from different perspectives: there are cross-border M&As and joint ventures, the establishment of subsidiaries or branches (direct investments), and, finally, lending or borrowing in a foreign currency and to non-residents. With regard to the latter, the European Central Bank is pointing to a steadily growing importance of international banking business for EU banks (ECB, 1999, pp. 21f). Somewhat surprisingly, EU banks are even taking a leading role as international lenders to emerging, transitional or developing countries. No numbers for individual countries are given, however.

More detailed information is presented in Table 5.4 on the establishment of subsidiaries and branches. The German banking system is currently raising more than 30% of its total assets from foreign branches and, to a lesser degree, from foreign subsidiaries. Actually, with about 300 branches or subsidiaries in other countries, the outward internationalisation of the German banking sector is more intense than in any other EU member state.

Table 5.4 Outward internationalisation of the German banking industry, 1998 *(% change against 1993 in parentheses)*

	foreign subsidiaries		foreign branches	
	number	assets as % of total assets	number	assets as % of total assets
in EC countries	81 (+40%)	7.4% (+20%)	94 (+42%)	12.6% (+158%)
in Luxembourg	30 (-3%)	3.8% (-7%)	32 (+10%)	1.4% (+23%)
in other EC countries	51 (+89%)	3.6% (+71%)	62 (+68%)	11.2% (+198%)
in non-EC countries	56 (+40%)	0.9% (+4%)	89 (+31%)	9.2% (+146%)
Total	*137 (+40%)*	*8.3% (+19%)*	*183 (+37%)*	*21.8% (+95%)*

Source: Deutsche Bundesbank.

As can be concluded from Table 5.3, direct investments in other EU countries are a more important reaction to the SMP than cross-border M&As. The high growth rates of the activities of foreign branches, which are by far outperforming foreign subsidiaries, are noticeable. It can be assumed that the Second Banking Directive, which introduced the principle of home country control for foreign branches, is one of the main forces for this pattern. The success of this regulatory milestone can also be observed in other member countries. More than 450 cross-border branches are currently established in the EU, up from 300 in 1992.

3.4 Cost changes: scale, efficiency, and input prices

Aside from M&As, cost reductions may also be realised from other sources, for example internal growth towards the optimal banking scale (see Section 1). However, no trend can be observed towards a more homogenous size distribution around this optimal scale. To illustrate this point, an average per bank growth rate of 13.9% between 1990 and 1998 in total assets should be kept in mind. Cooperative banks, which are typically far below the optimal firm size, could realise only an annual per bank growth rate of just 11.8%. The growth of savings banks, with 7.7% per year, was even lower. Credit banks, which are typically far beyond the minimum optimal scale, enjoyed the healthiest growth rate with 15.3% per year. Summing up, the size difference between cooperative banks and savings banks decreased, whereas the spread between these groups and the credit banks increased. This last result is in clear contrast to the hypothesis that the completion of the SMP would reduce the heterogeneity in bank sizes.

Figure 5.5 Distribution of X-inefficiency *(estimated percentage differences between actual and minimum cost)*

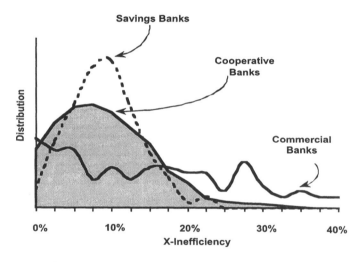

Source: Lang 1996.

On turning the focus to X-inefficiencies, we find one possible explanation for this somewhat surprising result. Compared to the cost disadvantage from having chosen the wrong size, managerial X-inefficiency has a much more negative effect on the cost situation. This impressive conclusion can be drawn from existing empirical work on the German banking industry (see, for example, ERE, 1997, p. 92; Lang, 1996; Tebroke and Wolf, 1998). As illustrated in Figure 5.5, a cost reduction in the order of 10% through a switch to best practice technology is realistic for the majority of German banks. The main reason for this deviation from the cost frontier is number of staff. It is important to note that cost savings from lowering input prices or from a reduction in the branch network are not included in the X-inefficiency measure because only input quantities are assumed to be under the control of the management.

Within the context of the SMP, the question of an occurring trend in X-inefficiency is of obvious interest. As a key hypothesis, increasing competitive pressure should have forced banking firms to reduce unit costs as far as possible. Actually, there is some empirical evidence that bank managers have reduced the level of X-inefficiencies since 1990 (ERE, 1997; Tebroke and Wolf, 1998; Lang and Welzel, 1999). However, the improvement seems small in comparison to the existing cost saving potential.

With regard to input prices, the recent changes were less drastic for German banks than for banks in other EU countries, especially for those in the eurozone. The general tendency in money market rates has been downward since 1992, with interest rates in other countries approaching the lower benchmark which was set by the German mark. The margin between the rate paid to customers and the money market rate has decreased due to increasing competition, but in a postal survey the SMP was made only slightly responsible for the higher competitive pressure (see also Table 5.2).

3.5 Revenue changes: quantities, prices and margins

The quantity growth of the non-commission business can be seen from Figure 5.6. Increasing ratios between deposits and GDP, as well as between loans and GDP, are a reliable indicator of an income-elastic demand for these outputs. The banking industry is obviously offering attractive products, with the German market somewhat overrepresented in relationship to other EU member countries. Interestingly, the loan side realised higher growth rate than the deposit side during the last years. In turn, the capital market became more important for refinancing the loan output.

The trend towards disintermediation finds its expression in increasing turnover on the securities markets. To some extent, as shown in Figure 5.7, banks could participate in these high growth rates. That was especially true at EU level when considering a representative bank. In Germany, the three largest German banks were also able to benefit. However, the smaller banks in Germany were not successful in strengthening their commission business; their non-interest revenue shares in 1998 were somewhat lower than in 1990, and the observed spread against the top three German banks, as well as against the EU average, even increased.

Figure 5.6 Non-bank deposits and non-bank loans as % of GDP, 1985-1998

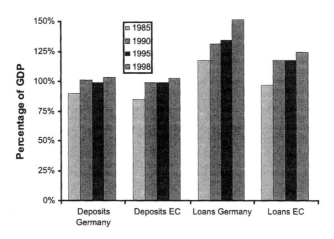

Note: EC data for 1997.
Source: Deutsche Bundesbank *and* ECB, 1999.

Figure 5.7 Non-interest income as % of total income

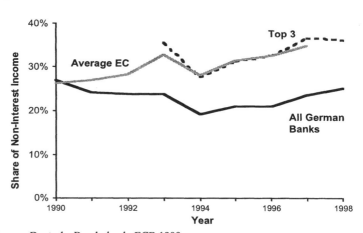

Source: Deutsche Bundesbank; ECB 1999.

With regard to output prices and margins, both drastically decreased since 1990. Figure 5.8 illustrates this trend for EU as well as for German banks. Most significant was the changing competitive environment for the large credit institutions, which topped the trend of shrinking margins. In contract to other EU member countries, disintermediation, technological changes (such as direct banking and better-informed customers), and overcapacity are the main reasons for increased competition in Germany. The SMP has strengthened this trend, but it is unlikely that it is solely responsible for the situation as outlined here.

Figure 5.8 Net interest margin, 1990-1998

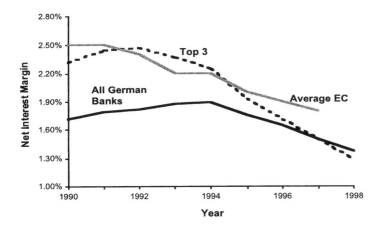

Note: Net interest income (interest revenues minus interest payments) as % of total assets.

Source: Deutsche Bundesbank *and* ECB 1999.

4   BANK PREPARATIONS FOR EMU

4.1 Effects of EMU on banking activities

The creation of a single European currency is affecting German banks more significantly than the SMP, because the latter is more or less a harmonisation-driven change within the regulatory framework. It is no easy task, however, to separate the effects of the SMP, EMU, and other changes in the market environment, such as growing disintermediation or technical progress. The reason for this difficulty is that, in many ways, these forces work towards the same direction: growing competition within the banking sector, and between banks and non-bank financial institutions. Summing up, many of the results outlined in earlier sections can also be applied here.

There are some specific effects of EMU on banking which are worth outlining. Obviously, the ending of the future and spot exchange markets for EMU currencies, and the general reduction in hedging needs, is reducing revenues, especially for the larger banks. This negative influence on bank revenues will be at least partly offset by the high growth rates of the integrated capital markets. The market capitalisation of the euro stock exchanges is now comparable to that of Japan (15% of the world market capitalisation) and has therefore become attractive to international investors. Still better is the competitive viability of the fixed income sector where euro-denominated loans from domestic borrowers account for about 25% of the world market.

A more liquid euro capital market will increase price transparency for loans and deposits. Together with an increasing liquidity of this large onshore market and the trend towards disintermediation, shrinking margins will continue. Falling prices and increasing volumes have a clear positive impact on borrowers as well as on the economies, but the outcome for banks is not clear. Only larger banks, typically those more engaged in non-interest business, can be expected to benefit fully from higher turnover of the securities market.

A specific advantage which German banks enjoy is the location of the European Central Bank (ECB) in Frankfurt. This will strengthen the informal links between central bankers and commercial banks, which may be important for future decisions regarding monetary or regulatory policy. Furthermore, a positive impact on the competitive viability of Frankfurt as a trading place for securities is probable. As a first indicator, Frankfurt has won the leading role in the trade of 'bund futures' back from London.

Finally, when analysing the effects of EMU on banking, the importance of the macroeconomic situation has to be mentioned. If governments and the ECB can successfully create an environment of exchange rate stability, low public deficits and low interest rates, then a significant positive effect, especially for banks, can be expected. Continuous and stable economic growth rates are accompanied by high growth rates in the lending business, while loan losses are low because of few firm defaults. This interrelationship is due to the price and income-elastic demand for bank loans.

4.2 Banking sector responses

The main consequence of the establishment of EMU will be a more competitive environment, and further pressure on bank margins can be expected. According to ECB 1999, the response of the banking system to EMU will be quite similar to what is expected from the SMP: improvements in services and procedures to reduce costs and enhance risk management; changes in the product range (for example, a shift to consulting or internationalisation); and mergers and acquisitions, which are driven by cost aspects or by the goal to change output mix and to expand geographically.

As far as retail banking is concerned, the single currency will reduce the customers' preferences for a home-country bank: prices, conditions and quality will determine the depositor choice, not nationality. Not all banks will be able to attract foreign customers, however. Because of low transaction costs, direct banks will have a comparative advantage in the cross-border retail business. The large German credit institutions have well established direct banks with attractive conditions which could gain significant market shares in the international retail banking segment. As a consequence, large banks may in general redirect their retail business towards direct banking where their technological leadership puts them at an advantage compared to medium-sized or small banks. At the same time, the branch network of commercial banks can be expected to be scaled down. In spite of high growth rates of direct banking, that strategy would reduce the significance of retailing for large commercial banks. Savings banks, as well as cooperative banks, could fill this gap, but at the cost of losing market shares in the commission business.

Currently, discussion about an appropriate response to EMU is strongly focused on megamergers, for example between Deutsche Bank and Dresdner Bank, number one and number two respectively in the German banking industry. From an official point of view, the degree of concentration within the EU can be regarded as low and no obstacles from the antitrust authorities should be expected. However, the economic success of M&As is guaranteed neither for defensive nor for strategic mergers. Although strategic mergers, as in the example cited above, offer big opportunities for saving costs, increasing revenues and reducing risks, the negative evidence from empirical banking studies should be kept in mind. To be more specific, the significance of managerial X-efficiency should again to be stressed at this point: unit costs are clearly more influenced by managerial quality than by the size of a bank. Wheelock and Wilson (1999) confirm the importance of low X-inefficiency values for the US market, where the probability of bank failure was significantly higher for inefficient banks than for well-managed firms.

4.3 Banking sector scenarios

To sum up, EMU will further speed up structural change in German and European banking. Large, stock-traded German banks, especially, are currently under pressure because of their relatively low profitability. This can clearly be seen by a comparison of market capitalisation and bank size: Europe's largest bank measured in terms of total assets, Deutsche Bank, can only reach rank seven in market value. Similarly, the other large German banks have reached an enormous size, but are valued significantly lower than comparable European competitors. For the majority of non-traded banks, their low performance can be seen from statistical material.

To maintain or enhance profitability in an environment of decreasing margins, all banks must increase their efforts to reduce costs. The reduction in capacity, especially in the number of branches and banks, will continue. According to empirical estimates, future efforts should concentrate on an increase in managerial quality which promises a higher potential for cost savings than scale economies. Increasing efficiency means fewer staff (about two-thirds of the theoretical cost savings) and a lower, but more efficient capital input (buildings, data processing). The economic gains from a more efficient input allocation will easily offset possible job losses in the banking industry.

On the product side, the disintermediation process is expected to speed up. As a consequence, the traditional system of universal banks could be somewhat changed. There is likely to be a partial retreat by savings banks, as well as cooperative banks, from investment banking, but both are likely to increase their market shares in the branch-based retail business. For commercial banks, the consultation-intense investment business looks very attractive. In the retail sector, a specialisation in direct banking allows for additional customers from abroad as well as for high growth rates in the brokerage business.

References

Akhavein, J.D., A.N. Berger and D.B. Humphrey (1997), 'The effects of megamergers on efficiency and prices: evidence from a bank profit function', *Review of Industrial Organization,* 12, pp. 95-139

Altunbas, Y. and P. Molyneux (1996), 'Economies of scale and scope in European banking', *Applied Financial Economics,* 6, pp. 367-75

Berger, A.N., G.A. Hanweck and D.B. Humphrey (1987), 'Competitive viability in banking: scale, scope, and product mix economies', *Journal of Monetary Economics,* 20, pp. 501-20

Berger, A.N. and D.B. Humphrey (1997), 'Efficiency of financial institutions: international survey and directions for future research', *European Journal of Operational Research*, 98, pp. 175-212

Deutsche Bundesbank, *Monthly Reports*

Economic Research Europe Ltd (1997), *The Single Market Review: Impact on Credit Institutions and Banking*, (Kogan Page, London)

Economist (1999a), 'Survey on international banking', 351, 8115

Economist (1999b), 'German banks' investments: untangling', 352, 8132, pp. 59-61

European Central Bank (1999), *Possible Effects of EMU on the EU Banking System in the Medium to Long Term*, (ECB, Frankfurt)

Kolari, J. and A. Zardkoohi (1987), *Bank Cost, Structure and Performance*, (Lexington Books, Lexington, Mass.)

Lang, G. (1996), 'Efficiency, profitability and competition: empirical analysis for a panel of German universal banks', *ifo-Studien* 42, pp. 537-61

Lang, G. (1997), 'Wettbewerbsverhalten Deutscher Banken: Eine Panelanalyse auf Basis der Rosse-Panzar Statistik', *Jahrbuch für Wirtschaftswissenschaften (Review of Economics)*, 48, pp. 21-38

Lang, G. and P. Welzel (1998), 'Technology and cost efficiency in banking: a 'Thick Frontier' analysis of the German banking industry', *Journal of Productivity Analysis*, 10, pp. 63-84

Lang, G. and P. Welzel (1999), 'Mergers among German cooperative banks: a panel-based stochastic frontier analysis', *Small Business Economics*, 13, pp. 273-86

Molyneux, P., D.M. Lloyd-Williams and J. Thornton (1994), 'Competitive conditions in European banking', *Journal of Banking and Finance*, 18, pp. 445-59

Neuberger, D. (1998), 'Industrial organisation of banking: a review', *International Journal of Business*, 5, pp. 97-118

Priewasser, E. (1985), *Die Banken im Jahre 2000*, (Fritz Knapp, Frankfurt)

Rode, M. and C. Moser (1999), 'Die neuen Basler Eigenkapitalanforderungen', *Zeitschrift für das Gesamte Kreditwesen*, 52, pp. 720-24

Schure, P. and R. Wagenvoort (1999), *Economies of Scale and Efficiency in European Banking: New Evidence*, Economic and Financial Reports of the European Investment Bank, 99/01 (EIB, Frankfurt)

Statistisches Bundesamt (1999), Einkommens- und Verbrauchsstichprobe 1998, Wiesbaden

Tebroke, H.-J. and J.B. Wolf (1998), *Structural Variations in the Efficiency of German Banks: Empirical Evidence*, (mimeo, University of Augsburg)

Vander Vennet, R. (1996), 'The effect of mergers and acquisitions on the efficiency and profitability of EC credit institutions', *Journal of Banking and Finance*, 20, pp. 1531-58

Wheelock, D.C. and P.W. Wilson (1999), 'Why do banks disappear? The determinants of US bank failures and acquisitions', (to be published in *Review of Economics and Statistics*)

6 Greece

Christos Gortsos

1 MARKET STRUCTURE AND PERFORMANCE

1.1 Size of the financial market

1.1.1 The situation before the Single European Act 1986
The structure of the contemporary Greek banking system was shaped in the 1920s with the foundation of a state-controlled monetary authority, the Bank of Greece (BoG), and two state-controlled specialised banks, one for financing housing investments (the National Mortgage Bank of Greece) and the other for agricultural production (the Agricultural Bank of Greece). These institutions operated, along with a handful of commercial banks, most of which had been established in the second half of the 19th century, within a comprehensive legal framework established by the 1931 Banking Law. During the 1930s several small banks went bankrupt and were closed down, while several others were absorbed as a result of the 1929 international monetary and financial crisis.

In the early 1950s, the Greek government, inspired by prevailing theory and practice about the role of the state in economic development, intervened heavily in the banking system, making it the main domestic vehicle for financing the country's restructuring projects. Monetary policy was shaped by a governmental body (the Currency Committee), for which the BoG acted simply as an executor of decisions. Most banking activities came under state control, either directly or indirectly. Even the largest banks and their affiliated institutions came under the control, or even the ownership, of the Greek government. The establishment of specialised credit institutions for long-term financing was especially encouraged, leading to the creation of three development banks in the 1960s: the Hellenic Bank for Industrial Development (ETBA), the National Investment Bank for Industrial Development (ETEBA), and the Investment Bank.

The most important result of these developments was the high degree of market share held by state-controlled banks dominating the market. Even though conditions did not favour the establishment of new banks,

128

during the 1970s several foreign banks established branch offices in Greece. This trend was reinforced by Greece's association with the European Economic Community and then its membership of the EEC in 1981. At the end of 1985 there were 40 credit institutions operating in the Greek banking market:

- the BoG, the country's monetary and bank supervisory authority
- twelve Greek commercial banks, ten of which were state-owned or state-controlled and only two of which were private
- branches of nineteen foreign banks and
- eight specialised credit institutions.

State control in the banking market (*see* Section 1.2 below) and the extent of preventive regulations on the operation of credit institutions (*see* Section 2.1 below) were unprecedented. In addition, credit institutions dominated almost totally the Greek financial system since, with the exception of brokers (individuals who were members of the Athens Stock Exchange), few other financial intermediaries were permitted to provide financial services in Greece.

1.1.2   The impact of the SMP
The SMP was implemented during the late 1980s and early 1990s in the banking sector of the member states of the European Union to encourage liberalisation and increase competition in European banking. Its impact on the structure of the Greek financial system was clearly positive. As a result of its extensive deregulation and liberalisation, the Greek financial marketplace started becoming attractive to institutional and private investors and induced several private commercial banks to establish a physical presence, either to offer a wide range of financial services or to act as niche players. In addition, legislation adapted to the requirements of the international financial environment, of which the Greek banking system started to become a member, made the operation of several types of financial intermediaries possible.

Depending on the financial activities in which they are permitted to engage, financial intermediaries under close prudential supervision by public authorities (the BoG and the Capital Market Committee) are classified into three groups: credit institutions, market intermediaries, and other financial institutions.

(a) Credit institutions
Credit institutions, the only deposit-taking financial intermediaries, provide the widest range of commercial banking and investment services. According to the prevailing three-pillar structure, credit institutions are divided into three sub-groups:

- *commercial banks;* including branches of foreign credit institutions (*see* (i) and (ii) below)
- *specialised credit institutions;* including one mortgage bank, two development banks (usually referred to as investment banks), two special purpose credit institutions, and a shipping bank (*see* (iii) below)
- *cooperative banks;* (*see* (iv) below).

(i) Commercial banks are the dominant category of all depository and credit-extending institutions operating in Greece. They are incorporated as stock companies under a licence provided by the BoG, which is valid throughout the EU. The number of commercial banks increased substantially during the first half of the 1990s, both in anticipation and as a result of the SMP. By the end of 1997 there were 19 commercial banks incorporated in Greece, compared with 12 in 1985.

Table 6.1 The size of the Greek banking system, 1987-1999

	1987	1990	1993	1996	August 1999
Commercial banks	12	14	19	20	16
Specialised credit institutions	8	8	9	8	6
Cooperative banks	-	-	-	5	13
Branches of foreign banks	19	17	19	21	20

The consolidation and restructuring taking place in the Greek banking system in 1998 and 1999, however, reduced again the number of commercial banks to 16 in August 1999. That number will be further reduced to 12 by 2000 when the banks that have been acquired by EFG Eurobank (Ergobank, Cretabank), Bank of Piraeus (Xiosbank and Macedonia Thrace Bank) and Alpha Credit Bank (Ionian Bank of Greece) will be absorbed and will cease to exist (*see* Table 6.2). However, the current picture will be modified in the near future since two new commercial banks have applied for a licence and also further consolidation cannot be excluded.

(ii) The number of branches of foreign commercial banks established in Greece remained stable during the last decade. By August 1999, the branches of eleven banks incorporated in other member states of the EU and the branches of nine banks from non-EU countries were operating in Greece. Compared to 1985, five foreign banks established a physical presence in Greece (Bayerische Vereinsbank, Instituto Bancario San Paolo di Torino, ING Bank, Bank of Cyprus, and Hellenic Bank) while three ceased operating.

(iii) Structural despecialisation has been one of the major features of the recent financial reform programme (*see* Section 2.3.2). Even though some specialised credit institutions are still operating in Greece, their number is declining. In 1991, the Agricultural Bank of Greece was transformed into a commercial bank and in 1992 the Investment Bank was absorbed by its parent institutions. In 1997, two specialised mortgage banks, the National Mortgage Bank of Greece and the National Housing Bank, merged to create the new National Mortgage Bank of Greece, a subsidiary of the National Bank of Greece. By October 1998, when the absorption of the new National Mortgage Bank by the National Bank of Greece was completed, only six specialised credit institutions remained in operation (*see* Section 1.2.2), compared with eight operating in 1985.

(iv) Since 1994 cooperative banks operate under legislation permitting Greek credit cooperatives the creation of credit institutions. The initial capital requirement for their incorporation is substantially lower than that of commercial banks and depends upon the territorial scope of their activity. By August 1999, there were 13 cooperative banks operating in the market. Their importance, however, is not yet significant and they are not going to be discussed further in this study.

(b) Market intermediaries
The principal activity of market intermediaries consists in providing investment services, either on a collective basis through investment portfolio companies and mutual funds, or on an individual basis through brokerage firms and other companies providing core and supplementary investment services.

Investment portfolio companies and mutual funds operate in Greece under a 1991 law which implemented into Greek law the provisions of the UCITS (Undertakings for Collective Investment in Transferable Securities) Directive (85/611/EEC, as amended). Investment portfolio companies are incorporated as stock companies and can be considered as closed-end funds to the extent that the amount of their shares, which must be listed in the Athens Stock Exchange, remains stable. The minimum initial capital of these companies, the assets of which are invested exclusively in cash and financial instruments, is GRD2 billion. In August 1999, 18 investment portfolio companies were operating in Greece, of which six were subsidiary companies of Greek credit institutions.

Mutual fund management companies are also incorporated as stock companies with an initial capital of GRD100 million. Their task consists in managing the assets of one or more mutual funds invested in Greek and foreign money market instruments, bonds, and stocks. In August 1999 there were 33 mutual fund management companies incorporated in Greece managing more than 160 mutual funds. The parent institutions of these companies are Greek credit institutions (18), foreign banks operating in Greece through branches (6), and insurance companies (9).

(ii) After implementation of the Investment Services Directive (93/22/EEC) into Greek law in 1996, core investment services can be provided only by credit institutions and firms providing investment services, known as 'EPEY' (after the Greek acronym). These firms, incorporated as stock companies and supervised by the Capital Market Committee, are classified into three groups:

- The first group consists of brokerage firms, which are still the only non-bank institutions allowed to become members of the Athens Stock Exchange and the Athens Derivatives Exchange. Their minimum initial capital is GRD200 million (even though contributions to the local investor protection scheme were increased in 1999 to levels that require an initial capital of at least GRD800 million for new entrants). In August 1999 there were 80 brokerage firms operating in Greece, of which 16 were subsidiary undertakings of Greek commercial banks.
- The second group consists of firms which are allowed to provide only the investment services of accepting and transmitting orders in organised capital markets as well as portfolio management. Their minimum share capital is also GRD200 million, while they are required to have a share capital of GRD1 billion to engage in securities underwriting.
- The third group consists of firms permitted only to accept and transmit orders for the conduct of exchange-traded activities. Their minimum share capital is GRD60 million.

(c) Other financial institutions
Financial institutions specialise in financial activities either not undertaken by credit institutions or complementary to them. This group consists of leasing and factoring companies, foreign exchange bureaux and foreign exchange brokers, all supervised by the BoG.

1.2 Ownership structure and privatisation

1.2.1 Commercial banks
Commercial banks can be divided into state-controlled banks and private banks. In August 1999, only 5 commercial banks were under the direct or indirect control of the Greek state, while the number of private banks amounted to 11. This is probably the most important recent development in the structure of the Greek banking system and can definitively be attributed to the competitive implications of the SMP and European monetary unification. In contrast, of the twelve Greek commercial banks operating in Greece in 1985, ten were state-owned or state-controlled and only two were private.

The state controls commercial banks either directly (Agricultural Bank of Greece) or indirectly (National Bank of Greece, Commercial Bank of Greece, General Hellenic Bank, Bank of Attica). The indirect control comes from the majority equity participation of public pension funds, municipalities and other funds.

Private commercial banks also can be divided into two groups, depending on whether or not controlling shares are held by a foreign institutional investor (in particular another credit or a financial institution) resident abroad. Greek controlled banks are Alpha Credit Bank, Bank of Piraeus, Egnatia Bank and Dorian Bank. Foreign controlled banks, that is subsidiaries of supranational financial conglomerates, are EFG Eurobank and European and Popular Bank.

The remaining banks are subsidiaries of other credit institutions (*see* Table 6.2). It is interesting to note that the majority of these banks were incorporated during the 1990s either in anticipation of the deregulation and liberalisation of the banking system brought about by the SMP (EFG Eurobank, Bank of Piraeus, Xiosbank, Egnatia Bank, Dorian Bank) or just after the system had been deregulated (European and Popular Bank).

1.2.2 Specialised credit institutions
After the absorption of the National Mortgage Bank of Greece by the National Bank of Greece, Aspis Bank is the only specialised mortgage bank operating in Greece. Aspis Bank, the subsidiary of an insurance

company, operates under the provisions of specific legislation permitting the establishment of mortgage banks with a lower initial capital than that required for commercial banks if the parent undertaking is a financial company.

Table 6.2 Ownership structure of Greek commercial banks (August 1999)

Bank	Status	Bank subsidiary (in Greece)	Merger and acquisition activity
National Bank of Greece	state-controlled	ETEBA (investment bank)	1998: merged with National Mortgage Bank of Greece 1998: sold participation in Macedonia-Thrace Bank 1994/1998: sold qualified participation in Bank of Athens
Agricultural Bank of Greece	state-owned		
Commercial Bank of Greece	state-controlled		1999: sold majority participation in Ionian Bank of Greece 1996: sold minority participation in Bank of Attica 1991: sold majority participation in Bank of Piraeus
Alpha Credit Bank	private		1999: acquired Ionian Bank of Greece
EFG Eurobank	private		1999: acquired a major participation in Ergobank 1998: acquired Cretabank 1998: acquired Bank of Athens 1998: acquired a qualified participation in Ergobank 1996: acquired Interbank of Greece
Bank of Piraeus	private (since 1991)	Macedonia Thrace Bank Xiosbank Piraeus-Prime Bank	1998: acquired Xiosbank 1998: acquired Macedonia-Thrace Bank 1997: acquired branch network of Credit Lyonnais (Grece) and NatWest
General Hellenic Bank	state-controlled		
Egnatia Bank	private		acquired Bank of Central Greece
European and Popular Bank	private		
Dorian Bank	private: controlled by the owners of a brokerage firm (Telesis Securities)		
Bank of Attica	state-controlled		

The National Bank of Greece is the parent institution of the National Investment Bank for Industrial Development (ETEBA), one of the two development banks operating in Greece. The second, the Hellenic Bank for Industrial Development (ETBA), is a state-owned credit institution. Both specialise in corporate and project finance activities.

The Postal Savings Bank is an administratively independent institution in the public sector supervised by the Ministry of Transport and the Deposits and Loans Fund is part of the Ministry of National Economy, although the decision-making process is to a certain extent independent.

Finally, Citibank Shipping Bank is a 100% owned subsidiary of Citibank Corporation S.A. and operates under the provisions of specific corporate and tax legislation pertaining to banks specialised in shipping finance.

1.3 Competition

1.3.1 Sources and uses of funds

(a) Commercial banks

Competition among Greek commercial banks is in four areas of financial services: (i) deposit taking and credit extension; (ii) payment services; (iii) investment services (including asset management); and (iv) off-balance-sheet activities. On the other hand, Greek branches of foreign credit institutions operate as niche players, specialising in such areas as shipping finance, corporate finance, private and personal banking, asset management, and capital market activities. They do this even though they are permitted by law to engage in all financial services provided also by Greek credit institutions, with the exception of real estate lending. Nonetheless, their market share has increased steadily during the last decade for both their on-balance and off-balance sheet activities.

(i) Primarily, commercial banks link collecting savings with supplying credit through traditional commercial banking services such as:

- soliciting and accepting retail and wholesale deposits in Greek drachmas and other freely convertible foreign currencies
- repurchase agreements
- short-term and long-term loans, both to large corporations and to small and medium-size enterprises
- services relating to corporate mergers and acquisitions
- debt and equity placements
- residential and commercial mortgage loans

- consumer loans and
- shipping finance.

(ii) The provision of payment services was, and still remains, part of the core business of commercial banks. These include:

- the issuance of cheques and credit cards (under conditions partly determined by the BoG)
- the remittal of credit for retail and wholesale payments, and
- the acceptance of standing orders.

(iii) Through their dealing rooms and private banking departments, commercial banks provide a variety of core investment services including:

- the reception and transmission of investors' orders with regard to primary and derivative financial instruments
- trading in and market-making of Treasury securities
- discretionary financial portfolio management in the course of private banking
- underwriting of debt and equity securities.

Banks also are permitted to participate directly as brokers and market-makers in the Athens Derivative Markets. Greek commercial banks also provide supplementary investment services, such as safekeeping and administration of physical financial instruments, custody services (especially for mutual funds and other institutional investors), as well as investment advisory services and services related to underwriting.

(iv) Commercial banks are undertaking significant off-balance sheet operations, including services linked to import and export finance (guarantees, letters of credit, endorsements), as well as transactions in OTC financial derivatives (forward rate agreements, interest rate and foreign exchange swaps, OTC currency options).

Table 6.3 Concentration among commercial banks with regard to total assets, 1990-1996

	1990	1993	1996
3 largest Greek banks	66.2	62.2	52.3
5 largest Greek banks	77.9	74.3	67.7
3 largest foreign banks in Greece	5.3	5.2	6.6

According to financial statements of credit institutions, the degree of concentration in the Greek banking system remains significant, even though it is constantly diminishing. The following tables present the evolution during the last decade of the market share of, respectively, the three largest and five largest Greek commercial banks measured on an individual and not on a group basis, and the three largest foreign banks in Greece with regard to their total assets.

(b) Specialised credit institutions
Traditionally, the main focus of specialised mortgage banks was to provide residential and commercial mortgage loans. They were mainly funded through short-term demand and savings deposits, as well as through mortgage bonds. With the deregulation of the system, these banks were permitted to accept interbank deposits, engage in secondary market transactions with retail and corporate customers, provide financing to tourist sector investments and short-term working capital to business enterprises, and conduct foreign exchange operations and operations on financial derivatives. They also have the privilege of providing subsidised housing loans to low-net-worth individuals. (This constitutes the only significant subsidy still existing in Greek banking).

Development banks were granting long-term loans to the industrial sector of the economy through savings collected by issuing long-term bonds. Since 1992 the scope of their activities has been broader because they were allowed to accept retail and interbank deposits, conduct foreign exchange operations, grant short-term loans, and invest in corporate bonds. Development banks are also active in corporate mergers and acquisitions, public and private equity and debt placements, and in financial consulting.

Because of its extensive branch network, the Postal Savings Bank has a considerable advantage in collecting retail deposits and providing payment services, enhanced by its deposits being fully guaranteed by the Greek state. These funds are used to finance low-risk development and social programmes, and purchase Treasury bills and notes. The Deposits and Loans Fund specialises in holding and administering every kind of consignation, which constitute a significant part of their liabilities. Funded also through deposits from various legal entities, it grants loans to individuals and legal entities, including housing loans to civil servants and pensioners.

1.3.2   Affiliation with other financial institutions
According to the 'firewalls' introduced by financial law, credit institutions operating in Greece are not allowed to provide the whole range of

financial services in-house. Hence, those wishing to exploit existing economies of scope in the provision of financial services in Greece have created, or participated in the creation of, market intermediaries or other financial firms in three areas of financial activity:

- credit institutions and Greek branches of foreign banks have been permitted to become members of the Athens Stock Exchange as of 1 January 2000. Until that date they were prevented from executing their clients' orders in relation to listed equities and dealing in equities for their own account. In addition, they could not execute orders in relation to equity-linked derivatives and deal in such derivatives for their own account in the Athens Derivatives Exchange. All these services could be provided only through subsidiary brokerage firms
- banks also are required by law to provide leasing, factoring and venture capital services through specialised subsidiary undertakings
- given the fast growth of the business of portfolio management on a collective basis, several Greek commercial banks, branches of foreign banks established in Greece, and specialised credit institutions have created subsidiary undertakings to manage mutual funds and/or subsidiary investment portfolio companies
- some Greek commercial banks have also chosen to create subsidiary credit card companies, while several others have majority and/or minority participation in life insurance and general insurance companies and are expanding rapidly in the field of bancassurance.

1.3.3   Geographical scope of activity

(a) Commercial banks
There are significant differences in the extent of the physical presence of Greek commercial banks in Greece. The large ones (including the National Bank of Greece, the Agricultural Bank of Greece, the Commercial Bank of Greece, the Ionian Bank of Greece, Alpha Credit Bank, Ergobank and, after the 1998 acquisitions, EFG Eurobank and Bank of Piraeus) have a substantial branch network dispersed throughout the country. Other banks (such as General Hellenic Bank and Bank of Attica) also operate in all major Greek cities but the overall scope of their activity is narrower, while the remainder have a small number of branches, mainly restricted to Athens, Thessaloniki and Piraeus.

Some Greek commercial banks have also established a presence abroad. Nevertheless, with the exception of the National Bank of Greece (which has a significant global network of branches and subsidiaries),

EFG Eurobank (which belongs to an international banking group), and Alpha Credit Bank, the international presence of other commercial banks is mainly directed towards other member states of the EU, the Black Sea region, and Balkan states. On the other hand, the branches of all foreign credit institutions, with the exception of Citibank, are based and operate exclusively in the three largest cities, Athens, Piraeus, and Thessaloniki.

(b) Specialised credit institutions
The geographical scope of activity of most specialised credit institutions is narrow. With two exceptions, none has more than 12 branch offices. Citibank Shipping operates exclusively through its headquarters in Piraeus, the country's principal shipping centre, while ETEBA has only two offices, both in Athens. The two exceptions are the National Mortgage Bank of Greece and the Postal Savings Bank which has the most extensive network in Greece consisting of 112 branches throughout the country and the 800 offices of the Greek Post.

1.4 Banking performance

1.4.1 A general assessment
In addition to its effects on the structure and size of the banking sector of EU member states, the SMP was also expected to affect the performance of EU-based credit institutions. According to a study published by the European Commission in 1997, European financial integration should affect bank performance in several ways. A principal aim of internal market integration was to increase competitiveness and the contestability of markets which, in turn, would reduce loan and deposit rates and fees.

The SMP was expected to affect the profitability of European banks by:

- reducing interest margins as well as staff and non-staff costs, because of intensified competitive conditions
- creating a higher proportion of income from non-interest income business (including off-balance sheet activities and securities trading) through portfolio diversification, and
- producing lower returns on equity.

It was also expected that implementation of the SMP would lead to more efficient management of banking firms and higher productivity. The deregulation of financial markets was expected to encourage banks to increase their production and diversify into new financial activities. Scale and scope economies should have resulted in lower average cost.

The effects of the SMP on the performance of Greek commercial banks can be summarised as follows (specific reference is made in Section 1.4.2 with regard to income, expenses, and efficiency):

• prices of loans and deposits fell significantly during the 1990s after implementation of the SMP in Greece. The price elasticity of loans was, however, higher than the price elasticity of deposits. Commissions charged by Greek banks also fell considerably. These developments clearly are the result of increased price competition in the market after deregulation.

• no thorough analysis (to the author's knowledge) has been published on how European financial integration affected scale and scope economies in Greek banking. Based, however, on the strategic responses of certain Greek banks during the period under review, and also taking into consideration the results of the 1997 study of the European Commission, it can be assumed that for smaller banks there existed some potential for increasing returns through changes in the scale of production. There was also some indication, particularly for larger banks, of potential unit cost reductions through economies of scope.

1.4.2   Income, expenses and efficiency

(a) Net interest income
The net interest margin of Greek commercial banks was very high during the 1980s, reflecting the inefficiencies of the heavily regulated market. Since 1992, however, it has been decreasing at a growing rate. This development is directly related to the impact of the SMP on the Greek banking sector.

It is worth mentioning that, because of the obligation imposed until 1993 upon Greek banks to finance the growing public debt by purchasing Treasury securities, the main source of interest income for Greek banks was Treasury notes and bonds (even though the Treasury securities held by state-controlled banks are significantly larger than those held by private banks). In addition, a recent study of the Hellenic Bank Association (1998) shows that the ratio of private loans to the private sector of the economy to total assets is comparatively low. This is mainly because of the unstable macroeconomic conditions of previous years such as high interest rates, the recession of the early 1990s, and the crowding out of private investments.

The income from interest on loans remains a relatively low percentage of the total operating income of Greek banks (Pantelias, 1998). This is reinforced by the fact that, after the abolition of interest rate controls, competitive conditions in the market caused the interest charges on loans to be reduced.

(b) Non-interest income

The ratio of income from commissions to total assets, on the other hand, ranks among the highest in the EU (Pantelias, 1998 and Massourakis, 1998). A significant portion of this income comes from traditional banking activities such as buying and selling foreign exchange, and the sale of government securities through bank networks. Income from financial activities, despite its fluctuation, is also a relatively high percentage of total income, but again it comes from the sale of government bonds at attractive prices during the current period of declining interest rates and not from transactions in innovative products, including financial derivatives.

(c) Costs

The ratio of costs to total bank assets is considerably higher in Greece than in other EU member states (Pantelias, 1998 and Massourakis, 1998). Staff costs, especially in state-controlled banks, are high and inelastic because of the considerable bargaining power of the banking employee union. Non-staff operating costs remain relatively constant. The cost-income ratio fell significantly in 1997 from its peak in 1996 of 65.3%.

(d) Efficiency

No study (to the author's knowledge) has been published analysing the degree of x-inefficiency (measuring how far production is from the efficient cost frontier) and total factor productivity for Greek banks. Based on a recent study by Pantelias (1998), the efficiency ratio of Greek banks (measured as the ratio of total operating expenses to net income) for 1995 was not among the highest in the EU. Of course, there are significant differences between state-controlled and private banks. By also assessing the ratio of total expenses to total assets, which was at the average European level, Pantelias concludes that the low productivity of Greek banks is mainly caused by inefficiencies in exploiting capacities and not by increased costs.

2   REGULATORY FRAMEWORK

2.1 Regulatory framework prior to the SMP

Greek government intervention in credit allocation since the early 1950s has been very extensive. The monetary authorities not only controlled nominal interest rates, but also determined the amount of credit available by economic sector. Credit programmes were mainly aimed at financing, under administratively determined conditions, state-owned and state-controlled firms, export-oriented producers, small- and medium-scale enterprises, the agricultural sector, the housing needs of a rapidly growing urban population, and the infrastructure in certain underdeveloped regions of the country. As in several other developing economies, direct credit controls in the banking system took several forms, such as lending requirements on credit institutions, granting loans at preferential and subsidised interest rates, providing credit guarantees, and directing long-term credit through the specialised development banks. The provision of loans denominated in drachma and foreign currencies was heavily regulated. In addition, credit institutions were required to invest a fixed 40% of their deposits in Treasury bills (yielding lower than market rates) in order to finance large public sector expenditures.

After 1987 the Greek financial system became a system under change. Allocative inefficiencies, initiation of the process for financial integration within the EU, and international trends toward globalisation and deregulation, all contributed to the start of a programme for modernising the system and adapting it to internationally acceptable standards. The structural deregulation of Greek banking and, in general, of the Greek financial market was carried out in three stages:

- the first stage (1982-1986) consisted of laying the foundations for the conduct of an independent monetary policy and rationalising the credit market
- the second stage (1987-1991) consisted of lifting constraints on the operation of financial markets, intermediaries, and financial services. Market deregulation and the liberalisation of services, as described in the benchmark Karatzas Committee's *Report on the Reform and Modernisation of the Greek Banking System (1987)*, were motivated by international developments and the need to prepare for participation in the single European market for financial services (*see* Section 2.3)
- the third stage (since 1992) involved the abolition of remaining direct controls and interventions, incorporation into Greek law of the

secondary community legislation on the establishment of the single European financial market (*see* Section 2.2), and preparing Greek credit institutions and the supporting mechanisms of the Greek financial system for the technical and operational modifications required for introducing the single European currency, the euro (*see* Section 3).

2.2 Main SMP legislation

Table 6.4 Implementation of EC banking legislation into Greek law

Regulatory measure	Council Directive	Greek Legislation
Capital movements	Capital Movements Directive (88/361/EEC)	Presidential Decrees 96/1993 and 104/1994 Acts* Nos. 2302-4/1994; 2416-7/1997
Authorisation requirements	First (77/780/EEC) and Second (89/646/EEC) Banking Coordination Directives	Law No. 2076/1992
Freedom to provide services and freedom of establishment	Second Banking Coordination Directive (89/646/EEC)	Law No. 2076/1992
Capital adequacy for credit risk	Solvency Ratio Directive (89/647/EEC)	Act* No. 2054/1992
Capital adequacy for market risks	Capital Adequacy Directive (93/6/EEC)	Law No. 2396/1996 Acts* Nos. 2291/1993; No. 2397/1996
Own funds for meeting capital requirements	Own Funds Directive (89/299/EEC)	Act* No. 2053/1992
Supervision of large exposures	Large Exposures Directive (92/121/EEC)	Act* No. 2246/1993 Law No. 2396/1996
Consolidated supervision	Second Consolidated Supervision Directive (92/30/EEC)	Presidential Decree No. 267/1995 Law No. 2396/1996
Deposit guarantee	Deposit Guarantee Directive (94/19/EEC)	Law No. 2324/1995
Money laundering	Money Laundering Directive (91/308/EEC)	Law No. 2331/1995
Accounting	Bank Accounts Directive (86/635/EEC)	Law No. 2190/1920 (modified periodically)

Note: *Acts instituted by the Governor of the Bank of Greece

2.2.1   An overview

With the gradual deregulation of interest rates (*see* Section 2.2.2), the liberalisation of cross-border capital movements (*see* Section 2.2.3), and the incorporation into Greek law of the benchmark Second Banking Coordination Directive (*see* Section 2.2.4), the introduction of regulatory measures to maintain market stability and protect consumers became a high priority. The Greek Parliament and the BoG closely followed developments in EU law, which required several regulations about the establishment and prudential supervision of Greek credit institutions to prevent excessive risk vulnerability and insolvency exposure (*see* Section 2.2.5).

A deposit guarantee system was created to protect depositors of failing banks and prevent bank runs (*see* Section 2.2.6) and legislation was passed to prevent the financial system being used for money laundering (*see* Section 2.2.7). Bank accounting standards were also harmonised with those in other EU member states according to the provisions of the Bank Accounts Directive (86/635/EEC).

When the programme for liberalising, deregulating and prudentially re-regulating the Greek banking system was completed in 1996 (*see* Table 6.4), all EU Council Directives pertaining to the operation of credit institutions had been incorporated into Greek law. The only remaining barriers to full financial integration are horizontal ones, resulting from the lack of harmonisation on the taxation of incomes from financial assets and from the comparatively (even by European standards) rigid labour legislation.

2.2.2   Interest rate deregulation

According to a three-year phase-in procedure, deposit and lending interest rates were fully deregulated in 1993. Rates are now determined by market forces which are, in turn, influenced by interventions by the BoG in the course of its monetary and foreign exchange policies.

2.2.3   Liberalisation of cross-border capital movements

The cross-border movement of capital between Greek residents and residents of other EU member states was almost fully liberalised in June 1994 in accordance with the provisions of the relevant EU Council Directive. In principle, the same provisions apply to cross-border capital movements involving Greek residents and residents of third, non-EU countries. The last remaining barriers for some short-term cross-border capital movements were lifted in July 1997. As of that date, Greek credit institutions were no longer required to hold 70% of their foreign-currency-denominated deposits with the BoG and could dispose of these funds without restriction.

2.2.4 *The Second Banking Coordination Directive*

The Second Banking Coordination Directive was enacted in 1992 by Law No. 2076, the so-called 'Basic Banking Law'. It provided for the free provision of cross-border financial services by EU-based credit institutions and the freedom of their establishment based on the single licence granted by their home country authorities. It also introduced the principle of mutual recognition of these licences and home country supervision of credit institutions. The BCCI Directive (95/26/EC), which substantially amended some provisions of the Second Banking Directive, was incorporated into Greek law in 1997.

All Greek credit institutions (commercial banks and specialised institutions), including the direct and indirect subsidiaries of EU and non-EU credit and financial institutions incorporated in Greece, are supervised by the General Inspectorate of Banks of the BoG. Exceptionally, the Postal Savings Bank is supervised by the Ministry of Transport and the Deposits and Loans Fund by the Ministry of Finance.

Prudential bank supervision, which is exercised both on an individual and on a consolidated basis, covers two broad areas, solvency and liquidity. Solvency, in turn, has two aspects:

* supervision of the capital adequacy of credit institutions with regard to their exposure to credit, country, and market risks
* supervision of the large exposures of credit institutions to single clients and groups of clients.

Bank compliance with the regulatory measures is controlled by the BoG through external audits and on-site examinations. In addition, under the provisions of the Basic Banking Law and other legislation, all credit institutions operating in Greece are also subject to the following supervisory requirements:

* providing the BoG with reports pertaining to their profitability, exposure to financial risks and their open currency positions
* establishing adequate internal control systems and procedures with regard to their financial operations
* establishing a good administrative and accounting organisation, and adequate systems for monitoring and controlling the interest rate risk arising from their on- and off-balance-sheet activities.

Under EU financial law, bank subsidiaries of EU credit institutions are also subject to the consolidated supervision of the competent authorities of the member state in which the parent credit institution is incorporated. The same applies if the parent undertaking of the Greek subsidiary is a financial institution, for example a holding company, incorporated in another member state.

Table 6.5 Competent authorities for authorisation and prudential supervision of credit institutions in Greece

Nationality of credit institution	Authorisation	Prudential supervision
Greek		
Greek establishment	Bank of Greece	Bank of Greece
Branches in other EU countries	mutually recognised services covered by single licence: Bank of Greece other services: host authorities	solvency: Bank of Greece liquidity: host authorities
Branches in third countries	host authorities	host authorities
Subsidiaries in other EU countries	host authorities	solo supervision: host authorities consolidated supervision: Bank of Greece
Subsidiaries in third countries		solo supervision: host authorities consolidated supervision: Bank of Greece
EU incorporated		
Branches in Greece	mutually recognised services covered by single licence: home authorities other services: Bank of Greece	solvency: home authorities liquidity: Bank of Greece in cooperation with home authorities
Subsidiaries in Greece	Bank of Greece	solo supervision: Bank of Greece consolidated supervision: home authorities
Non-EU incorporated		
Branches in Greece	Bank of Greece	Bank of Greece
Subsidiaries in Greece	Bank of Greece	solo supervision: Bank of Greece consolidated supervision: home authorities

Source: Gortsos (1998)

Greek credit institutions belonging to a financial group are supervised by the BoG on a consolidated basis, irrespective of whether the parent institution of the group is another credit or a financial institution, such as a holding company. As far as the form and extent of consolidation are concerned, in principle the BoG requires the full consolidation of all credit and financial institutions that are subsidiary undertakings of the parent institution. The consolidated supervision of credit institutions includes:

- supervision of their capital adequacy with regard to exposure to financial risks and the supervision of their large exposures
- control of compliance with the limits applying to their participation in other financial and non-financial firms
- verifying the existence of adequate internal control systems.

Greek credit institutions belonging to a financial group are supervised by the BoG on a consolidated basis, irrespective of whether the parent institution of the group is another credit or a financial institution, such as a holding company. As far as the form and extent of consolidation are concerned, in principle the BoG requires the full consolidation of all credit and financial institutions that are subsidiary undertakings of the parent institution. The consolidated supervision of credit institutions includes:

- supervision of their capital adequacy with regard to exposure to financial risks and the supervision of their large exposures
- control of compliance with the limits applying to their participation in other financial and non-financial firms
- verifying the existence of adequate internal control systems.

2.2.5 Prudential regulations

(a) Capital adequacy
Since December 1996 all Greek credit institutions (with the exception of the Postal Savings Bank and the Deposits and Loans Fund) have been subject to a comprehensive set of capital adequacy requirements as a cover against exposure to credit and market risks. The provisions of Greek law on the calculation of the value exposed to each of these risks and the level of own funds required for covering these exposures draw heavily upon the Capital Adequacy Directive. The most striking deviation from the common European denominator of regulations is the 10% capital requirement imposed on credit institutions as a cover against exposure to

foreign exchange risk, which results in a 25% higher cushion than in other member states.

A *de minimis* exemption from the capital requirements for position, settlement, and counterparty risk applies to credit institutions with a small trading book. These undertakings remain subject only to the provisions pertaining to credit risk (on both their investment and trading books) and foreign exchange risk. Greek credit institutions can only use Tier 1 and Tier 2 capital to meet their capital requirements. They are not entitled to make use of Tier 3 capital in meeting their capital requirements against exposure to market risks.

(b) Supervision of large exposures
In its aim to control bank excessive exposure to single borrowers and to induce portfolio diversification, the BoG requires that credit institutions continuously report excessive concentration of exposures and limit such exposures to a certain percentage of their own funds. Credit institutions must report to the competent authorities each large exposure to a single client or group of connected clients. An exposure is considered large if its value is equal to or exceeds 10% of the own funds of the credit institution concerned. All assets and off-balance sheet items taken into account for the calculation of the solvency ratio of credit institutions against exposure to credit risk are considered exposures in this respect. Two limits are applied to the large exposures of credit institutions:

- the value of each large exposure may not exceed 25% of their own funds
- the sum of all large exposures may not exceed 800% of their own funds.

Since January 1997 any credit institution subject to the legal provisions about capital adequacy with respect to market risks must also monitor and control its large exposures to clients and groups of connected clients from positions arising in its trading book subject to the modifications laid down therein. The limits on large exposures arising in the trading book are subject to a 'soft limit', but the excess must be covered by own funds.

(c) Prudential liquidity requirements
All credit institutions operating in Greece must provide the BoG with specific information concerning their overall liquidity on a quarterly basis. This obligation, in effect since 1993, applies equally to domestic credit institutions and the Greek branches of EU and non-EU credit institutions.

The BoG keeps records of the information collected but it does not impose specific target liquidity ratios on credit institutions. In fulfilling the prudential liquidity requirement, each credit institution must submit a series of liquidity tables in which all asset and liability items are inserted in seven maturity bands according to their remaining maturity.

2.2.6   The deposit guarantee system

The Greek deposit guarantee system began operating in September 1995 according to the provisions of a law which incorporated the EU Deposit Guarantee Directive into Greek law. It is managed by a fund administered by a seven-member board of directors representing the BoG, the Hellenic Bank Association (3 members each), and the Ministry of National Economy.

All credit institutions incorporated in Greece are required to participate in the deposit guarantee system. According to the prevailing home country rule adopted in the Directive, the Greek deposit guarantee system covers deposits in Greek credit institutions irrespective of whether or not these deposits were accepted in Greece, in branches established in other member states, or in branches in third, non-EU, countries. In addition, the deposits accepted by the Greek branches of credit institutions incorporated in other member states are covered by the deposit guarantee system established in the member state where the credit institution is incorporated. If the level and scope of coverage in Greece is more generous than in the home member state, however, these branches can ask to participate in the Greek system for additional coverage.

Greek law adopted the minimum level of coverage provided for in the Deposit Guarantee Directive, that is the drachma equivalent of 20,000 euro held by each depositor in the same credit institution. The system covers the deposits made by a wide range of individuals and legal entities, with exceptions being only those listed in the law. The deposit guarantee system is funded by annual contributions from the participating credit institutions and are calculated according to a rule linking eligible deposits to specific deposit brackets in declining orders of magnitude. The procedure for compensating persons or legal entities whose deposits are covered by the system is activated when the deposits of a participating credit institution become unavailable either because of a decision by the BoG or a court order.

2.2.7   Prevention of money laundering

In August 1995 the Greek parliament passed a law preventing the use of the financial system for money laundering. Greek legislation closely follows the terms of the relevant EU Directive and its provisions can be summarised as follows:

* any action undertaken by a person to legitimise or support the legitimisation of revenues from illegal activities is considered a criminal offence. The law differentiates three types of such actions
* there is an comprehensive list of sixteen criminal offences considered as the 'illegal activities' generating the funds to be money laundered. This list includes offences connected with the illegal trade of narcotics, weaponry, and antiquities, as well as the removal and transplantation of human organs
* to help prevent money laundering, credit and financial institutions, insurance undertakings, and several other types of financial intermediaries must carry out certain procedures. These include asking their customers and any counterparty to prove their identity; conserving the documents pertaining to contracts and transactions for at least five years; carefully checking any transaction that, by its nature, could be connected with money laundering; implementing adequate internal control and communication procedures to prevent transactions connected with money laundering; and notifying the authorities, under specific conditions, of any suspicious transaction. A derogation from the provisions of private law on banking secrecy is also introduced for this purpose
* to ensure proper implementation of the law, a public authority has been established with the participation of representatives from several ministries, the BoG, the Athens Stock Exchange, and the Hellenic Bank Association. The purpose of this authority is to collect, evaluate, and analyse the information transmitted to it by the above financial intermediaries as possible indications of money laundering transactions.

2.3 Other domestic regulatory landmarks

2.3.1   Abolition of direct credit controls
By the end of 1993, the system of direct credit controls on Greek credit institutions was fully lifted. The obligation imposed upon credit institutions to hold 10% of their deposits in a reserve for extending credit to small and medium-size enterprises was removed and the requirement to invest up to 40% of their deposits in low-yielding government Treasury bills has been abolished. The preferential access of the Greek government to the banking system for financing and the obligatory financing of public

enterprises and organisations (set at 9% of bank deposits) was lifted by the prohibitive provisions of the Maastricht Treaty. In addition, credit institutions are no longer required to redeposit part of their deposits in foreign currencies with the BoG and they have been allowed to issue credit cards without authorisation by the BoG. A quantitative cap, however, is still being applied.

2.3.2   De-specialisation of credit institutions

A major structural feature of the Greek banking system was institutional specialisation required by law and not dictated by market forces. However, the distinction between commercial banks and specialised credit institutions has become considerably less clear in recent years. As we have seen in the previous section, the playing field for specialised credit institutions and commercial banks has been levelled since commercial banks can now provide their clients with the whole range of commercial and investment banking services permitted by law and specialised credit institutions have almost unlimited financial powers.

2.3.3   Modernisation of money and capital markets

The process of financial disintermediation started in 1987 and peaked in 1990 with the quickly growing Athens Stock Exchange and development of the market for short-term public debt. Many firms went public in the late 1980s and several companies, including major financial institutions, took advantage of the booming stock market to issue new shares. However, the persistently high level of nominal interest rates (mainly caused by large fiscal deficits) and adverse tax incentives prevented the development of commercial papers, long-term treasury bonds, and almost any issue of corporate bills and bonds.

The Greek capital market developed rapidly during the second half of the 1990s, supported by an accommodating legal framework. Book-entry bonds and equity shares are replacing traditional paper-based securities traded in the Athens Stock Exchange; transparency requirements were implemented; the range of market intermediaries was widened and their functions clearly defined. A new financial centre was established in Thessaloniki, the second largest city of Greece, to contribute to the smooth functioning of capital market operations in Northern Greece and become the basis for a regional Balkan financial market. In addition, a new exchange, the Athens Derivatives Exchange, was incorporated and started operating in August 1999.

The depth of money markets increased as well. In addition, a reference interbank interest rate, the Athens Interbank Offered Rate

(ATHIBOR), was launched, calculated on the basis of quotes given by eighteen credit institutions operating in Greece.

2.3.4   *Modernisation of monetary policy*

Monetary policy in Greece is conducted by the BoG. Since the early 1990s its policy orientation has consistently focused upon maintaining price stability, while also supporting the overall economic policy of stabilising the Greek economy. Supported by an accommodating foreign exchange policy, monetary policy contributed much to the considerable reduction in inflation from a peak of 22.7% in December 1990 to 2% in August 1999, and to a gratifying improvement in the balance of payments during recent years.

In order to achieve its goals within the context of a gradually but extensively deregulated financial system, the BoG reduced its emphasis on direct controls and interventions and shifted to market-oriented policy instruments. Open market operations have now become the main means of controlling monetary aggregates and the BoG has enlarged the framework for providing lending and deposit facilities to credit institutions for liquidity enhancement and deposit absorption. The extremely high level of a 12% reserve requirement imposed on credit institutions (yielding returns well below those of the market) remains the only regulation reminiscent of the old interventionist framework.

3   BANK PREPARATIONS FOR EMU

3.1 Greece as a member state with derogation

On 2 May 1998, the Council of the European Union, in the composition of heads of state and governments of the member states, decided that 11 member states could adopt the single European currency, the euro, as their national currency on 1 January 1999. The heavy macroeconomic imbalances of previous years prevented the convergence of the Greek economy to the levels required for Greece to join the first members of the eurozone. Greece will join this group of countries at a later stage since it managed to meet the convergence criteria prescribed in the Maastricht Treaty in 2000. As a matter of fact, the Greek government applied for participation in the eurozone in March 2000 and is expected to adopt the single currency on 1 January 2001.

Table 6.6 summarises the figures pertaining to the convergence criteria as they applied to Greece at the end of February 2000. According to the 'Convergence Reports' submitted by the European Commission and the European Monetary Institute in March 1998, Greek legislation is already compatible with the provisions of the Maastricht Treaty and the statute of the European System of Central Banks. In particular, the statutes of the BoG were amended in December 1997 to provide for the personal, financial, and operational independence of the BoG.

Table 6.6 Maastricht Treaty convergence criteria as applied to Greece

Criteria	Reference rate	February 2000
Inflation rate (%)	2.4	2.0
Long-term interest rates (%)	7.2	6.4
Budget deficit/GDP (%)	3.0	1.6
Debt/GDP (%)	60.0	104.4 (but on a constantly declining path)
Participation in ERM (I and II) for two years		Yes

3.2 Banking sector responses

The procedure leading to European monetary unification was supported heavily by the Greek banking sector. After the introduction of the single currency it is expected that the macroeconomic environment will be characterised by satisfactory growth rates, low inflation, fiscal discipline and, in consequence, by lower real and nominal interest rates. This is expected to boost overall economic activity and, necessarily, demand for financial intermediation. A reliable single monetary policy will lead to stabilised, low interest rates, while the completion of the European internal financial market will enhance the efficiency of money and capital markets, thus reducing the cost and increasing the range of products and services offered.

Since prospects for the development of financial activity within the eurozone are positive, competition among financial intermediaries is expected to intensify, accompanied by increased penetration, even though selective, of the Greek market by foreign banks. This will induce changes in the functioning of money and capital markets and the structure of the banking sector of all EU member states, whether with or without a derogation. It will also stimulate the reallocation of market shares through mergers and acquisitions, developments already evident because of the

SMP, rapid technological evolution, and the internationalisation of finance.

Even though banks will profit from monetary unification, adjustment costs will also be involved. These will affect bank profitability in both the short and in the long term. During a transitional period, banks in Greece will have to cope with the costs associated with the withdrawal from circulation of existing banknotes and coins denominated in drachma and their replacement by euro-denominated banknotes and coins, the adjustment of their operating systems to the conditions of the single currency, and a reduction in the volume of several banking activities after the introduction of the euro. These costs were examined in a study by the Hellenic Bank Association (1998).

Approximately 3,500 money transports will be needed to transport the existing stock of drachma-denominated banknotes to the storage rooms of the BoG before their withdrawal from circulation. Transportation of coins to be withdrawn from circulation will require a further few thousand money transports. The volume of euro-denominated banknotes and coins to be transported for placing in circulation will be smaller because the smallest subdivision of the euro (the one cent) will be much greater in value than one drachma.

With the beginning of the third stage of EMU, and especially before 1 January 2001 (when Greece will join the eurozone), Greek banks also will have to undergo significant operational changes, such as adjusting transaction systems (ATMs, counting machines, electronic transactions), software programs, and information systems; settling a considerable amount of balances which will result from the conversion of assets from the drachma into the euro; changing contracts, accounting systems and stationery; training personnel; and informing both their customers and the general public. These changes will involve costs which, for a certain period of time, will increase the operational cost of banks.

Based on estimations made by European bank associations and individual banks, the adjustment costs involved for the Greek banking system has been estimated to range between GRD10.2 and GRD29.5 billion (*see* Table 6.7). The cost could reach the highest estimate because of the high percentage of cash transactions; the extensive use of stationery for conducting transactions and completing services; storing, and also withdrawing from circulation, a considerable amount of banknotes in monetary units of the member states of the eurozone (accumulated mainly from tourist-related activities); and the relatively low level of development and use of electronic and remote means of payment. In addition, since

Greece did not join the eurozone on 1 January 1999, considerable adjustments will be made only towards the end of the transitional period.

Table 6.7 Estimated adjustment costs to the Greek banking system from the changeover to the euro

	Amounts in billion GRD	Amounts in billion GRD
Total assets	26,902	
Estimated cost for 0.072% of total assets		19.37
Cost range:		
+ 1 standard deviation		28.52
(0,072 + 0,034 = 0,106%)		
1 standard deviation		10.22
(0,072 - 0,034 = 0,038%)		
Total operating costs	737.4	
Estimated cost for 3,37% of total operating expenses		24.85
Cost range:		
+ 1 standard deviation		29.50
(3,37 + 0,63 = 4,00%)		
1 standard deviation		20.20
(3,37 - 0,63 = 2,74%)		

Notes: The estimations on the adjustment cost of the Greek banking sector are based on the sum of total assets of Greek commercial banks and specialised credit institutions. Operating expenses include general management expenses, depreciations and all other operating expenses

Source: Hellenic Bank Association (1998)

Introducing the euro also will affect banking activities and will lead to a reformation of the sources from which banks earn income. The financial activities associated with currency trading in particular (spot and forward foreign exchange transactions for commercial and tourist activities, speculation or risk hedging, swap transactions, capital transfers, currency deposits, maintenance of current accounts of foreign banks by Greek banks, and custodian services), will shrink after the changeover to the euro. In addition, it must be taken into consideration that about 80% of Greek imports and exports are conducted with other EU member states. On the basis of a small sample of the larger Greek banks, the income loss from the above was estimated to be about 10% of their total net commission income, or about 3% of their net income.

3.3 Banking sector scenarios in the run-up to EMU and beyond

As already mentioned, the severe macroeconomic imbalances of the 1980s and the early 1990s negatively affected Greece's prospects of becoming a member of the eurozone on 1 January 1999. In recent years, however, the Greek economy has improved considerably. Inflation was tamed, the levels of nominal and real interest rates were reduced and, most importantly, public spending was kept under control and the public debt stabilised, though both at comparatively high levels. The current stability provides a solid basis for the growth of banking activity and the improvement of banking performance.

Conditions will further improve during the year 2000, and even more so in 2001 with the introduction of the euro and the application of the Stability and Growth Pact. Interest rate levels will converge even further towards those of the other member states of the eurozone and the foreign exchange risk of drachma-denominated assets will be eliminated. In addition, fiscal consolidation will lead to a significant reduction of the country risk premium paid by Greek issuers, including the Treasury, for their debt. The credit rating of Greek banks and, accordingly, their funding cost, will depend heavily on the country's macroeconomic performance.

The expected effects of the introduction of the euro upon the European banking sector are well known: intensified competition, internationalised activities, easier penetration by foreign banks in domestic markets without establishing a physical presence. Since cross-border financial activity within the eurozone is expected to increase even further, some large Greek export-oriented companies may explore opportunities for more cost-efficient funding from credit and financial institutions incorporated in other member states. This means that internationalisation and intensified competition will adversely affect at least some Greek bank activities such as:

- investment banking services (including debt and equity underwriting, financial consulting, management of syndicated loans, custody services, listing in stock exchanges, project finance, sophisticated banking products and services)
- dealing room activities (such as foreign exchange and interbank transactions, dealing in securities, and operations in financial derivatives)
- asset management (mainly through private banking, mutual funds and trust management, either for institutional clients or for individuals with or without discretionary power)
- financing and providing services to large companies and organisations.

On the other hand, to the extent that branch networks, knowledge of the local market, and long-term relationships with customers retain their importance, retail banking operations will continue to be sheltered from international competition even after the introduction of the euro. This is confirmed by the fact that, despite their local presence, often for more than two decades, foreign banks in Greece have not become major competitors in the fields of mortgage finance, consumer lending, or in providing services to small and medium-sized businesses.

In addition to adapting their operations to the requirements imposed by the introduction of the euro, Greek banks will have to reappraise their strategies for survival in the single European financial market. In the years to come, some of them will retain a domestic orientation by exploiting the comparative advantages of their local presence. Since Greece's ratio of consumer and housing loans to the gross domestic product is the lowest among the member states of the EU, the expected growth in these markets will provide opportunities for Greek banks to grow and profit. Some Greek banks, however, will attempt to compete on a European scale by penetrating the markets of other member states and/or resist the increased competition from other EU-based banks in Greece (which may choose to provide services in Greece only on a cross-border basis).

All Greek banks will need to undergo major restructuring. In particular, the banks exposed to international competition are urged to undertake one or more of the following courses of action:

- exploit economies of scale by rationalising their operations, to achieve adequate size for competing on a Europe-wide basis
- exploit economies of scope by establishing efficient financial groups with high solvency ratios and creating strategic cross-border alliances to control networks for distributing products internationally
- create a considerable capital basis which would allow them to be funded at low cost and to carry out large-value financial transactions
- invest in technology and human capital
- reduce their (comparatively high) operating costs
- develop modern methods and infrastructures for managing their exposure to financial and operational risks
- and participate actively in banking activities in the peripheral areas of the country.

Recent and pending mergers and acquisitions in the banking sector and the efforts undertaken by all financial intermediaries operating in Greece to rationalise their operations are the best indicators of the impact European monetary unification will have on the Greek banking system in 2001, when Greece will become a member state without derogation. The structure of the Greek banking system and the performance profile of financial intermediaries operating in this system will be definitively different from what has been described in this paper.

Note

The study is updated to March 2000. Statistical data were available only until 1999.

References

Bank of Greece, *Annual Report of the Governor* (various issues) (Bank of Greece, Athens).

Committee for the Reform and Modernisation of the Greek Banking System (the Karatzas Committee) (1987), *The Committee's Report on the Reform and Modernisation of the Greek Banking System* (Hellenic Bank Association, Athens).

Economic Research Europe Ltd (1997), *The Single Market Review: Impact on Credit Institutions and Banking*, (Kogan Page, London)

European Central Bank (February 1999), *Possible Effects of EMU on the EU Banking Systems in the Medium to Long Term* (ECB, Frankfurt).

European Commission (1998), *Convergence Report* (EC, Brussels).

European Monetary Institute (1998): *Convergence Report 1998* (EMI, Frankfurt).

Gortsos, C. V. (1998), *The Greek Banking System*, Hellenic Bank Association (Ant. N. Sakkoulas Publishers, Athens *and* Bryulant, Brussels).

Hellenic Bank Association (1998), *Euro: Adaptations and Implications for the Greek Banking Sector from the European and Monetary Union and the Introduction of the Euro* (Ant. N. Sakkoulas Publishers, Athens).

Kostis, K. (1986), *Banks and the Crisis*. (Studies of Contemporary Hellenic History, Historical Archive, Commercial Bank of Greece, Athens).

Massourakis, M. (1998), 'EMU and the Greek banking system', *The Bulletin*, Hellenic Bank Association, 14, pp. 48-54.

Moschos, D. and D. Fragetis (1997), *The Present and Future of Greek Banks* (Institute of Economic and Industrial Research (IOBE), Athens).

Organisation for Economic Cooperation and Development (1996), *Bank Profitability* (OECD, Paris).

Organisation for Economic Cooperation and Development (1995), *Greece: OECD Economic Surveys* (OECD, Paris).

Pagoulatos, G. (1997), *Institutions and Public Policy Making: the Politics of Greek Banking Deregulation and Privatisation,* Doctoral Thesis, Oxford University (unpublished).

Pantelias, S. (1998), 'Profitability sources of Greek banks after the introduction of the euro', *The Bulletin*, Hellenic Bank Association, 14, pp. 62-7.

Provopoulos, G. *ed..* (1995), *The Greek Financial System* (Institute of Economic and Industrial Research (IOBE), Athens).

White, W. R. (1998), *The Coming Transformation of Continental European Banking*, Bank for International Settlements Working Papers No. 54 (BIS, Basle).

Zavvos, G. S. (1989), *EEC Banking Policy in View of 1992: Strategic Targets for the Greek Banking System,* Hellenic Bank Association (Ant. N. Sakkoulas Publishers, Athens).

7   Ireland

Ray Kinsella and Philip Bourke

1   INTRODUCTION

The Irish financial system, at the heart of which are credit institutions, has experienced a period of unprecedented expansion and structural change since the mid-1980s. There was a broadening and deepening in the key services provided by banks, both domestic institutions as well as those from other EU countries and from outside the European Economic Area (EEA), in intermediation, deposit taking and money transmission, financial and investment services, and portfolio management and related services.

This change process has been accompanied by institutional (including regulatory) and structural change. It is reflected in the transformation of the balance sheet of credit institutions. This has been facilitated by major investment by banks in management competencies, particularly in risk management, technology, marketing and compliance.

The key drivers of change include:

- the completion of the SMP
- the process of internationalisation, reflected particularly in the overseas expansion of the two major domestically-based banks, AIB and Bank of Ireland, as well as the process of portfolio diversification which followed the abolition of exchange controls in 1992
- the establishment in the docklands of the capital city, Dublin, of the International Financial Services Centre (IFSC) in 1987. The IFSC has attracted several hundred global financial service providers.

The SMP contributed substantially to the further liberalisation of what, since the late 1960s, had ostensibly been a relatively open banking market. Global competitive pressures reinforced the effects of the SMP and thereby contributed to the process of deregulation of credit institutions and also to the emergence of bancassurance as the dominant institutional structure.

The impact of the SMP has been enormously leveraged by technological innovation, especially in the latter half of the 1990s, just as the effects of the Single Market worked their way through the market. Technology has increased the contestability of the Irish banking market. It has facilitated entry on a cross-border basis and the creation, and marketing, of a whole new generation of distance-independent financial services. Domestically, it has allowed non-traditional banking service providers (notably retailers) to attack the franchise of the major banks in core savings and payments markets. Equally, it has created new opportunities for joint ventures. The banks have developed technological delivery systems alongside their branch network in order to broaden their product range. Having said that, there is little doubt but that technology has made it easier for non-banks to enter banking/financial services than for banks to expand outside of their core markets.

2 MARKET STRUCTURE AND PERFORMANCE

2.1 Developments in the number of institutions

Table 7.1 shows developments in the number of credit institutions in 1985, 1990, 1995 and 1997. The table also highlights developments in a progressively wider range of institutions now supervised by the Central Bank. Perhaps the first point to note is the increase in the number of credit institutions now operating within, and from, Ireland. The effects of the Second and Third Banking Directives – the Single Market – are clear. Equally clear is the enormous growth, particularly since the early 1990s, in a much wider set of investment services (Table 7.2). This reflects both the effect of the SMP as well as the growth in global financial markets over the period, and also the extent to which the IFSC has, through effective government intervention in taxation, infrastructure and education, successfully exploited this environment.

The data should be interpreted with some caution. Firstly, it is only since the late 1980s, and more generally into the 1990s, that certain important institutions (notably investment intermediaries) have been licensed. Concurrently, there was a progressive devolution of regulatory responsibility to the Central Bank. Secondly, the single banking licence means that responsibility for market entry is now shared with the regulatory authorities in other EU and EEA countries. Thirdly, there have been other definitional and compositional changes. All of these should be borne in mind when interpreting Table 7.1. Nonetheless, the main picture is clear: there has been an unprecedented expansion in banking and financial services, and in supporting infrastructure in Ireland, between 1985 and the late 1990s. And the implementation of the SMP was, directly and indirectly (in combination with other factors), a major factor in this expansion.

2.2 Branch network

Up to the end of the 1980s, the branch network was central to the distribution strategy of the associated (clearing) banks. The building societies also operated a branch network as did, in a more abbreviated form, the two state banks. The branch network underpinned the money transmission system operated by the clearing banks. Importantly, it served as an effective entry barrier, protecting the retail franchise of the associated banks.

The 1990s have seen fundamental developments in regard to the branch network in Ireland and other EU countries. Table 7.3 shows the branch network density (population/branch) for Ireland compared with other EU countries. In Ireland there has been a rapid development of IT-based distribution platforms that both complement (for the associated banks) and compete with the branch network. Between 1990 and 1995, there was a small rise in the branch network of the clearing (and state) banks, from 705 to 729. Concurrently, the number of ATMs rose from 484 to 853, and by 1977 to approach 1000. The number of ATM cards doubled to over 2 million. So, too, did the number of transactions, to 90 million. More recently, there has been a rapid growth (from zero) in real-time IT-based payments transfers. The clearing banks operate direct telephone banking, and credit institutions (including building societies) now provide banking facilities over the internet. The growth of internet-based distribution systems since 1998 has been especially notable, a characteristic Ireland shares with other EU countries.

These developments constitute a fundamental shift in the role of the branch. As IT-based payments and distribution systems have become relatively more important, bank branches have evolved primarily into marketing outlets for financial services. This is reflected in investment in, and the configuration of, branches. Increasingly, this has been reinforced by other developments. The first is the impact of the EMU-related low interest rate environment on traditional branch-centred savings products. Irish banks, like their EU counterparts, have by necessity had to develop a range of higher-yielding (including equity-backed) savings products. Secondly, the evolution of the major clearing banks into bancassurance has given banks additional impetus and opportunities to sell a broader portfolio of products through the branch network. Processing activities have largely been taken out of branches.

Table 7.1 Development in financial institutions, 1985-97

Year ended 31 Dec	Licensed by Central Bank				Investment intermediaries authorised by Central Bank	IFSC companies regulated by Central Banks	Collective investment schemes authorised by Central Bank[1]	Other financial services		Money brokers
	Cross-border basis	Operating in the State	Branch basis					Non-discretionary investment intermediaries	Stock-brokers	
			EU	EEA & Other						
1985		30			NA	NA	-	-	-	-
1990		47	3	2	NA	NA	-	-	-	-
1995	59	48	11	2	21[2]	96	759	-	10	6
1997	92	53	18	2	141[3]	73	1,221	500	15	6

[1] Includes sub-trusts
[2] Of which 15 are IFSC companies
[3] Of which 95 are IFSC companies

Table 7.2 IFSC Collective Investment Schemes, 1990-1997

	UCITS		Unit trusts		Designated investment companies		Management companies	Trustee
	No.	TNAV	No.	TNAV	No.	TNAV	No.	No.
1990	18	611	26	1356			18	10
1995	120	9314	78	2026	90	2745	75	17
1997	176	16337	101	5024	234	12075	128	26

Note: TNAV = Total net asset value (£million)
Source: Central Bank

In the 1980s, as noted, the branch network was a major barrier to market entry and, it should be said, to the completion of the SMP. This is much less true today. Competition has increased from both non-bank domestic suppliers of services (such as retailers) and from overseas institutions. To take one example: in 1997 almost 100 credit institutions from EEA countries had notified the central bank of their intention to provide services on a cross-border basis.

Table 7.3 Branch network density ratios, 1995

	Population/Branch	*Employee/Branch*
Belgium	1324	9.93
Spain	2199	8.26
Netherlands	2330	15.67
Portugal	2640	15.79
Italy	2720	15.93
Ireland	*3716*	*21.78*
Greece	3834	16.52
Sweden	3919	17.43
UK	4999	26.37
France	5539	19.24
Finland	6766	28.02
Norway	9603	30.77
Germany	10860	21.99
Austria	10850	28.92

Source: IBF/IBES

2.3 Ownership structure and privatisation

Irish banking has long exhibited a diversity of ownership structure. Over the last decade, three of the largest building societies have demutualised, while the Government has privatised the largest insurer. In 1998 the Government announced the sale of ICC Bank, the first such privatisation. In practice, the sale of both ICC Bank and the other state bank, ACC Bank, has proved difficult. By the beginning of 2000 the Government had not yet completed their disposal. However, the most obvious division is between, on the one hand, domestic credit institutions which are subsidiaries and, more recently, as a result of the SMP, branches of overseas institutions.

Broadly, one can distinguish four categories of institutions:

- the two major Irish-based banks, AIB and Bank of Ireland, are listed on the Irish and UK stock exchanges and have a broad shareholding base. So, too, does Irish Permanent, which demutualised in 1994 and in 1998 'merged' with Irish Life to form a major bancassurance force, Irish Life and Permanent. Woodchester, formerly owned by Crédit Lyonnais and recently acquired by GE, is also listed, as is Anglo Irish Bank. Two of the large clearing banks, Ulster Bank and National Irish Bank, are subsidiaries of major overseas banking groups, NatWest and National Australia Bank respectively. The takeover of NatWest by Royal Bank of Scotland in 2000 involved the disposal of Ulster Bank, which is still to be completed
- the state sector comprises ICC Bank Ltd and ACC Bank. Both were set up in the 1930s to foster industry and agriculture. By the 1980s, with the growth of financial markets, their original rationale had largely disappeared. In the early 1990s, a proposal by the then Government to establish a so-called 'Third Banking Force' comprising these banks and also the TSB, stymied the privatisation/acquisition process. This proposal was subsequently dropped. More recently, in 1998, the Minister for Finance announced his intention to sell ICC Bank. It is likely that ACC Bank will also be disposed of as soon as market conditions permit. The Government is also likely to approve a strategic initiative by the Trustee Savings Bank (TSB) to participate in the consolidation process that is already under way. The rationale for state participation in banking no longer exists
- in the early 1980s a strong mutual building society sector existed in Ireland. The Building Society Act 1989 allowed, inter alia, for demutualisation. The Irish Permanent, the largest mutual building society, availed itself of this option in 1994. Another large mutual, First National Building Society, completed this process in 1998. The scope for building societies to provide banking services and the fact that they are now supervised by the Central Bank on the same basis as other licensed banks, together with the extraordinary growth in the mortgage-related business by licensed banks, has focused attention on the future of other mutual building societies. The Educational Building Society (EBS) has indicated that it will retain its mutual status and has used its non-profit status to compete with the banks on the basis of margins. In many ways, the debate on the ownership structure of the building societies in Ireland mirrors that in the UK
- the importance of cooperative banks, a feature of some continental EU countries, is not evident in the Irish banking market. On the other hand, there is a large credit union sector. Credit unions accept deposits and

make advances to members. They are not-for-profit organisations, owned by members, and have a common governance structure. The Credit Union Act 1997 enhanced their profile and scope to compete with banks in their specialised niche.

2.4 Competition

The last decade or so has seen an intensification of competitive pressures in a radically transformed set of financial markets in Ireland. The key features of the Irish banking market in the mid-1980s were:

- the high level of market concentration associated with the dominance of the clearing 'associated' banks
- an institutionally segregated market characterised by regulatory and structural entry barriers
- a regulatory/supervisory regime that muted the impact on the major banks by ensuring that they generated an adequate rate of return
- an attenuated set of capital market services with limited access to non-debt forms of finance.

The SMP has progressively transformed this structure, working with the grain of developments in global financial markets, specifically deregulation, financial innovation, and technology. The Irish banking market is now more contestable and, so, competitive. What may be termed 'endogenous' entry barriers (networks, reputations, and so on) remain. But it is clear that bank management strategy is predicated on the fact that banks now operate in an essentially global market place. This will be reinforced by the prospective impact of EMU in terms of minimum efficient scale and price transparency in banking.

Domestically, a number of factors have, since the early 1990s, reinforced the competitive impact of the SMP:

- in retail banking, the consolidation of the hitherto regionally based Trustee Savings Banks into a single entity
- the effect of the Building Societies Act 1989 that provided building societies (now categorised as credit institutions) with additional scope to compete with the banks
- the demutualisation and listing of the Irish Permanent, which rapidly developed as a domestic conglomerate before merging with Irish Life.

These developments have contributed directly to competition across the marketplace: individually, the business re-engineering associated with demutualisation and listing contributed to a culture of competitiveness and a strong focus on shareholder value across the finance services spectrum.

The banks' intermediation role has come under pressure from the substantial, and latent, capability of retailers in providing niche existing products. For large banks in a small domestic market this poses particular problems: either accept an erosion of market share from strategically placed service providers (with brand name/reputation/location/'loyalty culture'/masters of marketing strategy and excellent informational advantages and IT systems) or seek joint ventures with them in the knowledge that retailers will capture most of the value embedded in service processes and, they may, in the process, cannibalise their own customer base.

In their core savings markets, these developments have brought considerable pressure on the banks. There is an additional pressure, one which is evident across the face of banking in the EU: the sustained low interest rate environment has, as argued, seriously eroded the attractions of banks' individual savings products. Returns are simply too low. Consequently, banks have had to develop a wider portfolio of savings products. In Ireland, equity-backed savings products, such as tracker bonds in various forms (for example with capital guarantees and embedded options), now offer greater attractions than traditional current and time deposits.

In Ireland, no less than in other countries, there are clear indications of disintermediation. The growth in capital market services, both domestically and in the wider EU, creates three forms of competitive pressure for banks:

- the need to compete for domestic business with other EU banks
- the need to offer progressively better terms to mid-sized corporates
- the possibility of an erosion in the risk profile of corporate customers, a classic 'adverse selection' process.

The emphasis so far has been on emerging competitive pressures on banks right across the spectrum of asset- and fee-based activities. It should not, however, be inferred that banks have been passive in these circumstances. Quite the contrary. The evolution of the associated banks as bancassurance organisations, the internationalisation of the two major domestic groups, the rapid expansion in growth markets such as fund management, and also the rapid expansion of IFSC-related activities which now generate, in the case of AIB, Bank of Ireland and Ulster Bank, in excess of 10% of total revenues, is evidence of a strong competitive capability.

2.5 Market concentration

Analysis of the market structure of Irish banking at the start of the 1980s suggested that the major clearing banks had significant market power and, also, that this was reflected in above normal profitability. The latter was a function, not simply of the market structure, but also of institutional and other de facto entry barriers. The SMP was a major factor in the transformation of this structure though it was not until the early/mid-1990s that the full effects had worked their way through. Even then, the effects of the SMP in dampening the impact of domestic market concentration are overlain by other powerful structural factors.

Dias attempted to measure concentration and competition in the mid-1990s using the Rosse-Panzat H statistics[1]. Her analysis indicated that the behaviour of bank revenues for the period 1993-95 corresponded to monopolistic competition. Notwithstanding the scope, *in principle,* for entry, the data indicated the absence of conditions for free and unconstrained entry and exit. Dias infers that this may have reflected:

- the fact that the full impact of the Second Banking Directive had not yet worked its way through
- the existence of non-legal entry barriers, including the small size of the market from the perspective of major EU groups and, more especially, the branch network, networking and switching costs.

While, in principle, high market concentration was reflected in the relatively weak level of competition, the relationship was complex. Other factors were also important, including the method of central bank supervision which aimed, inter alia, at ensuring an appropriate level of profitability for prudential purposes. Also important in terms of market structure were the facts that the dominant associated banks were 'too big to fail' and the substantial entry costs into retail banking in a small open economy (especially in the light of the defensive mergers of the 1960s/early 1970s in the face of entry by UK banks).

2.6 Banking performance

The total assets of the clearing banks rose from £39 billion to £55 billion between 1990 and 1995. By end-1997 they exceeded £70 billion. Total after-tax profits of the clearing banks rose, over the same period, from £174 million to £670 million. Over the period 1990-97, and more specifically since 1994, the share prices of AIB and Bank of Ireland have consistently outperformed the market (ISEQ) index and also their UK peers. More recently, and in part because of sector-specific factors, there has been a sharp decline from these buoyant levels.

There are a number of factors which need to be borne in mind in assessing this performance, especially into the mid-1990s:

- a strong emphasis on cost control reflected in a progressive decline in the cost/income ratio. In the case of Bank of Ireland this was associated with a period of domestic retrenchment and consolidation in the early 1990s, following what proved to be a costly (at least in the short-/medium-term) acquisition of Bank of New Hampshire (BNH) in the US in 1988
- a strong emphasis on shareholder value 'as a core business principle'[2]. This has served as a catalyst for a 'performance culture' and strategic and management processes have been build around this culture. The Irish Permanent, prior to its merger with Irish Life, is a good example. At the same time, the emphasis on shareholder value has, in the case of AIB and Bank of Ireland, served to protect (so far) the banks from overseas predators by driving up the acquisition premium to book value
- a systematic and strategically driven process of overseas expansion, providing both geographical and sectoral diversification. Both AIB and Bank of Ireland have learned from their recent history in the 1980s and 1990s the importance of protecting their domestic franchise. At the same time, both need to escape the constraints of what is a small domestic market. The twin strategy of organic growth and focused expansion through acquisition pursued by both banks in the 1990s helps to explain their ROE and their share price performance.

Recent overseas acquisitions need to be seen against the backdrop of highly problematic acquisitions, leading to difficulties, in the 1980s. AIB's purchase of ICC (with large unanticipated exposures arising from its London activities) in 1984 left the bank vulnerable. Bank of Ireland's acquisition of BNH in 1988, cost the bank dearly in the early 1990s. Lessons were learned.

In 1995, AIB acquired Dauphin Deposit, positioning it in the top 50 banks in the US. This was a highly strategic response by AIB to the emergence in the mid-1990s of inter-state banking and the 'super-regionals'. This required, in effect, the bank either to invest in building market share to protect its franchise or, alternatively, to exit the market. In 1997, AIB acquired a controlling interest in Weilkopolski Bank Kredytowy in Poland. This, again, was an innovative entry strategy in the heartland of the rapidly evolving banking market in Eastern Europe.

By early 1993, Bank of Ireland had turned around BNH. This was achieved against the background of an intensively focused domestic strategy of reducing costs and getting the domestic market right. In management terms, it was a singularly impressive performance by then Chief Executive, Patrick Molloy. This provided a robust platform on which to build value-creating options in regard to BNH while also resuming a more positive approach to the bank's regional hinterland. It merged BNH with Citizens Bank (in which Royal Bank of Scotland has a majority shareholding). In 1997, Citizens Bank made some local acquisitions intended to reinforce its market share. This opened up a range of options for Bank of Ireland in the US market. Meanwhile, in 1997 it felt free to acquire the UK's Bristol and West Building Society and, in the Irish market, New Ireland Insurance Company.

It will be clear that, in the 1990s, there have been both defensive and, more especially, strategic dimensions to overseas acquisitions by both AIB and Bank of Ireland. Both have been highly rated by the financial markets as enhancing present and prospective growth. They have contributed materially to the transformation of both banks as bancassurance organisations within the EU, and also US, markets. They explain, to an important degree, the robust performance of both banks in the 1990s. But there are additional factors which cast light on banks' performance.

Firstly, there has been a buoyant domestic economy, with real growth in excess of 6% for the middle and late 1990s. This has boosted credit, especially mortgage, demand while simultaneously reducing bad loans and provisions. Ireland's macroeconomic performance, so central to the value of the major banks' domestic franchise, has been shaped by an unequivocal commitment to EMU and to adherence to the Maastricht convergence criteria. This constituted an essential foundation for economic growth.

Net EU transfer facilitated major capital investment in the central areas of public infrastructure (pivotal, given Ireland's peripheral nature) and research and development. Ireland's favourable demographics, together with high educational standards, served to attract foreign direct investment (FDI) on a scale wholly disproportionate to Ireland's size within the EU market. A strong emphasis on social partnership helped moderate wage demands, helping Ireland cope with the effects of movements in the punt against sterling and protecting cost competitiveness.

These, and related factors, generated a 'virtuous circle' of low inflation, high real growth and a declining debt burden, quite unlike anything experienced elsewhere in the EU. Financial institutions have benefited enormously from these conditions.

This provided the background for the deregulation and expansion of domestic financial markets and institutions. Performance has been enhanced by the demand for asset-based and fee-based activities. Competition from overseas and domestic non-banking institutions, and a low interest rate environment, reduced the demand for, and margins on, traditional savings products. On the other hand, it generated a significant demand for mortgage and insurance-related products, and for asset management services. Asset quality has been improved by the economic environment and by investment in credit management systems.

3 REGULATORY FRAMEWORK

3.1 Developments since the Single European Act 1986

The Irish regulatory and supervisory framework has been transformed since 1985. The key factors have been:

* developments in the regulatory framework which now encompasses in Irish statute law the EU Directives arising both from the SMP and developments in international banking
* the rapid expansions in depth, scale and scope of Irish financial markets. The break in the one-for-one, no-margins link between the Irish pound and sterling in 1978 was an important catalyst. So, too, was the establishment in 1987 of the IFSC. The calibre of global financial institutions attracted to the IFSC[3], together with the range and complexity of the activities, has contributed to the critical mass of the Irish financial sector and in expertise and support functions.

3.2 Main SMP legislation

The statutory framework for the supervision of banks developed very rapidly in the 1990s. It encompasses a very wide range of legislative measures, including Acts, Regulations and Statutory Instruments, some of it extending beyond banking, for example the Companies Act 1990 and the Criminal Justice Act 1994. Nonetheless, by far the most important influence has been the SMP. Thus in 1992 the Central Bank noted that 'The Bank exercises its supervisory functions against the background of an evolving financial services sector, both domestically and internationally. In particular, emphasis was placed on the implications of the completion of the internal market in Europe'[4].

To an increasing extent, the criteria and standards applied by the Bank are set by the EU in the form of Community Directives. They are the:

- First and Second Banking Co-ordination Directives
- Capital Adequacy Directive, Own Funds Directive and Solvency Ratio Directive
- Annual Accounts of Credit Institutions Directive
- Consolidated Supervision Directive
- Large Exposures Directive.

The Second Banking Co-ordination Directive (89/646) came into effect on 1 January 1993. In early 1993, on foot of the Directive, notifications were received from the Bank of England indicating that a number of UK credit institutions proposed to provide banking services in Ireland on a cross-border basis. There has been a rapid growth in the number of such notifications[5].

Table 7.4 Central Bank supervision of credit institutions

Credit institutions	*National legislation*	*EU Directives (relating to all credit institutions)*
Licensed banks	Central Bank Acts 1971, 1989 & 1997	First Banking Directive Second Banking Directive Annual Accounts Directive
Building societies	Building Societies Act 1989	Branch Accounts Directive Own Fund Directive
Trustee Savings Bank	Trustee Savings Banks Act 1989	Solvency Ratio Directive Consolidated Supervision Directive
ACC Bank plc	ACC Bank Act 1992	Large Exposures Directive Capital Adequacy Directive
ICC Bank plc ICC Investment Bank Limited	ICC Bank Act 1992	Deposit Guarantee Scheme Directive Money Laundering Directive Post BCCI Directive

Source: Central Bank

Table 7.4 shows the extent to which the EU Directives arising principally from the SMP have been incorporated within the supervision of banking.

3.3 Present supervisory structure

The Central Bank of Ireland is responsible for the supervision of a wide range of financial institutions including banks, building societies, collective investment schemes, stockbrokers, money brokers, investment intermediaries, IFSC companies, the Irish Stock Exchange and futures exchanges. The types of institutions, other than credit institutions, for which the Bank has supervisory responsibility, and the legislation from which those responsibilities are derived, are summarised in Table 7.5.

Table 7.5 Supervision of non-credit institutions

Nature of institutions/markets	Relevant legislation
Futures and options exchanges Money brokers Certain institutions established in the International Financial Services Centre (IFSC) not engaged in activities requiring authorisation under the Investment Intermediaries Act 1995	Central Bank Act 1989 (as amended by the Central Bank Acts 1997 and 1998
Certain institutions established in the International Financial Services Centre (IFSC) Certified persons as defined in the Investment Intermediaries Act 1995 Investment business firms Restricted activity investment product intermediaries	Investment Intermediaries Act 1995 (as amended by the Central Bank Act 1997 and the Investor Compensation Act 1998)
Irish Stock Exchange Member firms as defined in the Stock Exchange Act 1995	Stock Exchange Act 1995 (as amended by the Investor Compensation Act 1998)
Collective Investment Schemes	European Communities (Undertakings to Collective Investment in Transferable Securities) Regulations 1989 (UCITS Regulations) Investment Limited Partnership Act, no. 24, 1994 Unit Trusts Act 1990 Companies Act 1990 (Part XIII, investment companies)

Source: Central Bank

This amounts to a total transformation of the situation which prevailed in 1985 at the outset of the SMP when, within a much smaller banking and financial services sector, responsibility was fragmented across a number of agencies and government departments. The Central Bank is at present the de facto single regulatory authority (with the notable exception of insurance, for which the Department of Enterprise, Employment and Trade retains, for the present, responsibility). This is set to change with the establishment of a single regulator in late-2000 (if in fact the proposal goes ahead) whose mandate and structure is not yet clear.

The principles and processes of supervision employed by the Central Bank encompass the 'core principles' drawn up by the Bank for International Settlements (BIS).

3.4 The future of the supervisory system

There have, at the same time, been a number of parallel developments that continue to shape the supervisory structure. These include:

- an increased emphasis on corporate governance and on internal controls[6]. The Central Bank's criteria for licensing now include an assessment of the adequacy of an applicant's internal controls. This also reflects lessons learned from the BCCI failure and from the collapse of Barings bank in 1994. More generally, the Central Bank's focus on internal controls corresponds to the requirements of the EU Directives
- consistent with the objectives of the SMP, a significantly greater emphasis through the 1990s on the need to ensure the transparency of bank charges and to ensure the consumer is adequately informed and protected. Prior to 1997 the Central Bank was responsible for monitoring bank charges. It had, indeed, played an analogous role in the 1970s and 1980s in relation to the impact of interest rates. However, under the Consumer Credit Act 1996 responsibility for bank charges was transferred to the Office of the Director of Consumer Affairs
- an extension, beyond the traditional usages of banking law, into areas such as company law and those relating to the criminal justice system. The latter, reflecting international practice, aims at preventing money laundering and, more generally, the criminal subversion of the financial sector.

4   IMPACT OF THE SMP

4.1 Bank strategies

The SMP has had a pervasive impact on the structure, competitiveness and also management of Irish banks. The harmonisation of prudential standards, together with the 'single passport' aimed at creating a 'level playing field', was at the heart of this impact. The increased contestability of Irish banking within the EU Single Market, together with greater price transparency, has reshaped the perspective of bank management. The entry of Bank of Scotland into the mortgage market in late 1999 had an immediate impact on margins, and on management's strategic thinking. This process has been reinforced by a new, more demanding, corporate and retail customer base. It is worth noting that the creation of a single capital market has put new pressures on the intermediation role of banks.

The imperative for Irish banks has been to defend their domestic market. This is the platform on which both major domestic banks have had to rebuild, following setbacks in the 1980s. Equally, the Single Market has created new options for further building a market presence within the EU, not least given the prospective growth dynamic behind the SMP.

Irish banks, like their EU counterparts, have been required to adapt their strategic thinking to the need for increased scale: a focus on 'shareholder value' is a strategic imperative. In this new environment, both of the major banks are vulnerable to EU and other predators. The premium arising from strong performance may provide only temporary protection as the logic of scale asserts itself across Europe into the new millennium. This will require both major banks to enhance their competencies, weaned on expansion in the US and UK, in relation to valuation, acquisition and market entry strategies within the Single Market.

4.2 Mergers and acquisitions

There is unambiguous evidence that the SMP has contributed to a process of consolidation through mergers and acquisitions across the EU. In Ireland the impact has been less evident. There have been mergers, notably among Trustee Savings Banks in the early 1990s, and acquisitions. Irish Permanent, for example, acquired Irish Progressive (formerly owned by the Prudential) in their development as a bancassurance organisation and subsequently merged with Irish Life. Equally, Bank of Ireland acquired New Ireland Assurance in 1997. These, and smaller domestic acquisitions, were more related to a secular trend towards bancassurance than to the SMP.

Table 7.6 International business of all licensed banks: liabilities

Non-residents analysis by currency (millions)

	1995	1997
US$	7945	17194
Sterling (£)	4005	8855
DM	6039	9564
DCr	994	1154
Other	4873	8874
Total (IR£)	*25857*	*45531*

Residents in foreign currency: analysis by currency (millions)

	1995	1997
US$	2166	5016
Sterling (£)	2134	3424
DM	1948	1490
DCr	245	345
Other	1546	2690
Total (IR£)	*8037*	*12964*

Source: Central Bank

Table 7.7 International business of all licensed banks: assets

Non-residents in foreign currency: analysis by currency (millions)

	1995	1997
US$	8271	18469
Sterling (£)	4357	8285
DM	6989	10367
DCr	575	837
Other	5589	10833
Total (IR£)	*25781*	*48818*

Residents in foreign currency: analysis by currency (millions)

	1995	1997
US$	2961	5630
Sterling (£)	2535	4542
DM	1747	1391
DCr	910	1271
Other	1694	2731
Total (IR£)	*9847*	*15565*

Source: Central Bank

4.3 Internationalisation

The most notable examples of acquisitions have, as already noted, been by AIB and Bank of Ireland in the US, the UK and in Eastern Europe. These initiatives reflected the growing internationalisation of Irish banking, motivated by the small size of the domestic market and the need to diversify both risk and earnings streams. The Bank of Ireland's consolidation in New Hampshire and its acquisition of the Bristol and West Building Society in the UK represent the progressive strengthening of the bank's strategic vision. Equally, AIB's acquisition of Dauphin Deposit represented an unambiguous strategic response to developments in the US and the consequent need to grow its franchise. Both banks have more recently made acquisitions in Europe: AIB in a highly strategic initiative in Poland and Bank of Ireland in Hungary.

4.4 Prices and margins

Over the decade 1985 to 1995, and more especially since, here has been a clear trend towards the 'unbundling' of banking services and the elimination of cross-subsidisation. This reflects a number of factors. The emphasis on price transparency, which is at the heart of the SMP, is one such factor. This will be reinforced by the single currency. There are other factors. The decline in nominal interest rates has put pressure on net interest income. There has been a narrowing in recent years of margins that, compared with other EU countries, had been on the high side. The new contestability of the banking franchise, partly stemming from the SMP, has acted to compress margins. At a more fundamental level, the development of capital markets (not least as a result of the SMP) has put pressure on the banks' intermediation role.

There are no easy options: there is a real and pressing need to develop non-interest income. And this means looking more vigorously than hitherto (certainly than in the 1980s) at prices. More generally, increased surveillance of bank charges in the 1990s has, perhaps paradoxically, worked alongside cost management strategies to focus banks' attention on full cost pricing. Equally, in the face of pressure on traditional savings products, banks are seeking to develop strategies which allow them, so far as possible, to maintain margins.

5   BANK PREPARATIONS FOR EMU

5.1 Introduction

An evaluation of Irish banks' preparations for EMU must be cognisant of
the key interfaces within which the preparatory work has progressed:
EU/domestic and Central Bank/commercial banking. The scale and
complexity of the exercise is such that any evaluation of banks'
preparation for EMU must be crafted around these interfaces.
Accordingly, this section reviews preparatory work by the EU regulatory
authorities, including the Commission, and also the Fédération Bancaire.
The Central Bank of Ireland and the Irish Bankers' Federation contributed
to, and drew from, developments in these EU forums. Against this
background, preparation for EMU by the Central Bank of Ireland and the
Irish banking sector is reviewed. The section concludes by highlighting
key aspects of the prospective impact of EMU on Irish financial
institutions and markets.

5.2 Background

The Maastricht Treaty was signed in February 1992. Almost immediately
banks in EU member countries, including Ireland, began formulating a
response to the prospective introduction of a single currency. Indeed, some
banks undertook preparatory work as early as 1991[7]. Following
Maastricht, and well before the unification process was completed,
national central banks directly and through the Committee of Governors
began the process of identifying and addressing the key issues. The
Committee of Governors undertook work, inter alia, on the design of bank
notes and payments systems in 1993.

Four points emerged from the initial post-Maastricht flurry of
discussions in various national and EU forums:

- it was recognised that banks, in particular, had the pivotal role to play
  in the successful transition to the single currency
- the transition would be unprecedented in scope and complexity. The
  nearest, and quite inadequate, comparator was decimalisation in
  Ireland and in the UK in the early 1970s
- banks at national and European levels would have to work together to
  develop a common strategy. In practice the Irish Bankers' Federation,
  its national counterparts in EU countries, and the European Banking
  Federation had a central role in this regard

- this strategy would have to be developed by the banks in collaboration with national monetary authorities and with their commercial hinterland (retail sector, public sector, and industry). In this regard, developing a co-ordinated response involved a massive and sustained exercise in strategic planning under conditions of uncertainty.

Moreover, the banking sector's response, encompassing technical, administrative, and logistical challenges, had to be accommodated by the banks:

- within their national day-to-day commercial activity
- against the backdrop of structural and technological change in global financial markets and within an EU hinterland that was being reshaped by the SMP
- at the same time (though this was not initially recognised) as the adaptation of bank systems to the millennium 'bug'.

5.3 EU regulatory response

The early and mid-1990s were characterised by considerable uncertainty at the political level as to whether EMU would become a reality within the timeframe envisaged in the Maastricht Treaty or, indeed, at all. What is quite fascinating is that, at the technical level within banking markets, there was no such uncertainty. National central banks, EU forums (including the Committee of Governors, the Commission, and the commercial banking sector) at EU and national level, as well as the level of individual banks, simply got on with the job.

The Committee of Governors presented a study on the technical issues involved in the design and manufacture of EU bank notes in 1993 and also on the payment systems for securities in relation to monetary union. By 1994, intense preparatory work was well under way within the Committee of Governors, as well as in national central banks, on the key issues including:

- the design and logistics of the single currency
- payments arrangements
- information systems
- monetary policy
- regulatory and supervisory issues. It should be said that the focus here was on the formation of statistical reporting while the practicalities of supervision were, in effect, devolved to national central banks
- the operation of the European Monetary Institute (EMI).

The Commission's perspective was, basically, that the single currency was the essential component of the Single Market and that the political theatre surrounding the ratification process had obscured the benefits of the single currency. The costs to the banking sector of making the transition were to be seen in the context of these benefits. At the same time, EU President Jacques Delors, who had seen through the SMP, was clear on the scale of the response required by the banking industry and the wider financial services sector. All areas of banking would, he noted, be affected[8].

The President proposed the setting up of a Study Group on the changeover to the single currency and, parallel with this, an Interdepartmental Working Party within the Commission. This work built on a 1993 study by KPMG in which the Commission participated.

5.4 EU commercial banking response

The Fédération Bancaire played a key role in EU (and Irish) banks' preparations for EMU. 'The Fédération has an undivided commitment to the success of the single currency and intends to participate in all possible ways in which will contribute to the smoothest possible changeover process...' The role of the Fédération Bancaire, acting with national federations, including the Irish Bankers' Federation, encompassed:

- liasing with the Commission and other regulatory forums
- establishing specialised working groups composed of member banks
- more generally, developing an EU-wide consensus drawing on banking systems of member states and thereby minimising any 'information deficiency' within the EU banking system that could undermine confidence in the preparatory process.

As early as 1992 the Fédération Bancaire set up three working groups, made up of experts nominated by member associations, to study three key dimensions of the consequences for banking of the introduction of the single currency. These were its impact on treasury/forex business, on monetary policy, and on organisation/logistics.

In 1994, the Fédération Bancaire published the first systematic study[9], based on a survey of 100 European banks, of the time likely to be necessary, and the finance required, to effect the transition. The study was interesting and important for a number of reasons.

Firstly, the methodology specified cost in terms of impact on products and functions. Products included notes and coins, ATMs, card-based payments, forex/dealing and treasury management, loans/deposits, and capital markets, as well as certain other products. Key functions included legal systems, audit/security systems, marketing/communication systems, training systems, stationery systems, external reporting systems, and compliance systems. Importantly, this provided, for smaller banks, a template around which in-house planning could be developed.

Secondly, a number of conclusions were inferred from the data in regard to the logistics. The survey indicated that, given adequate time for preparation and implementation, 'the banking industry would be able to accommodate the changeover to a single currency in an orderly, cost-effective way, without disruption of services'. The complexity of the transitional arrangements were highlighted. 'Although multi-currency settlement and accounting systems are in place in most countries, the relevant mainframes are highly complex and interface with many diverse trading systems. Banks will need to alter software so that trades can continue to be processed, validated and settled during the transition'.

Thirdly, the survey provided detailed estimates of the likely costs, and also the timeframe required to effect the transition. The estimated minimum cost (8-10 billion ECU or up to 2% of annual operating costs) was an underestimate, for number of reasons. But it did provide a baseline for planning purposes. For the majority of banks, three to four years was the minimum time required to change operations and systems to the single currency in time for the 1 January 1999 deadline.

5.5 Role of the Central Bank of Ireland

The Central Bank of Ireland played the pivotal role in the technical preparations for participation in EMU by Irish financial institutions and markets. This reflects the Bank's position at the centre of markets and the supervisory system, and its proactive approach over the years to the development of Irish financial institutions and markets. It also reflects the fact that the Bank interfaces with both domestic markets and the EU institutions and processes which will underpin EMU[10].

The preparatory work undertaken involving the banking system involved a number of dimensions:

- internal preparations bearing on the systems which support the Bank's mandate. These included, inter alia, market operations, settlements, and statistical reporting (including harmonisation of accounting formats). It also included the development of a communications infrastructure involving operations with the European Central Bank and other participating national central banks
- management and co-ordination (directly and through participation in specialised working groups) of domestic financial markets' adaptation to the single currency

- collaborative work with other national central banks (NCBs) both through the EMI and in specialised forums such as the Monetary Committee and the recently formed Banking Supervision Committee[11].
- modification of monetary policy instruments and procedures which impact directly on banking institutions and markets
- development of systems required for: conversion of accounts to euro (this was central to the transition to the single currency for the whole network of markets and institutions); harmonisation of accounting techniques with other NCBs, which was necessary for the preparation of consolidated accounts by the European Central Bank; transfer to, and management of, foreign exchange assets for the European Central Bank
- development of a national Real Time Gross Settlement (RTGS) and its integration with the EU TARGET, which handles large-value cross-border payments in euro and underpins EMU-wide monetary policy
- detailed planning for the production, storage and distribution of euro notes and coins
- enhancement and harmonisation of a statistical reporting system which was central for a wide range of functions and processes which support the operation of the single currency, including prudential supervision.

On the domestic front, the Central Bank liased with the Central Statistics Office (CSO) in regard to presentation of balance of payments data and sectoral finance accounts.

The pace of preparatory work intensified and came into sharper focus in 1995. The Central Bank established a European Affairs Committee which held a number of plenary services with credit institutions. These complemented bilateral meetings, and also initiatives by the Central Bank, aimed at informing commercial banks of required changes.

5.6 Preparations by commercial banks

Preparations by the commercial banking sector progressed at two levels. Task force/working groups were established within most banks, the precise mandate depending, inter alia, on the nature and scope of a bank's activities and also on the bank's status, for example whether it was a domestic institution or a subsidiary of an external bank. At a second, and closely related level, the Irish Bankers' Federation and Irish Mortgage and Savings Association (IMSA) established an EMU Steering Committee.

Joint working groups were established in key areas: Financial and Capital Markets, Payments, and Statistics. The Steering Committee worked closely with the Central Bank and with the Government to inform and advise business. More generally, the Steering Committee played a major role in identifying key issues and coordinating and helping manage an industry-wide response[12].

The EMU working groups established by individual banks were initially operating in conditions of uncertainty. Close coordination with the Central Bank, directly and through the Irish Bankers' Federation, contributed to the development of the necessary infrastructure to run systems applications, including cross-border payments (RTGS) and new reporting arrangements. Some of the banks were highly proactive. AIB capped its forex earnings in the run-up to EMU as a means of smoothing the revenue impact as well as developing customised software and a highly visible information strategy for its customers and the public[13].

5.7 Prospective impact of EMU on Irish banks

The scale and complexity of the transition to the single currency is unprecedented in the monetary history of Europe. There were no guarantees that the transition would be seamless and trouble free on 1 January 1999.

Watson provided a sensible summary of the position prior to the transition. 'The areas which will come under most customer pressure are the wholesale areas. There is reasonable certainty about what needs to be done to prepare wholesale money and foreign exchange markets for 1 January 1999. For credit institutions with a significant presence in retail payments markets, however, the 'no delegation, no prohibition' principle creates much greater uncertainty...If the demand (for the euro accounts and euro payments facilities) extends to a significant number of customers who wish to generate substantial volumes of payments in euro, credit institutions could find themselves unable to meet it unless their retail payments infrastructure and their internal accounting facilities have been approximately adapted...The extent to which they may cease to be significant in a domestic Irish context will vary depending on the degree of competition they face from the centralising forces within the monetary union'[14].

The prospective impact of the introduction of the single currency on the Irish banking system, and the wider financial services sector, is difficult to assess[15]. The preceding sections have identified certain impacts. What can be said is that the single currency, coming on the top of the SMP, has transformed Irish banking.

Dowling has provided an insightful analysis of the possible effects of EMU. He notes that the key issue is whether there will be a future for certain financial activities within a single currency zone. 'The areas which will come under the most contractionary pressures are in the wholesale sector...This is because the market influences in these areas will be Euro-wide...the information content of making an investment in Irish instruments...will drop sharply'[16]. He argues that the extent to which such wholesale activities may cease to be significant in a domestic Irish context will depend, amongst other things, on the degree of competition they face from the centralising forces within the single currency area.

Notes

1.   Dias, F. (1995), *Bank Competition in Ireland*: thesis submitted to UCD for MBS degree. The model used by Dias was similar to that used by P. Molyneux, D.M. Lloyd-Williams and J. Thornton (1994), 'Competitive conditions in European banking', *Journal of Banking and Finance,* 18, pp. 445-59. It had a single product (loan) output, with deposits, labour and capital as inputs. It did not take account of deposit services, hence of non-interest income, which has become progressively more important as a proportion of total revenues throughout the 1990s. Kinsella (1980) used the Herfendahl index to measure market concentration in 'Market concentration in banking: structure, conduct and performance', *Journal of Statistical and Social Inquiry Society of Ireland,* 24 (3) 1980/81, pp. 31-70.

2.   *Bank of Ireland Report and Accounts 1998*, p. 4

3.   See P. Bourke and R. Kinsella (1998), 'Globalisation, cross-border trade in financial services and offshore banking: the case of Ireland' *in* C. Schoz and J. Zentes, *Strategisches Euro-management* (Schaffer-Poeschel, Stuttgart).

4.   Central Bank of Ireland Annual Report 1992, p. 37.

5.   See *Central Bank of Ireland Annual Report 1998* (Statistical appendix) for details.

6.   See R. Kinsella (1996) in *Internal Controls in Banking* (Wiley, London) for Irish case studies and for EU and regulatory perspectives.

7.   The Association for the Monetary Union of Europe.

8.   *Practical problems in introducing the single currency:* memo to the Commission from the President and Vice President (11/39/1994).

9.   This study can be found on the website of the Fédération Bancaire (www.fbe.be) under Documents: euro and is entitled *Survey on the Introduction of the Single Currency: a First Contribution on the Practical Aspects.*

10. The most detailed and incisive summary of preparations in Irish banking for EMU is to be found in *Preparations for Economic and Monetary Union* (Central Bank Annual Report 1996) and *Economic and Monetary Union,* (Central Bank Annual Report 1997). Both papers provide an extensive bibliography of relevant Irish and EU papers.

11. The Central Bank Act 1998 gives statutory effect to the banks' participation in the European System of Central Banks. This complements

previous legislation which makes statutory provision for relevant operations, such as the Central Bank Act 1997 which, inter alia, authorises the Bank to regulate payments systems.

12. A major example was the conference held by the IBF in 1997, the proceedings of which were published in Irish Banking Review 1997.
13. See, for example, *The ABC of EMU* (AIB Bank, Dublin, 1996). In 1998, AIB launched a multi-currency conversion software package (X Changer) customised for euro applications.
14. Watson, *Irish Banking Review*, EMU Special Issue 1997.
15. Terry Baker, Joan Fitzgerald and Patrick Honohan (1996), *Economic Implications for Ireland and the EMU* (Economic and Social Research Institute, Ireland, Policy Research Theories, 28).
16. Dowling, *Irish Banking Review*, EMU Special Issue 1997.

8   Italy

Franco Bruni, Andrea Balzarini and Daniele Fox

1   EFFICIENCY V. PROFITABILITY

Returns on assets (ROA) and returns on equity (ROE) of Italian banks compare rather unfavourably with those of other banking systems in Europe. The impression one derives looking at these yields is that, as a consequence of the introduction of the single currency, increasing Europe-wide competition could see Italian banks as hopeless losers, in spite of the restructuring process in which they are currently involved.

But the information available on the comparative profitability of Italy's banking system is insufficient to put together a clear picture of its competitive strength and understand its implications for the years to come. In fact, the corporate governance of Italian banks is still insufficiently market oriented, with many banks still publicly owned or indirectly controlled by the public sector. Moreover, the degree of competition in domestic banking markets has been increasing during the last decade, following deregulation, but is still low in some regions and in several sections of the industry, with significant rents accruing to inefficient institutions.

Therefore, to assess the impact of the Single Market on Italy's banks and to evaluate their competitive strengths and weaknesses, somewhat sophisticated measures are needed of their technical and scale efficiency, which are of much more value than the usual indicators of profitability. After some brief comments on the comparative profitability of Italian banks (Section 2), these notes describe such measures of efficiency (Section 3). The results of efficiency calculations are then shown for Italian banks (Section 4), and compared with corresponding institutions in Germany, France and Spain (Section 5). An analysis of the evolution over time of the efficiency of Italian banks is then presented in Section 6. Finally, some conclusions follow (Section 7) on the strategic response of the Italian banking system to the increased competitive pressure coming from the single market for banking services and from the European currency unification.

2   PROFITABILITY

The average ROE of Italian banks has been between 2% and 3% in recent years, half that of French banks and almost one-third that of Germany and Spain, while UK and US levels of bank ROE are beyond comparison. Ten years ago Italy's banking profitability was ranking much better, both in absolute value and in international comparisons. The basic cause of the deterioration is easily identified as the narrowing of the interest rate spread on the traditional interest-based intermediation activity. This phenomenon was already strong and evident at the beginning of the 1990s. In 1992 and 1995 two major currency crises resulted in higher levels of interest rates which favoured a widening of banks' spreads (see Figure 8.1).

Figure 8.1   Difference between spread at indicated dates and spread in June 1997 *(= 4.82)*

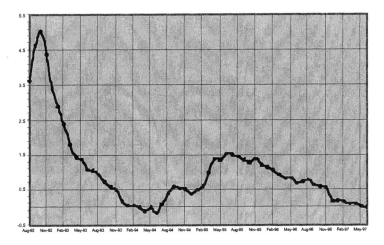

Note: Spread = average lending rate – average rate on deposits at indicated dates.

The structure of Italian banking markets, in fact, is such that a general upward movement in interest rates gets transmitted faster to the rates on loans than to the rates on banks' deposits: the opposite happens when the general level of interest rates decreases. On both occasions the long-run decline of the interest margin was thus temporarily interrupted with an artificial limitation of the profitability crisis. The pressure to devise a strategic reaction by both bankers and financial authorities was weakened and restructuring was postponed. We think the comparative situation of the Italian banking system is still suffering from this delay even if now, after some years of steady decline in interest rates, narrowing margins and insufficient profitability, the pressures for change are strong and restructuring has started. Some further easing of the pressure, to be sure, was caused in 1996 by a different consequence of the sharp decrease in interest rates, that is the very large capital gains earned on banks' portfolios of long-term bonds.

As we just observed, interest margins were already weakening at the beginning of the 1990s. This was not a direct consequence of the EC provisions to foster the single market. The major cause has been a general process of internal financial liberalisation, of which the most important measures were the liberalisation of bank loans in 1988 and of bank branching in 1990. The latter was a much delayed consequence of the EC's First Banking Directive and had an impressive impact on Italian banks' strategic plans, comments on which will follow later. As far as bank loans are concerned, their growth was previously limited by direct administrative controls that froze market shares and prevented competition. After liberalisation the supply of loans increased at an average yearly rate of 17% (nearly 12% in real terms) between 1989 and 1992 with substantial consequences on interest rates, especially for low-risk borrowers.

The behaviour of interest margins is not the only cause of problems for Italian banks' profitability. High labour costs, taxes and provisions for bad loans are also depressing the ROA, while a comparatively high degree of capitalisation (low leverage) tends to make the picture in terms of ROE even worse than in terms of ROA. In 1997, for instance, Italian banks showed an average cost-to-income ratio almost 5% higher than that of other European competitors. But here we do not want to conduct a systematic analysis of the individual components of profitability since a thorough study has been conducted by the Italian Banking Association (ABI, 1997). We prefer to concentrate on the more general concept of 'efficiency' according to a scheme that we describe in Section 3.

3   MEASURES OF EFFICIENCY

Applying data envelopment analysis (DEA) to an IBCA data bank containing balance sheet data up to 1997 produced some interesting results that are in part summarised in the following sections (see also Balzarini, 1996 and Pieggi, 1996-7).

Given a set of banks, the DEA methodology uses linear programming to detect their input-output technology and to locate the position of each bank with respect to the production possibility frontier (ppf), assuming both constant (CRS) and variable (VRS) returns to scale. By comparing the results under the two assumptions, scale (in)efficiencies can then be distinguished from pure technical (in)efficiencies. An easy geometrical intuition (Figure 8.2) can be obtained for the one-input/one-output case. Five banks are represented in the figure by points A,B,C,D,K. With VRS, an input-oriented efficiency measure can be obtained as the (ratio)-distance of each bank from the non-linear envelopment: HJ/HK for bank K. With CRS, the same measure yields HI/HK. The ratio of the latter (total X-efficiency) to the former (pure technical efficiency) is a measure of scale efficiency: HI/HJ. All these measures are non-negative and reach a maximum of 1 for a bank located on the ppf.

Figure 8.2 Measures of efficiency with data envelopment analysis

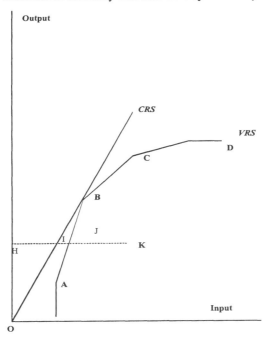

With linear programming, corresponding measures have been calculated in multi-dimensional spaces, considering technologies with three inputs (fixed assets, personnel expenses, other non-interest expenses)

and three outputs (loans, deposits and commission fees). We chose to include deposits in the output vector as a measure of banks' supply of liquidity services for which the market is willing to pay a substantial opportunity cost.

International and intertemporal comparisons can also be obtained for each measure of efficiency using Malmquist indicators. Let $E(x,y)$ be the efficiency of bank y with respect to the technology (frontier) x; and let B be a benchmark technology (calculated in a certain period for a given country or for a group banks of different countries). Finally, let α and β indicate two banks (and two technologies) of different countries, or let them indicate the same bank in two different periods (with possibly different technologies). Then:

$$E(B,\beta)/E(B,\alpha) = [E(\beta,\beta)/E(\alpha,\alpha)] \cdot \{[E(B,\beta)/E(\beta,\beta)] / [E(B,\alpha)/E(\alpha,\alpha)]\}$$

is larger than 1 if bank β is more efficient than bank α with respect to the benchmark technology. (Note that measures such as $E(B,\beta)$ could exceed unity if B is from a banking system where bank β does not belong). The first multiplier is the relative X-efficiency of the two banks with respect to their own ppf, while the second bracketed ratio is a measure of the relative efficiency of banking technologies with respect to the benchmark.

4   EFFICIENCY OF ITALIAN BANKS

Table 8.1 gives a first set of results obtained in analysing the Italian banking industry in isolation, that is measuring the efficiency of Italian banks with respect to the national ppf. Under the CRS hypothesis the average level of 'total efficiency' is around 0.7 and is quite similar for all size classes, while 'pure technical efficiency' (assuming VRS) is U-shaped with respect to size and reaches a maximum for the largest banks. This suggests that even if scale efficiency is highest for medium-sized banks, for larger banks the improvement in X-efficiency is sufficient to compensate for diseconomies of scale. As a consequence mergers might enhance the productivity of the system even if the resulting bank has decreasing returns to scale. A word of caution is in order, to be sure, on this latter conclusion because we are using measures of efficiency that tend to be biased upwards for larger banks, especially with the VRS assumption. (In Figure 8.2, by construction, a bank like D lies on the VRS frontier).

Table 8.2 compares the efficiency of the largest Italian banks, calculated as in Table 8.1, with similar measures obtained for three other countries that we consider to be interesting benchmarks for evaluating the international competitiveness of Italy's financial industry. Comparing average national efficiency measures calculated with respect to national ppfs, that is with respect to different benchmarks, could be misleading and more accurate procedures are used in the following paragraphs. However, some basic facts already appear from Table 8.2: under the VRS hypothesis Italian banks are less efficient than those of Germany and Spain. France's banks have the lowest performance, but mainly because of scale reasons.

Table 8.1 Efficiency measures for Italian banks, 1997

Size (Total assets in DM millions)	CRS	VRS	Scale efficiency (CRS/VRS)
<500	0.75	0.81	0.94
500-1000	0.71	0.71	0.99
1000-2000	0.68	0.69	0.98
2000-10000	0.70	0.73	0.96
>10000	0.80	0.88	0.96
10 largest	0.77	0.97	0.79

Table 8.2 Comparing efficiency measures of the 10 largest banks in each country with respect to national PPFs, 1997

Country	CRS	VRS	Scale efficiency (CRS/VRS)
Italy	0.77	0.96	0.79
Germany	0.65	0.97	0.68
France	0.60	0.88	0.70
Spain	0.80	0.99	0.81

As we have already noted, efficiency can be better than profitability as an indicator of banks' competitive strength in the single European market. Table 8.3 shows that in Italy the correlation between efficiency and profitability is peculiarly low, and statistically insignificant when measured both with respect to ROE and to ROA. The correlation is substantial in Germany and Spain, where there is a lower percentage of small banks, while for France it is significant only in the case of ROA. Part of the explanation may be that in Italy local monopoly rents are often at the origin of inefficient banks' profits, thus weakening the link between efficiency and profitability.

From the evidence of Table 8.3 we feel encouraged to go one step further in analysing the efficiency measures that we derived with the DEA methodology.

Table 8.3 Correlation between profitability (ROE and ROA) and efficiency (CRS and VRS) (*1997 linear correlation coefficients in parenthesis when statistically insignificant*)

Country	(TA<1000 DM millions)	ROE with CRS	ROE with VRS	ROA with CRS	ROA with VRS
Italy	27	(0.12)	(0.02)	(0.11)	(0.01)
Germany	24	0.27	0.20	0.35	0.21
France	20	(0.03)	(-0.12)	0.16	(-0.01)
Spain	13	0.45	0.42	0.39	0.34

5   INTERNATIONAL COMPARISONS OF EFFICIENCY

A correct comparison between the efficiency of different banks taken from different countries requires reference to a common benchmark and thus to a common ppf. We first pooled the banks of four countries (Italy, Germany, France and Spain) per size category and then derived an international ppf for each size. Table 8.4 shows the average values of efficiency scores obtained for the large banks, the largest banks and the ten largest banks of each country. We leave aside smaller institutions for which direct international competition will be much less relevant.

It is a striking fact that Italy always ranks last. France and Germany are clearly the best in all the three size classes, with France slightly better than Germany (both under CRS and VRS) for the largest banks with total assets above DM10 billions. France's good performance in terms of pure technical efficiency, however, is spoiled by large diseconomies of scale that reduce the overall level of X-efficiency. This result, referred to 1997, partially changes the picture if compared with the first half of the 1990s when the gap between French and German largest banks was in favour of Germany. The efficiency of Spanish banks, when measured with respect to a common ppf, appears to be close to that of France and Germany and always higher than the efficiency of Italian banks. The last part of Table 8.4 shows that before 1990 this was not the case: the relative efficiency of Italy's banks with respect to Spain's has been deteriorating rapidly during the 1990s. Is it because Spain had a better reaction to the challenge of the single market? We have more evidence on this later in this paper.

Table 8.4(a) Efficiency measures with respect to an international PPF, 1997 (*averages of efficiency measures of banks in each country*)

Large banks (total assets DM2-10 billions)		
	CRS	VRS
Italy	0.30	0.38
Germany	0.55	0.67
France	0.51	0.70
Spain	0.48	0.64

Largest banks (total assets >DM10 billions)		
	CRS	VRS
Italy	0.22	0.28
Germany	0.27	0.36
France	0.30	0.41
Spain	0.29	0.39

10 largest banks in each country		
	CRS	VRS
Italy	0.22	0.41
Germany	0.32	0.66
France	0.32	0.72
Spain	0.30	0.47

Table 8.4(b) Efficiency of Italy's and Spain's largest banks compared over time: ratio of Italy's to Spain's efficiency measures

	CRS	VRS		CRS	VRS
1988	1.25	1.23	1994	0.86	0.85
1990	1.00	0.99	1995	0.87	0.81
1992	0.89	0.92	1997	0.76	0.71

To obtain a deeper and more eloquent comparison between the four banking systems on which we have been concentrating the analysis, we calculated an 'average bank' for each country and made use of Malmquist indicators, as described in Section 2. We chose German technology as a benchmark on the basis of the good performance shown by German banks both in terms of X-efficiency and of scale, and because of the quantitative importance of the German banking system in the Single European Market. Malmquist indicators then allowed us to divide the resulting efficiency gaps into two parts: the part depending on the different efficiency of national technologies and the part depending on the different position of the average national bank of each country with respect to its own national technology (ppf). Table 8.5 summarises the main results of these calculations.

Table 8.5 Ratio of the efficiency of the Italian 'average bank' to the efficiency of the average bank of Germany, France and Spain, 1997 (*when < 1 Italy's bank is less efficient*)

	Total relative efficiency		National technology		X-efficiency with respect to domestic PPFs	
	CRS	VRS	CRS	VRS	CRS	VRS
Germany	0.69	0.86	0.48	0.72	1.46	1.20
France	0.68	0.64	0.37	0.57	1.83	1.14
Spain	0.83	0.73	0.84	0.76	1.00	0.96
ranking						
1st	F & G	F	F	F	S & I	S
2nd		S	G	G		I
3rd	S	G	S	S	G	F
4th	I	I	I	I	F	G

Italy has the lowest total relative efficiency, both with the CRS hypothesis and with VRS. Italian banks perform well in terms of X-efficiency (that is with respect to domestic ppf), ranking first or second depending on which returns to scale are considered, but their production technology is clearly poor. Indeed, as far as X-efficiency is concerned, Spain is the top performer, both under CRS and VRS. This result might depend on the presence in the Spanish banking system of a higher competitive pressure coming also from size distribution of banking units: in our sample, only 13% of Spanish banks are smaller than DM1,000 million while the same percentage is around 23% for the average of the other three countries we are comparing.

A wide and worrying technological gap between the French and the Italian banking systems can also be detected from Table 8.5, with France clearly holding the technological leadership among the four countries. This suggests that, if France keeps improving its relatively low X-efficiency, it could become a strong competitor not only for Italian banks but also for other European institutions. Italy's technological gap with Germany is also a substantial one, under both the hypotheses on the returns to scale.

There are important differences between the results in Table 8.5 under CRS and under VRS. The reasons for these differences only indirectly impact on Italy's banking competitiveness, however they can offer interesting insights. For instance, it is clear that France suffers a less efficient scale distribution of its banking units, resulting in much higher scale diseconomies and in an lower overall level of X-efficiency. The opposite seems to be true for Italy and, in part, for Spain. A better scale distribution can be diagnosed from the fact that the relative X-efficiency is better under CRS, while the opposite is true for technological performance. In terms of Figure 8.1, the intuition goes as follows: the whole VRS frontier is closer to the CRS ppf, so that the distance of the 'average bank' (relative to the Italian bank) from its CRS frontier can be smaller than its distance from the VRS frontier, while the average distance between the CRS frontiers (for instance, the technological superiority of France over Italy) is larger than between the VRS frontiers.

6   RELATIVE EFFICIENCY OF ITALIAN BANKS 1988-1997

The picture drawn so far shows that the Italian banking system performs poorly in terms of efficiency with respect to the other countries that we have been considering. As has already emerged from Table 8.4, this has not always been the case: the relative efficiency of Italy's banking system started deteriorating after 1988. Let us now take a closer look at the evolution of efficiency figures of Italian banks from 1988 to 1997. In order to do this, we look first at early 1990s, focusing our attention on the largest banks with total assets above DM10,000 million and then move on to more recent developments in 1994-97. This is important in order to analyse the impact of the single market on Italian banks and to discuss the process of bank restructuring that is currently taking place in Italy, and which started before the introduction of the single currency.

We compare the 'average bank' of each country in the 'largest' size class using Malmquist indicators with reference to the benchmark technology derived for an international pool of these banks. Table 8.6 shows that Italy has worsened its position in the five years preceding (preparing for) the single market. This deterioration was mainly due to technological reasons: there was too much fixed capital because of too many branches, and too few commission-based activities. In the next paragraph we will see how this is connected to the strategic reaction of Italian banks to the single market and to deregulation, which has been of a defensive nature.

During the three years after 1992, a 15% improvement in Italy's banking technology took place but the average X-efficiency of the country's largest banks worsened, so that the total efficiency index did not improve. A tempting interpretation of this result is that only a small group of the 'largest' Italian banks were able to move their technology towards significantly higher levels of productivity following the arrival of the single market. This was sufficient to produce an outward movement of the country's ppf but it also increased the average X-inefficiency of the other banks.

Table 8.6 Evolution of technological productivity and X-efficiency in the largest Italian banks, 1988-1995 *(Total assets >DM10,000 millions)*

	Total efficiency	Technological	X-efficiency
1988	100	100	100
1992	87	84	104
1995	86	97	87

Table 8.7 Efficiency measures for Italian 'average bank' and 'largest bank' between 1994-1997

	Average bank		Largest banks	
	CRS	VRS	CRS	VRS
1994	0.68	0.70	0.75	0.85
1995	0.66	0.67	0.72	0.84
1996	0.68	0.73	0.75	0.87
1997	0.71	0.74	0.80	0.88

In Table 8.7 we compare the efficiency measures for the average and largest Italian banks obtained by applying DEA to a constant sample of banks for the years 1994-97. In order to have a significant comparison of efficiency measures through time we looked at the same banks for all four years, taking out of the sample those institutions whose nature changed during this period because of mergers, acquisitions and takeovers. Efficiency measures show an upward trend during the whole period, with the relevant exception of 1995, when the average bank, and also the largest (at least under CRS), reached the lowest level of efficiency. As we have remarked, in that year the widening of interest margins and the consequent temporary recover of banks' profitability may have caused a break in the restructuring process that had been started in the system, with negative consequences that are still felt today.

A more accurate picture of the dynamic evolution of banking efficiency during 1994-97 can be derived from Table 8.8, where we have calculated Malmquist indicators for each year with respect to the 1994 ppf, and where we have been able to break up the overall efficiency gain (or loss) into its technological and X-efficiency components. The results, referring to largest banks, prove that substantial changes occurred in Italy's banking industry during this period. The level of total efficiency grew substantially between 1995 and 1997, CRS by +32% and VRS by +27%. A relatively fast outward movement of the national ppf, and thus an improvement in the industry production technology, took place as is signalled by a remarkable rise in commission revenues over the four years (up by 68% in real terms). This outward movement, however, has not been followed by an adequate increase in the level of X-efficiency which, after the 1995 slump, stayed almost flat. This suggests that the gap between the small group of frontrunners who reacted first to the new challenging scenario (and whose action explains the movement of the national ppf), and the majority of the banks in the system, is hard to overcome.

Table 8.8 Evolution of efficiency in the 'largest' Italian banks relative to 1994 *(Total assets > DM10,000 millions)*

	Total relative efficiency		Technology		X-efficiency	
	CRS	VRS	CRS	VRS	CRS	VRS
1994	100	100	100	100	100	100
1995	114	110	127	109	89	101
1996	124	118	124	114	100	104
1997	132	127	125	122	105	105

Comparing the behaviour over time of Italy's banking efficiency with those of the other countries in the same period, explains why Italy still ranks last in 1997 international comparisons. German banks' total efficiency increased by approximately 20% from 1988 to 1995 at a time when Italy's fell; two-thirds of the improvement (which was evenly distributed between technology and X-efficiency) took place in the five years before 1992. In 1996 and 1997, instead, large German banks have suffered a reduction (around 10%) in the average level of X-efficiency and, as a consequence, seem to have lost part of their advantage over French banks. Over the same period Spain has shown a large growth in efficiency, obtaining a 20% improvement in the total efficiency of its largest banks both from 1988 to 1995 and from 1995 to 1997. This increase was mainly concentrated in technology, which was good because technology was the weak aspect of Spain's banking competitiveness, while its X-efficiency has been, and still is, comparatively strong. As far as France is concerned, data for the 1992-95 period (no previous data were available) show a formidable improvement in technology (+58%, mainly due to the increased weight of commissions in banks' income accounts) together with a smaller decrease in X-efficiency: total efficiency improved by 14%. This trend also characterised the period 1995-97 when the French banking sector further increased its technological potential (+27%) but it was not able to improve its performance in terms of X-efficiency. This still appears the main weakness of France's large banks, acting as an obstacle to them becoming leaders in the European market.

In spite of its evolution in 1996 and 1997, Italy's banking has not yet succeeded in closing the efficiency gap with other major European systems. The reason is probably due to the size of the lag it had accumulated in the first half of the 1990s. An impressive confirmation of the evidence on the inferiority of Italy's banking efficiency and of its evolution in the years around the introduction of the single market, comes from observing the only important foreign bank which made a substantial and successful effort to enter the Italian domestic market, also in the retail section, Deutsche Bank. In 1995 the Italian subsidiary of Deutsche Bank was the most efficient bank in Italy, having increased its efficiency by 20% since 1992.

7   BANK PREPARATIONS FOR EMU

It is our opinion that the European banking market is still segmented along national boundaries, even if a 'single market' has gradually developed in certain sections of bank activities and in certain parts of the continent. We believe that the existence of national currencies has been the main reason for the slow progress in European banking competition and that only with the adoption of the euro will a major boost to cross-border competition take place. In view of this potential increase in cross-border development, the current state of Italian bank efficiency is dangerously weak.

Our view is also supported by the results obtained in a clustering analysis conducted on the 62 largest banking groups (10 of which were Italian) of nine European countries using the 1996 IBCA data bank. This is not the place to describe in detail our statistical exercise. A similar exercise was carried out by Resti (1996). We will only give brief information on the input data and on the results obtained. Sixteen variables were used to create seven clusters where the 62 groups appeared, together with the nine 'average' national banking groups. Profitability variables entered the analysis, together with efficiency indicators obtained with the DEA methodology, as well as measures of capital adequacy, of size and growth rate of total assets, of credit risk, and of product diversification, together with Moody's ratings.

The characteristics of the clusters obtained were sufficiently evident, but we will not describe them here in any detail. One cluster, for instance, could be labelled 'Will they be euro?' and included largest banks with good efficiency and satisfactory rating but weaker profitability and product diversification. Another cluster included 'high tech growing banks', others were called 'too small to bite' and 'competition profile'.

We want here to point only at two aspects of the overall result of the clustering. First, the clustering tends to reproduce the national distribution of the banking groups, with nearly all the banks from each country belonging to one cluster. In other words, the clustering exercise produces very strong evidence of the still high current segmentation of the European banking industry along national boundaries. Second, Italian banks are concentrated in two clusters that deserve the label of 'first category regional banks' and 'second category regional banks'. Both groups are characterised by bank sizes too small to compete at a continental level, while banks in the 'second category' also have weak performances in most of the 16 variables used to make up the groupings. It is comforting that the 'average Italian banking group' falls into the 'first category' regional cluster. What are the strategic explanations and implications of this relative position of the Italian banking system in the perspective of the single market and of the single European currency?

As a matter of fact, the reaction of many Italian banks to the increasing international competitive pressures has been the search for a stronger position in the domestic banking market. The threats stemming from the integration of the European banking market were considered strategically more important than the opportunities offered by the single market. The main strategic reaction was therefore of a defensive nature. This looked to be the only feasible alternative, given the huge amount of capital and skills required to enter foreign markets in a profitable way.

Along these lines, following the liberalisation of branching, several banks started important programmes of network expansion, aimed at increasing (and defending) their share of the domestic market for financial services, their collection of funds and their placing power. The result was that the Italian market, primarily in the north, became crowded with bank branches (see Figure 8.3), leading to an overwhelming increase in the supply of retail banking services and in the search for deposits. This caused an increase in fixed costs and diverted attention from the need to revise the basic model of the banking business and to increase the efficiency of banking technology. After years of administrative controls protecting Italian banking from both external and internal competition, the first strategic reaction was, in some sense, naive and short-sighted.

The rigidity of the labour market played its role in constraining the decision process. Sometimes one of the main reasons for opening new branches was to avoid dismissals and, until 1994-95, an increase in the number of branches could not take place at the same time as any substantial shrinking of their average size: only in few cases was a consistent strategy pursued to move rapidly to a model of 'light' branches.

The basis for the protective strategy that we have discussed was the fear of foreign bank competition in the single market. But this source of competitive pressure has, until recently, remained mainly 'potential' and relevant only in specialised niches of the corporate finance segment where most Italian banks had neither substantial amounts of business nor important plans of action. As far as the acquisition of Italian banks by foreign banks are concerned, they did not reach the level and intensity that could have been predicted on the basis of the estimated efficiency gaps. Cross-border M&As mainly involved minor banks, and did not cause a substantive modification of the competitive environment. The only significant acquisition was by Deutsche Bank, but the acquired institution was already a foreign bank.

This scenario started to change during 1996 and 1997, and this change is becoming increasingly rapid. The Italian banking system is currently abandoning the protective strategy, while the competitive pressure from abroad and the interest in cross-border acquisitions of Italian banks are becoming much more relevant. Moreover, things seem to be changing so rapidly, and the present situation is so different, that proposing a well researched scheme for interpreting the current status of the impact of the European single currency on the Italian banking system is impossible at the moment.

In concluding this chapter we can only briefly suggest some hypotheses about the factors that are causing a change of scenario from the one that described the impact of the SMP in the years around 1992, and about the new strategic attitude of Italian banks. When it comes to the factors of change, there can be little doubt that the fact that the single currency was approaching and was becoming more probable and credible, played the dominant role. In this respect, the higher probability of the inclusion of the lira in the euro was obviously a crucial point.

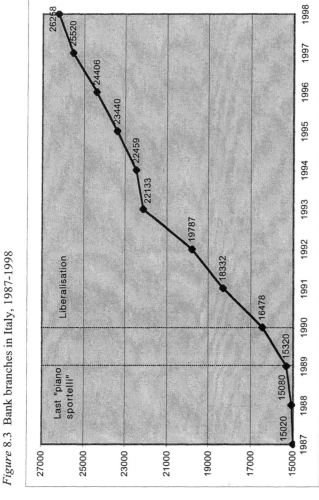

Figure 8.3 Bank branches in Italy, 1987-1998

It is becoming increasingly clear in the financial industry that the single market has been a rather incomplete object without a single currency, and the euro is causing a surge in the internationalisation of various aspects of banking, from the provision of payment services to the management of portfolios. Banks are therefore preparing for a corresponding jump in their strategic attitude towards the single market.

Other factors are contributing to the rapid modification of the scenario of the Italian banking industry and of its international integration. Among them we would like to stress the gradual progress towards a more private and market-oriented corporate governance of Italian banks. This goes together with the increase in the pressure to restructure that is evident in the Italian banking industry. This pressure comes, first of all, from the persistent tendency towards a shrinkage of interest margins, but the increasing importance of the shift towards managed portfolios in the relationship between banks and savers is also very important, as well as the treatment of non-performing portfolios of loans that is becoming, albeit much too slowly, a little more transparent. Changes are also beginning in banking labour markets where some signs of increasing flexibility can be detected. All these pressures to restructure originate from the increasing domestic competition that, as we have said, was already characterising the first 'protective' reaction to the SMP. But the pressure also comes directly from Europe, for instance when the Commission opposes the recourse to (explicit or implicit) public subsidies to preserve inefficient and insolvent institutions.

A more contestable and flexible Italian banking industry within a single currency market must be linked to a new strategic perspective by individual banks. Here a distinction must be made between smaller and larger banks. For the best institutions in the small to medium-size group, a potentially successful 'protective' strategy can still be viable. If they have a niche in providing retail services at a local level, they can survive in a profitable way, even in a world of global players from which they will buy the services to be sold to their local retail clients.

But when the bank has a national dimension, and no regional niche strategy is available, the single market plus single currency does not allow avoidance of the game of global competition. This game requires a certain rather large critical dimension: this is a widespread intuitive idea of both bankers and economists that cannot be tested on the basis of data from the past, in other words from a 'regime' that is going to change.

It is very difficult for an Italian bank to reach this critical dimension without merging with other national large banks. And, even after a merger, the resulting institution will not be able to play a genuinely global game:

the services it will provide will necessarily be deeply characterised by its nationality. The only alternative is to be acquired by a much larger foreign financial group. In any case, the new larger banks will need rapidly to adopt an updated banking technology, a model of the banking business that can survive global competition. In this respect, the most urgent strategic change is the acceleration of the shift from interest-based, traditional intermediation activities to commission-based, innovative activities with a strong concentration on portfolio management services. This newly emerging strategic scenario is at the root of four facts that are worth mentioning to describe what is currently happening in the Italian banking system.

First, in many Italian banks a new emphasis on strategic planning is becoming evident and internal reorganisation is starting. Earlier in this paper we have seen how the shape and the relative efficiency of the technological ppf of Italian banks changed between 1995 and 1997. We expect that the picture will improve further when data for subsequent years are available in complete form. But we also think that the new results will not be completely comparable with the previous ones as it is not possible to reject the hypotheses of a substantial discontinuity in the path of technological progress in the Italian banking sector after 1998.

Some of the weaknesses of the Italian banking system in the new international context that have been shown by 1997 data are already stimulating a laborious and difficult change and, to the extent that parts of the system will be able to survive, they will certainly look stronger. To understand the timing of restructuring it must also be recalled that mergers and acquisitions involving small and medium-sized banks peaked in 1994 and 1995 (Giorgino and Porzio, 1997). This has a lagged effect on reorganisations. It is only during 1996-97, when the number of M&A operations is again smaller, that previous operations are giving rise to substantial organisational changes.

A second fact to be mentioned is that plans for merging large national banks have been announced, forecast or simply hypothesised with increasing frequency and insistence in recent years. Some of these plans have started to be implemented and will give rise to institutions of a substantially larger size than those now operating. To mention only some examples, with different degrees of advancement and concreteness: Istituto Mobiliare Italiano with Istituto Bancario San Paolo di Torino; Ambroveneto with the Cariplo group (Banca Intesa); Istituto Nazionale delle Assicurazioni (an insurance company) with Banco di Napoli; and, more recently, Banca Intesa with Banca Commerciale Italiana. It is interesting to note that, while in some cases one of the merging institutions has had serious problems of bad loans and illiquidity, the major driving force towards this process of merger and acquisition is not a need for help by some problem banks but, as we said, a more general search for larger size in a larger European market. It is also worth stressing that in several cases the planned mergers are connected to the process of privatisation of one or more of the institutions involved.

A third fact which is related to the new competitive scenario is the increasing weight of foreign shareholders in the capital and, sometimes, in the governance of Italian banks. We do not have the appropriate figures to analyse the extent of this phenomenon but it is a fact that a bullish market for bank stocks has benefited from strong demand from abroad and foreign shareholders have increased their involvement in the governance of some large banks like, for instance, Banca Intesa, Credito Italiano, and Banca di Roma during recent years.

The fourth fact is a consequence of the previous ones: the price of bank stocks increased during 1997 and the first two months of 1998, much faster than the general stock exchange index (see Figure 8.4). There is also evidence that the market tends to react favourably when news of merger plans are released: this did not happen in previous periods, when the strategic scenario surrounding the possible merger was much less clear.

The market seems to share the basic conclusion of this paper, that the impact of the single market and the single European currency on Italian banks will be a very strong shock causing major risks for a relatively weak and still inefficient system, but also bringing interesting opportunities.

References

Associazione Bancaria Italiana (febbraio 1997), *Gli Svantaggi Competitivi Delle Banche Italiane Nella Prospettiva Dell'Unificazione Monetaria* (ABI, Roma)

Balzarini, A. (1996), Efficienza ed Integrazione: Prospettive per Alcuni Sistemi Bancari Europei, ricerca di base su 'Gli intermediari finanziari nelle prospettive dell'economia aziendale e dell'economia politica: verso un'integrazione', Università Bocconi, quaderno n. 24, luglio.

Giorgino, M. and C. Porzio (1997), 'Le concentrazioni bancarie in Italia: alcuni fattori interpretativi', *Bancaria,* dicembre.

Pieggi, M. (1996-7), *Efficienza Comparata dei Sistemi Bancari: Una Analisi Empirica* (Tesi di laurea, Università Bocconi)

Resti, A. (1996), *Fallen Angels or Money-Pumps? Trying to Draw a Map of the Main European Banks* (Banca Commerciale Italiana, Ricerche, n.8.)

205

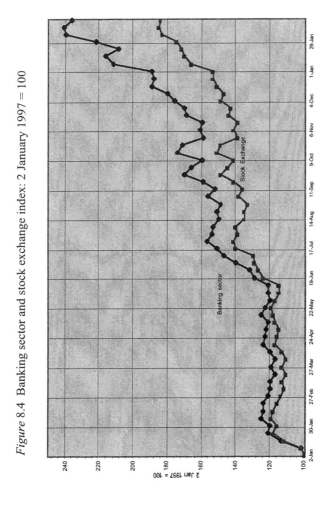

Figure 8.4 Banking sector and stock exchange index: 2 January 1997 = 100

9   Netherlands

Harald A. Benink and Jacques J. Sijben

1   INTRODUCTION

In this chapter we focus our attention on the banking sector in the Netherlands. The Dutch banking sector represents an interesting case study since the Dutch market has been, well before the adoption of the EU regulations related to the SMP and the Europe 1992 target date, relatively small, open, liberal and efficient. At the same time, the SMP has had a profound impact due to bankers' anticipatory reactions to internal market legislation. Moreover, the introduction of the euro is likely to have significant consequences for the banking system in the Netherlands. These consequences will be dealt with in the following paragraphs.

In Section 2 we present an overview of the Dutch banking sector in terms of market structure and performance. Attention is paid to the main players and market positions, the degree of competition, the entry barriers, and the banking performance and condition[1]. Section 3 contains a description of the regulatory framework for banks in the Netherlands, both before and after implementation of the SMP. In Section 4 we analyse how the SMP has affected the strategic behaviour of Dutch banks. Special attention will be paid to the strategy of the ING Group, based on interviews we had with high-ranking officials of ING. Moreover, using key results of the Economic Research Europe report, empirical evidence on the Single Market's impact on Dutch banks will be presented. Section 5 deals with the preparations by Dutch banks for the planned introduction of EMU with a common currency, the euro. For this purpose, we conducted a postal survey on the impact of the introduction of the euro on the banking sector in the Netherlands. The survey was conducted among three large banks and two small banks. In Section 6 we draw some conclusions.

2   MARKET STRUCTURE AND PERFORMANCE

2.1 Main players and market positions

On 4 April 1990 the Dutch financial newspaper *Het Financieele Dagblad* reported data on the market shares of the three largest banks in the

Netherlands. From these data it can be concluded that already in 1990, and well before (and possibly in anticipation of) the Europe 1992 target date, the market share of the three largest banks together is rather high. Therefore, the Dutch domestic banking industry seems to be highly concentrated (see Table 9.1).

Table 9.1 Market shares of the three largest banks

	NMB-Postbank	ABN-AMRO Bank	Rabobank	Total
Short-term private savings accounts	42%	17%	28%	87%
Mortgages	22%	18%	46%	86%
Consumer credits	19%	38%	13%	70%
Short-term business savings accounts	24%	40%	19%	83%
Deposits	24%	50%	17%	91%
Credit services to companies	18%	44%	21%	83%

Note: In 1989 NMB Bank and Postbank merged into NMB-Postbank which, after its merger in 1991 with the insurer Nationale Nederlanden into the ING Group, came to be called ING Bank. ABN-AMRO Bank is the result of a merger in 1990 between ABN Bank and AMRO Bank.

Although the top three banks in Table 9.1 represent the lion's share of the Dutch banking market, there are two other large financial institutions, namely AMEV and Aegon. These five institutions own, with all subsidiaries, at least 80% of the banking market (credit services for individuals and companies) and around 40% (indemnity market) to 70% (life insurance) of the insurance market.

Three of these financial institutions banks are insurance banks (ING, Rabobank and AMEV), while ABN-AMRO and Aegon are, respectively, 'pure' bank and insurance company. ING conducts its insurance activities under the name of Nationale Nederlanden. Rabobank cooperates with insurers Interpolis and Avero/Centraal Beheer. The latter also has a collaboration with Zilveren Kruis. AMEV is the smallest insurance bank. It has taken over VSB (United Savings Bank) and has merged with the Belgian insurer AG (Assurance Générale) to form Fortis AMEV. Thereby, AMEV is the first Dutch financial institution to form a truly European bancassurance company. In 1996, Fortis bought MeesPierson Bank from ABN-AMRO.

In the past few years some important mergers, acquisitions and takeovers were carried out in the Netherlands. At the end of 1997, ING Group merged with Banque Bruxelles Lambert from Belgium, thereby increasing its activities by 60%. In this way the strategic objectives of extending the investment banking activities and creating a second 'home market' in Europe were realised. In August 1999, ING Group further enlarged its activities through the takeover of the German investment bank BHF (Berliner Handels und Frankfurter Bank), so boosting its position in the German market.

In 1997, ABN-AMRO strongly increased its participation in the Brazilian bank Banco Real in order to create an important 'home market' outside Europe. In 1998, both ABN-AMRO and Fortis were trying to buy the Belgian Generale Bank. After a battle with regard to a public bid by ABN-AMRO, ultimately Fortis merged with Generale Bank. In this way, next to ING Group, a second big 'Benelux bank' was created. Generale Bank Netherlands is the result of the takeover of Crédit Lyonnais Bank Netherlands by Generale Bank in 1995. Again in 1997, an integrated financial concern, SNS-Reaal Group, emerged through the merger of SNS Bank and Reaal Group (insurance). The next step was that SNS-Reaal Group merged with Banque de Suez Netherlands. Finally, in 1999, two big pension funds (ABP and PGGM) took over National Investment Bank (NIB), bundling their portfolio activities.

2.2 Competition

Despite the increased international mobility of capital, certain segments of the Dutch financial market are still protected from international competition. Inquiries were held into seven Dutch commercial banks that account for more than 75% of the value of total bank assets in the Netherlands. None of the respondents complain about foreign competition in any of the segments (Swank, 1994). Prices can be set by banks, within certain limits, without a negative impact on profits. Only highly rated large companies can borrow easily on international capital markets, therefore the competition in this segment is larger. In markets where others, such as insurers and institutional investors, are operating, competition is greater.

Competition in the mortgage market has increased due to new entrants like pension funds and Postbank. Another reason for increased competition in the mortgage market is the attempt of banks to match the duration of their assets and liabilities to reduce interest rate risk. This results in banks trying to negotiate mortgages on a floating-rate base.

Competition in the deposits market declined due to the large increase in concentration of the banking sector. The banking sector is among the most protected and least dynamic sectors in the Netherlands. Gual and Neven (1992) find in their research on the impact of deregulation on the European banking sector that Dutch banks charge higher margins to private individuals, as well as to companies, than banks in Belgium, France, Germany, Spain and the UK.

A keyword in the Dutch financial market is consolidation. The large banks are increasing their competitive strength and investments abroad while mainly focusing on cost reductions in their home market. Almost every week they open new branches abroad while closing branches in the Netherlands. The decreasing need for labour is caused by new technology and mergers. Banks are trying to divide this process into several phases in order to achieve gradual changes. This will lessen the resistance of employees and make changes easier. Expansion abroad is mainly possible because of earnings made in the sound home base of the large banks where they could afford, until recently, to change only gradually and delay large, necessary investments because there was hardly any competition. In serving large international companies or institutional investors, naturally they have to compete with global competitors. But, in the private customer market and middle and small companies market, the three largest banks are relatively safe. The costs to a foreign competitor to break into this market are enormous. Whether the large banks make arrangements with each other or just watch each other's moves constantly is not relevant: in practice the result is that they seem to have the same policy priorities. Large investments, such as the chip card (electronic wallet), could be delayed without any penalty because there was, until recently, no real competition in this segment. In the meantime, the financial sector in the Netherlands is lagging behind in the field of technological developments compared to other European countries. Foreign competitors may find ways to penetrate the Dutch market if banks do not take measures to improve their domestic services (Haenen, 1994).

The Dutch government has allowed the mergers to take place because it expects globalisation of competition. This competition will certainly reduce monopoly powers in the future but at the moment banks can still profit from their monopoly powers in the small and medium-sized business segment and in the private customer market. Access to distribution channels is probably one of the most significant barriers to enter the Dutch banking market. Therefore, if one seeks to enter the Dutch market, a niche strategy or a take-over/merger strategy would be the most feasible option.

2.3 Entry barriers

One of the driving forces for mergers and takeovers is the need to increase scale. In post-1992 Europe internal borders vanished, but most mergers in the Netherlands are still performed on a local scale. Domestic mergers are a defensive strategy. The home market is closed as much as possible to new entrants. A strong home base is required to be competitive abroad. This leads to the fact that entering the Dutch banking market with the goal of achieving a large market share is unlikely to succeed. The only successes have been companies penetrating the Dutch market in specialised financial services such as brokerage, derivatives, and takeovers. However, even these possibilities are limited by the fact that Dutch distribution channels are not easily captured, thus leaving little room for penetration.

However, there are some opportunities for new competitors. Dutch banks are vulnerable in profitable market segments because they compensate incurred losses on non-profitable services, such as transfer of payments, with higher tariffs on profitable services: so-called cross subsidies. A new entrant can start competing in these high tariff segments, giving Dutch banks a hard time. However, the three big financial institutions can reduce losses on, for example, transfer of payments by using their market power to make better arrangements. This may lead to less competition and raise penetration barriers (Tamminga, 1991).

As already mentioned above, entering the Dutch financial market is quite difficult due to high concentration levels. It is difficult to gain considerable access to distribution channels in order to obtain large market shares. The internal market programme has triggered the legislation changes in the Netherlands. Former barriers between insurers and banks have vanished. Furthermore, bank legislation in general became less restrictive and these developments resulted in merger waves. The resulting increase in concentration made it even more difficult than before to enter the Dutch market.

A good example of a recent entry to the Dutch banking market was the takeover in 1995 of Crédit Lyonnais Bank Netherlands (CLBN) by Generale Bank. Generale Bank, the largest bank in Belgium, is now an important player in the Dutch banking market but is still much smaller than the three largest banks, ABN-AMRO, ING and Rabobank, which have about 80% of the banking market between them. The name Crédit Lyonnais Bank Netherlands has disappeared and has been replaced by Generale Bank Netherlands. Generale Bank declared that it does not have ambitions to become as large as the three biggest banks. It will position itself as 'second bank' for small and medium-sized companies, as well as for the top 30% of wealthy individuals. However, Generale Bank declared that it would not hesitate to penetrate profitable segments where possible. Generale Bank can be much more competitive in the Netherlands than CLBN because it can borrow against lower interest rates. CLBN was bothered by its bad reputation, due to scandals and financial problems, and had to compensate for this by paying higher interest rates.

In summary, one can conclude that the Dutch banking market has some characteristics that increase entry barriers: it is a relatively small market, highly concentrated, highly efficient, and only moderately profitable with relatively low prices on average. However, there are also some vulnerable areas within the Dutch banking sector which foreign competitors could take advantage of: lack of innovative strength, low degree of specialisation, high prices for some specific services, high number of independent intermediaries, and frequent use of cross subsidies (Nederlandse Vereniging van Banken, 1990).

2.4 Banking performance

The Dutch banking sector had an excellent year in 1996. ABN-AMRO Bank generated a net income of 3.3 billion guilders (26.3% up compared with 1995), ING Bank had a net income of 1.4 billion guilders (27.5% up), and Rabobank realised a net income of 1.6 billion guilders (14.4% up). The balance sheet total was 595.3 billion guilders for ABN-AMRO, 311.4 billion guilders for ING Bank, and 331.3 billion guilders for Rabobank. With respect to capital adequacy, ABN-AMRO and ING had a BIS ratio of 10.9% and Rabo had a ratio of 11.3%. These numbers are well above the required minimum ratio of 8%.

Brouwer (1997) notes that ABN Bank and AMRO Bank had a stagnating profit flow before the merger of 1990. Since then the newly formed ABN-AMRO has been able to more than double its profits. Also ING Bank, almost half the size of ABN-AMRO, has been able to double its profits during the 1990s. As noted before, this development was made possible by increasing its competitive strength and investments abroad while mainly focusing on cost reductions in the Dutch home market. Rabobank exhibited a lower net income growth, the reason being that it is not so strongly represented in the fastest growing markets such as international loans and the securities business.

After the takeover of Crédit Lyonnais Bank Netherlands by Generale Bank in December 1995, 1996 was the first full year that the bank was active under its new name of Generale Bank Netherlands. Net income increased by 43% compared with 1995. However, this figure is somewhat misleading since it is largely caused by a reduction of incidental costs.

Nevertheless, Generale managed to increase substantially its loan and securities activities while reducing its costs at the same time.

1996 was also an excellent year for other Dutch banks, with significant net income increases. Their BIS ratios are in the range of 12% to 15%. A high-flyer is the investment bank Kempen & Co., which doubled its net income in 1996 and had a BIS ratio of 30% at the end of 1996.

3   REGULATORY FRAMEWORK

3.1 Regulatory framework prior to the SMP

The Economic Research Europe report identifies possible business restrictions for EU countries in their banking markets. The categories of possible business restrictions include interest rate restrictions, capital controls, bank access to stock exchange membership, bank ownership restrictions, branching restrictions, foreign bank entry, credit ceilings, mandatory investment requirements, restrictions on insurance, underwriting and brokerage, portfolio management, and leasing and factoring. At the beginning of 1986, well before the signing of the Single European Act in February 1986, only one of the restrictions mentioned above was still applicable to the Netherlands, namely banks' involvement in insurance business. Thus, already in the mid-1980s the Netherlands had a liberal and open banking market resembling a true universal banking model.

3.2 Main SMP legislation

Completing the Internal Market, the title of the White Paper discussed by the European government leaders during their meeting of June 1985 in Milan, set the date of completion of the single market for 31 December 1992 ('Europe 1992'). For this purpose a detailed timetable was presented, with approximately 300 proposals to be implemented before 1 January 1993. An important part of these proposals dealt with the liberalisation of the banking and financial services market in Europe. The completion of the internal market was elevated to the status of a Treaty commitment as a result of the signing of the Single European Act in February 1986, which came into effect on 1 July 1987 and entails an amendment to the Treaty of Rome.

The Second Banking Directive for universal banks (called 'credit institutions' in the directive) forms the cornerstone of all Directives for the business of these institutions in the context of the achievement of the single (or internal) banking market. The directive was adopted by the EU Council of Ministers in December 1989 and was implemented on 1 January 1993. At the heart of the Directive is the requirement of a single licence, along with an agreed list of banking activities covered by this licence. Notwithstanding its key character, the Second Banking Directive is supplemented by a large group of coordinating Directives in the fields of consolidated supervision, annual accounts, large exposures, deposit guarantee schemes, consumer credit, capital adequacy requirements, and capital movements[2]. As noted above, the banking market in the Netherlands was already open and liberal in the mid-1980s, the only exception being banks' involvement in insurance business (see also subsection 3.3). Nevertheless, the Netherlands has implemented into its national banking laws all the EU directives referred to above.

3.3 Other domestic regulatory landmarks

As far as bank holdings in non-banking institutions (the so-called concept of 'banque d'affaires') are concerned, the Second Banking Directive introduces two limits. First, a credit institution may not have a qualifying holding (that is a holding embodying 10% of shares held or voting rights in an individual non-bank) exceeding a total of 15% of its own funds in such an undertaking. Second, the amount of all holdings in such undertakings may not exceed 60% of the own funds of the credit institution. However, the member states need not apply the limits to holdings in insurance companies. Currently, no EU member state is doing so, which enables banks to have insurance subsidiaries and to operate as a bank-insurer, the so-called concept of 'bancassurance'.

The Netherlands, in anticipation of the implementation of the Second Banking Directive at the end of 1992, fully liberalised its structural regime for banks and insurance companies at the beginning of 1990. Until 1990, the structural regime limited the mutual share holdings of banks and insurance companies up to 15% of total share capital. Moreover, banks and insurance companies were not allowed to operate within one legal entity. The full liberalisation of the structural regime in 1990 implied that the limits on mutual holdings were abolished. This made it possible for banks to own fully an insurance company and for insurance companies to have 100% of the shares of a bank. However, it remained prohibited for banks and insurance companies to combine their activities in one legal entity. In this way it remained possible to have separate supervision and supervisors for banks and insurance companies. This element of separate supervision was considered as desirable for two reasons. First, there are huge differences between banks and insurance companies in the type of business and the structure of the balance sheet. Second, in the case of banking supervision, there is an important interaction between prudential and monetary aspects of supervision.

3.4 Remaining barriers to the SMP

From the point of view of implementation of EU Directives, the Dutch banking market is fully open and liberalised. Although from a legal point of view there are no remaining barriers to a single banking market with its related competition, efficiency, and low prices and margins, the Dutch banking market still has some characteristics that increase entry barriers (as we noted in subsection 2.3). In particular, the combined effect of a relatively small size and a high degree of concentration makes it difficult for foreign financial firms to enter the Dutch banking market. However, as we will argue in section 5, the introduction of the euro is likely to change this situation by opening possibilities for increased market integration, greater uniformity in market practices, and more transparency in pricing.

4   IMPACT OF THE SMP

4.1 Bank strategies

Possible strategic results from financial services regulation, in terms of opportunities and threats, are mainly caused by four coherent developments. First, the internal market legislation by the EU. Second, global market developments in general which are accelerated by Europe 1992. Third, anticipatory behaviour of banks' clients and, finally, anticipatory behaviour of banks and other financial institutions (Nederlandse Vereniging van Banken, 1990).

General market developments, such as shorter product life cycles, trends towards universal banking, declining customer loyalty, and the appearance of bancassurance, are accelerated by the process of European unification. Dutch banks, which still have a comfortable position in their home market, may find some developments resulting from the unification process to be threatening. Lagging behind in terms of product innovation can be dangerous. Additional emphasis on cost control of branches will be necessary. Customers switching to non-Dutch and/or non-banking financial institutions pose another threat. Furthermore, profit margins, mainly on servicing large companies and institutional investors, are continuously under pressure. In-house banking is becoming more popular among large companies. Finally, the competition between insurance companies and insurance intermediaries is increasing because of the blurring of bank and insurance products.

Anticipation of global competition by banks' corporate clients causes developments such as strategic alliances, mergers and cross-border takeovers of these corporate clients. One reason for these is to gain strength in the negotiation process in the buying market and in the distribution channels. This increase of scale leads to larger volumes of supply and demand. Because their clients are growing, banks also have to find ways to increase their scale.

Anticipatory behaviour by private individuals consists mainly of higher mobility by certain labour groups in the EU and a changing customer attitude with respect to companies and financial institutions in other EU countries. Opportunities might exist in serving private individuals at a European level and in 'sheltering' foreign workers who are employed in the Netherlands. However, barriers caused by the lack of knowledge of local structures remain for foreign banks trying to penetrate markets abroad.

Anticipatory behaviour by banks and other financial institutions, and the legislation aimed at liberalisation, are mutually reinforcing each other. Cross-border as well as national forms of collaboration are being formed between banks, insurers, investment institutions, and securities traders.

4.2 The strategy of ING[3]

In anticipation of internal market legislation based on the legislative measures envisaged in the 1985 White Paper, the management of ING made some important strategic decisions. The merger between NMB Bank and Postbank was a reaction to the expectation that foreign banks would enter the Dutch banking sector after 1992. NMB Bank was a rather small bank and wanted to increase its scale in order to be able to compete with larger foreign banks. NMB Bank's management expected many cross-border mergers and takeovers. The second merger, between NMB-Postbank and Nationale Nederlanden to create ING Group, was also driven by anticipatory reactions to internal market legislation. The need for this merger was even strengthened by the merger between ABN Bank and AMRO Bank, a main competitor, which forced NMB-Postbank to increase its scale within a national context.

In 1993, when important legislation came into force, nothing really happened: the expected cross-border mergers and takeovers did not take place. However, the anticipatory impact of the 1985 White Paper and internal market legislation on ING and other members of the Dutch domestic banking sector has been very large and has resulted in consolidation, increase of scale, and cost control in the Dutch banking market. With respect to the non-domestic activities of ING, the significance of the Second Banking Directive is regarded as rather small, although the concept of home country control is certainly convenient. In practice it is almost impossible to start a completely new network of branches in another EU member state, and the freedom of establishment does not change this. ING was already established in many foreign markets even before liberalisation came into effect. This limits the impact of European legislation even further. ING is mostly interested in emerging markets, such as Eastern Europe, the Soviet Union, Latin America and Asia, because it can earn higher returns on equity in these countries. Still, one desirable goal remains to be achieved: ING would like to have a second domestic market and its attempts to take over the Belgian Banque Bruxelles Lambert (BBL) illustrated this very well.

As described above, the anticipatory response of ING to EU banking legislation has been substantial. Two mergers increased the scale of ING Group tremendously over a short period of time. This increase of scale was found necessary in order to avoid hostile takeovers by foreign banks. The domestic merger wave in the Netherlands was, to a large extent, triggered by these expectations. However, cross-border mergers and takeovers did not occur, so it could be argued that the actual impact of internal market legislation was rather small.

One of the most important factors influencing ING's strategy independently from EU-initiated legislation is the trend towards globalisation which started in the early 1980s. This trend is viewed by ING as mostly autonomous. It is driven more by, for example, technological developments than by European legislation, or any legislation for that matter. The trend towards globalisation is observed all over the world and not only in Europe. Globalisation forces clients to increase scale, as a result of which banks are required to grow themselves as well. Banks adjusting to the increasing scale of their clients were first observed in the US, but European banks are now adopting this strategy too.

4.3 Evidence of the SMP's impact

In Sections 2 and 3 we described the Dutch banking market as having some characteristics which increase entry barriers. In particular, the combined effect of a relatively small size and a high degree of concentration makes it difficult for foreign financial firms to enter the Dutch banking market. At the same time, the Dutch market is only moderately profitable, with relatively low prices on average. However, there are also some vulnerable spots within the Dutch banking sector which foreign competitors, particularly in the case of increased market integration after the introduction of the euro, could take advantage of: lack of innovative strength, low degree of specialisation, and high prices for some specific services.

The Economic Research Europe report explored for each EU country the question of whether prices and margins relating to banking services, costs and revenues of banks, banks' efficiencies, and economies of scale and scope have changed since the completion of the Single Market Programme (SMP) at the end of 1992. This period is called the post-SMP period. Next, the report tries to establish the extent to which the SMP has been responsible for the changes. The reason for this analytical and empirical distinction is that certain developments and changes would have occurred in the absence of the SMP.

For the Netherlands, given its small size and the already high degree of concentration at the beginning of the 1990s, it is not unreasonable to expect small changes in the banking sector after the completion of the SMP. This expectation is confirmed by the empirical results in the Economic Research Europe report. For instance, in the prices of loans category, where 'prices' are defined as the margin between the rate charged on loans and the three-month inter-bank rate, only small price decreases can be observed since the full implementation of the SMP. This result is obtained from a postal survey among a group of large and small banks in the Netherlands. Moreover, confronted with the question to what extent the SMP has been responsible for the reported price decreases, the respondents to the postal survey indicate that the SMP has had only a slight influence. The same conclusion is reached for the decrease of deposit prices, where 'prices' are defined as the margin between the rate paid on deposits and the three-month inter-bank rate.

5   BANK PREPARATIONS FOR EMU

Since the early 1980s the international banking system has experienced a strong restructuring and consolidation process, driven by the rapid developments in information technology and the liberalisation of financial markets. These structural changes were associated with a reduction of transaction and information costs in the financial intermediation process on the one hand and with a sharpening of competition and a substantial squeezing of profit margins on the other. Over the last two decades, the value of the banking franchise, characterised by collecting deposits and bank lending, with a special role for risk management, has declined.

The introduction of EMU with a common currency, the euro, is the final stage in the process of European financial and monetary integration, creating a fully integrated European financial market with related benefits. This also implies that the financial landscape in Europe will change drastically. In this context McCauley and White (1997) point out: 'The starting point is that European-based financial firms are already under significant competitive pressure to restructure. Moreover, existing forces of technological change and deregulation affecting cross-border activity must eventually cause these pressures to intensify even if the effects to date on international competition in corporate and retail banking have been limited'. With regard to financial intermediation, new challenges, possibilities and risks will undoubtedly arise for the players in European and international financial markets. Schinasi and Prati (1997) suggest that '...the introduction of the euro is likely to encourage the further securitisation of European finance, and it opens possibilities for increased market integration, greater uniformity in market practices and more transparency in pricing'.

5.1 Banks as financial intermediaries

Traditionally, the theory of financial intermediation stresses as a rule that, within the spectrum of alternatives to finance investment projects, bank loans play a special role. The modern theory of financial intermediation, based on asymmetric information and the associated market imperfections, provides the microeconomic foundation of the bank lending channel in the monetary transmission process. Davis (1994) points out that, owing to asymmetric information between the ultimate lender and borrower, banks render assistance in solving the ex-ante asymmetric information problems. Initially, banks will have to judge the creditworthiness of the potential borrower (screening) and, subsequently, will have to watch carefully that the borrower makes use of the loan in accordance with the debt contract (monitoring). The banks' special role in comparison with other lenders is based on their comparative advantages with respect to reducing the asymmetric information problems in the intermediation process.

In this context Davis mentions three informational advantages. First, banks have information about the financial status of the borrower, often because of an established customer relationship. Moreover, financial markets have no incentive to monitor the borrower's behaviour, because information has the characteristics of a public good, giving rise to the 'free rider' problem. This means that individual lenders are expecting that other lenders will monitor the borrower's behaviour and will take advantage, without paying, of the information-gathering process of other lenders.

According to Diamond (1984), this monitoring function will be delegated by the ultimate lender (depositor) to the bank, which takes care of a diversification of the asset portfolio. The need for monitoring and the arising of moral hazard problems may be reduced if, in case of misbehaviour, the borrower will be faced with a loss of reputation. In this context Davis puts forward that '...for these borrowers, such as large, established companies with a reputation for repaying debt, it is a capital asset (as it facilitates borrowing at low cost) which would depreciate in the case of non-repayment'. The moral hazard problem will also be reduced in proportion to the value of the collateral. A second comparative advantage refers to the fact that, in case of bankruptcy, the bank can keep control of the borrower's assets. Because of the free-rider problem, the bank is better qualified to keep control than the individual lenders. Moreover, the bank can try to change the borrower's behaviour very early on by requiring additional collateral or by the threat of credit constraints. Finally, because of 'relationship banking', the bank has private information about the borrower and, therefore, will help him in less favourable circumstances by extending the original loan. In this way a 'customer market' exists, making it very costly for the borrower to look around for financial support from another lender or financial institution.

Apart from these informational advantages, the bank also has comparative cost benefits compared to other financial intermediaries. In this context the bank has the disposal of economies of scale by collecting deposits with several maturities and then transforming these funds into loans and investments. According to the Gurley-Shaw (1960) analysis of this transformation process, banks are appearing as information brokers between ultimate lenders (depositors) and ultimate borrowers and transform liquid assets into illiquid debt contracts[4]. Although at present many alternatives for bank loans exist, such as commercial paper, it has to be noted that these financial instruments cannot be used very easily by small and medium-sized firms because these firms are unknown to financial markets.

Finally, in this context, mention should be made of the quite different relationship that exists between banks and their clients in the US and the UK on the one hand and in Germany and Japan on the other hand. In the last two countries, banks not only play the role of central lender in the external financing of the corporations but they are also actively involved in the management of these firms. This means that a strong intertwinement exists between the banking system and industrial firms. It is obvious that, because of this close relationship, agency costs will be lower and bank loans play a special role. Banks are active participants in the management decision processes of corporations. In Germany this is usually done by the Hausbank (the main bank used by the corporation); in Japan banks are usually part of big industrial groups, the so-called Keiretsu. The impact of the bank lending channel in the monetary transmission process will probably be stronger in these countries than in the market-oriented Anglo-Saxon financial intermediation model. Therefore, the empirical results with regard to the quantitative significance of bank lending in the monetary transmission are strongly dependent both on the institutional and financial environment and on the characteristics of financial markets in the countries concerned. In this context Tsatsaronis (1995) remarks that '...the greater dependence of non-financial firms on bank-intermediated credit in Germany and Japan and the active involvement of banks in the governance of corporations are factors that mitigate the agency costs of financial relationships in these countries', and further on, that '...bank loans are relatively more special in these countries and the credit-channel of monetary policy transmission could therefore be expected to be, if anything, stronger'.

Before the wave of deregulation processes in the early 1980s the banking sector was operating in a regulated and protected environment, with rather fixed spreads to strengthen its solvency position and with a continuous inflow of cheap deposits. In the financial intermediation process, banks fulfilled a central role and they were strongly involved in the transmission process of monetary policy implementation (Boot and Greenbaum, 1995). In the early 1980s this situation started to change.

5.2 A new financial environment

Since the 1980s the traditional role of banking in the financial intermediation process has changed substantially. The driving forces of these changes can be summarised as follows. At first, the financial regulations dating from the 1930s gave an incentive to avoid these rules, so resulting in financial innovations. Subsequently, this process was intensified by erratic fluctuations of interest, inflation and exchange rates during the 1970s. Finally, both the internationalisation of finance, characterised by an increasing financial intertwining, and information technology have accelerated these structural developments. All these trends have delivered explosive growth and enormous power to financial markets, confronting the banking system very sharply with the marketplace and deteriorating the traditional comparative advantages in the intermediation process. In this context Llewellyn (1994) clearly points out: 'In effect banks are no longer the exclusive suppliers of banking services. There are many traditional activities of banks that can now be undertaken equally well by markets, non-banking financial institutions, and non-financial companies' (see also Gardener, 1996).

In this way, the blurring of the role of financial institutions and the associated disintermediation process has intensified. The strengthening of competitive pressures is manifesting itself on both sides of the banks' balance sheets. On the liabilities side, banks have to compete with other institutions to collect savings deposits, thereby increasing their funding costs. On the assets side, they are confronted both with a well developed international capital market and other financial institutions as strong competitors in their lending activities. In this context mention has to be made of the phenomenon of securitisation, which can appear in two ways. At first, owing to asymmetric information on credit markets 'good borrowers' with a high reputation (credit rating) will finance their activities by the issue of commercial paper and medium-term notes on the money and capital market. So, based on the principle of adverse selection, these borrowers switch to direct external financing thus leaving the banks' balance sheet. Next to this kind of disintermediation a new intermediation technology has come about. This refers to the phenomenon of asset securitisation, when banks sell their assets to another financial institution which is financing itself in the capital market (such as mortgage-backed securities). In this context Boot and Greenbaum (1995) remark: 'The monitoring and screening role of banks point to the complementarity of bank and public capital market funding'. According to this semi-disintermediation, illiquid assets are removed from banks' balance sheets. However, although the bank no longer funds the securitised assets, the loan-originating, servicing and risk-processing activities remain with the banks. In this way an integration of the banking loan market and the capital market arises. Llewellyn speaks about deconstruction (the unbundling of the lending activities) making a better use of the comparative advantages of the different participants in the intermediation process. He points out: 'The overall conclusion is that banking will not be as protected as it has often been in the past, and that as a result the value of the banking franchise is likely to decline. In many respects, banks are losing some of their competitive advantages in the provision of services and, increasingly as entry barriers come down, they are losing monopoly power' (Llewellyn, 1994 and 1997).

In its 1997 Annual Report, the Bank for International Settlements (BIS) pays attention to the effects of global competition in a world which is overbanked and where traditional intermediation faces intense competition from collateralised lending and securitisation. In this context the BIS concludes: 'Indeed, we already seem to be well on the way towards a world with no barriers to universal banking and significantly greater competition from securities markets than hitherto. The introduction of the euro is likely to reinforce all of these trends in Europe'.

5.3 The euro and the capital market

In this section attention will be given to the consequences of the introduction of the euro for the development of the bond market in EMU. Owing to the disappearance of exchange rate risk and a reduction of transaction costs, the advent of the euro will reduce the costs of supply and demand of government bonds and increase market transparency. The current market segmentation is related to the existence of national currencies but will disappear because, in the new eurozone, institutional investors can make a portfolio choice between various government debtors. This implies that governments will be faced with a broad group of investors and will be less dependent on financing through the domestic capital market. This also means that market participants will have to focus on the credit risks of the government securities concerned. In this context Schinasi and Prati (1997) point out: 'The refocus on credit risk by both issuers and investors is likely to increase cross-border competition between financial intermediaries for bringing new issues to market, for rating new credits, and for allocating investment funds across the national markets'.

The degree of desegmentation of government bond markets in Europe will be dependent on the pricing of the credit risks and the credit rating of the potential borrowers. After the introduction of the euro and the denomination of the bonds in the new currency, interest-rate spreads will be determined by the quality of the respective securities supplied. Schinasi and Prati (1997) hold the view that '...from a pricing perspective, credit risk will become the most important risk and will make up the largest part of the remaining interest rate spreads among EMU issuers after the introduction of the euro'. It is obvious that competition between issuers with regard to the benchmark for the yield curve in the euro market will increase. The benchmark status for the issuer is very important because it reflects the lowest cost of capital in a very broad, deep, efficient and liquid capital market. Finally, the 'no bail out' clause in the Maastricht Treaty will strengthen the disciplinary mechanism of governments both to improve public finance and to reduce moral hazard.

Contrary to the market for government bonds, the market for corporate bonds is still relatively small and strongly segmented. This is caused by the fact that, traditionally, European corporations overwhelmingly are dependent on intermediate bank lending to finance their activities. In contrast, US entities have relied more heavily on bond and equity financing. However, the introduction of the euro might change this situation. First, the market for corporate bonds will develop very rapidly when the credit risk culture is strengthened. Also, the potential group of investors will be enlarged and, in this way, institutional investors will contribute to intensify the disintermediation process in the banking system. A disciplinary mechanism will therefore arise because corporations will have the incentive to improve their credit rating in order to reduce the cost of capital.

This behaviour is also related to a switch in the corporate governance culture, emphasising the shareholder's value in the financial behaviour of firms. It is obvious that this process can be strengthened by the introduction of a European rating institute. However, although the introduction of the euro will create possibilities to develop further and broaden the market for corporate bonds, this will be a gradual process. This is caused by regulatory restrictions in the individual countries, such as fiscal policy, issue requirements, and so on, and the relatively small group of institutional investors that is willing to invest in corporate bonds (heterogeneity of securities, costs of credit assessment, etc.). This means that, because of the competitive advantages of local and national banks in the securities industry, for some time to come the 'customer relationship' and the understanding of credit risk will remain two sources of strength for domestic banks.

5.4 The euro and disintermediation

From the preceding sections it may be concluded that the introduction of the euro will imply strong changes in the European banking system, in particular with respect to ongoing disintermediation trends. The creation of more liquid European capital markets is likely to encourage small and medium-sized firms to access securities markets thereby affecting the competitive position of banks. Moreover, credit evaluation and local market underwriting skills will become extremely valuable. The sharpening of competitive pressures will give an incentive for cross-border mergers and acquisitions in the banking system in order to get the power to compete with other global players to supply financial services to multinational corporations (Sijben, 1997).

As was stated earlier, European institutional investors will have the incentive to increase cross-border investments because of the disappearance of currency risks. In this context European, but also non-European, banks will have the possibility of increasing their investment banking activities. The advent of the euro will also result in a restructuring and consolidation of wholesale banking activities in other financial fields, such as the rationalisation of treasury functions and the payments system, because corporations will concentrate their euro-business in a small number of banks. Moreover, international corporations will have more possibilities for netting and pooling, centralising their treasury activities and reducing bank costs.

The need for consolidation will also emerge in the field of retail banking activities because of 'overbanking' in Europe. European banks provide services at non-competitive prices, making them vulnerable to competitive pressures. Although in the recent past profit margins have been reduced owing to the wave of deregulation, the consolidation processes have been postponed or failed to materialise. Schinasi and Prati (1997) hold the view that this behaviour is caused by '...factors such as home-currency advantages, legal and regulatory restrictions, ownership structures that inhibit entry and exit, extensive branch networks, and strong traditional and cultural relationships'. However, without doubt the growing intra-European trade will result in a demand for EMU-wide banking services, which can only be supplied by big financial institutions. This implies that banks will meet a very competitive European financial marketplace. The potential for competition from new entrants can act as a disciplinary mechanism for established market participants and may lead to more consolidation. In these circumstances, big banks will try to protect themselves against the acceleration of disintermediation processes by increasing the diversification of their activities through, for example, bancassurance. This behaviour can be supported by information technology, utilising the economies of scale. However, the implementation of the consolidation processes might be delayed or even prevented by many current regulatory restrictions in the eurozone, such as fiscal policy, accounting principles, and so on.

It is obvious that the present big European universal banks with great experience with regard to credit risk assessment can oppose the consequences of the disintermediation trends, on the one side by operating as the lead manager of securities issues by potential borrowers preferring direct external finance and on the other side by making credit available to units in need of financing by actively participating in the corporation concerned.

It is evident that in the changing European financial environment the market orientation of the banking industry has to be strengthened because other non-bank institutions will also be very active in the wholesale and retail market as suppliers of broad financial services. This also implies that, because of a greater diversification of financial services, the relative share of non-interest income in total bank income will further increase in the near future. Finally, the introduction of the euro will also confront banks with a new competitor at the liability side of the balance sheet. This refers to the fact that the implementation of a common monetary policy by the European Central Bank will imply the introduction of the euro-repo market. Essentially this refers to a money market instrument, collateralised against government bonds, which will compete with bank deposits for short-term funds.

5.5 The euro and the Dutch banking system

The introduction of the euro and the associated achievement of one integrated European financial market is likely to have significant consequences for the corporate sector and the banking system in the Netherlands. The disappearance of exchange rate risk (hedging costs) and the reduction of transaction costs will stimulate cross-border investment activities, thereby increasing overall efficiency.

The international trade of the Netherlands is very strongly Europe-oriented. The Netherlands sells almost 80% of its exports to the EU and nearly 65% of its imports come from EU countries. From a recent inquiry among 800 corporations by De Nederlandsche Bank (the Dutch central bank) it appears that the direct benefits from the introduction of EMU will annually amount to 2 billion guilders. Moreover, indirect benefits resulting from greater market transparency and less price uncertainty will also result after some years. Furthermore, the corporate sector can realise economies of scale in a big, uniform and transparent 'local Euromarket' through mergers and acquisitions. From the inquiry it appears that these indirect benefits will amount to 4 billions guilders annually in the near future.

It is evident that the banking system will also benefit from the strengthening of the corporate sector. Naturally, substantial increases in trade flows, rising investment activities, strong economic growth in a more dynamic environment, and an increase in the purchasing power of the biggest consumer market in the world will influence banking activities very positively. In this context mention can be made of the possibilities of cross-border private banking activities and of new opportunities in the issuing of securities, mergers and acquisitions, and portfolio management. Dutch banks will also benefit from the broadening, deepening and transparency of the integrated European financial market. Treasury management activities of banks can be concentrated by making use of economies of scale. All these activities will compensate both for the permanent loss of income associated with the disappearance of currency transactions and for the substantial short-term costs of the introduction of the euro. Without doubt the Dutch banking system, with its great international reputation and experience, will play an essential role as an intermediary between the growing dynamic corporate sector and the new European financial home market.

Recently, we conducted a postal survey on the impact of the introduction of the euro on the banking sector in the Netherlands. The survey was conducted among three large banks and two small banks. The results are described below.

With respect to the impact on market opportunities, the banks hold the view that retail banking will see a slight reduction in activities. The three big banks also expect a small reduction in corporate customer loans and deposits. With regard to the government bond market, expectations are divided rather strongly, but the two small banks expect a slight reduction of their activities in this product area. The big banks are expecting an increase of activities both in the corporate bond and equity markets, and in the area of fund management. Furthermore, banks expect a reduction of their foreign exchange activities and an increase of corporate advisory services.

On the subject of EMU threatening the domestic market share, the following results can be reported. The big banks expect a moderate impact on customer loans and deposits, on the government bond market and on the corporate bond and equity markets. However, on average, the big banks expect a greater impact on fund management and foreign exchange transactions than the small banks. All banks expect an increase of the domestic share with regard to corporate advisory activities, and one bank is even expecting a substantial growth in this product area. The impact on retail banking activities will be rather small.

Small banks are of the opinion that the introduction of EMU will not threaten their market share in other EU countries. However, big banks are expecting a slight increased threat in the field of retail banking activities and a rather strong threat in the areas of the government bond market, the corporate bond and equity markets, fund management and foreign exchange.

With regard to the development of the market share outside the EU, no effect is expected in the retail market. However, the big banks do expect a slight rise in their market share relating to government bonds, corporate bonds, and equities. In these areas small banks do not expect any changes. In the area of foreign exchange, the big banks are expecting a rather strong reduction. Moreover, a slight increase of fund management activities is expected. Big banks hold the view that increased competition in the areas of capital markets and investment banking will come both from domestic insurers and from foreign banks and foreign security houses. Small banks are expecting competitive pressures from domestic banks and insurers. On average, big banks expect a small increase of their activities in other EU countries in the field of mergers, alliances, acquisitions and joint ventures. However, one bank expects a rather large decrease in these activities.

With respect to competitive advantages within the domestic market, the banks see advantages in the area of long-term historical access to customers and credit-risk evaluation. The big banks are emphasising both economies of scale and scope, and product innovation and differentiation. They also hold the view that the introduction of EMU will threaten the sources of competitive advantage in the fields of economies of scale and product innovation and differentiation.

All banks are expecting increased competition from Belgium, the UK and Germany. The banks expect collaboration with banks in Belgium, France and Germany. Moreover, two big banks also see opportunities to collaborate with institutions in other EU countries such as Italy, Portugal and Spain.

On average, banks expect a slight change in their strategy with regard to retail banking and a significant change in the field of wholesale banking. All the banks will focus on customer and service quality, both domestic and abroad. Moreover, mergers and alliances will become more important and there is an increased focus on cross-border activities through product diversification and innovation. No bank is expecting a significant influence from the introduction of the euro on potential distribution channels of selected bank services. However, the big banks expect an increase in internet banking, TV-screen banking and telephone banking with regard to retail banking activities.

Finally, there are no other ways in which the introduction of EMU might stimulate the banks to operate in other EU countries. However, one big bank expects a relative ease in using its present distribution capacities in other countries.

6   CONCLUSIONS

The Dutch banking sector represents an interesting case study because the Dutch market has been, since well before the adoption of the EU regulations related to the SMP and the Europe 1992 target date, relatively small, open, liberal and efficient. At the same time, the SMP has had some profound effects due to bankers' anticipatory reactions to internal market legislation.

In anticipation of internal market legislation based on the legislative measures envisaged in the 1985 White Paper, the previous management of ING and ABN-AMRO made some important strategic decisions. The merger between NMB Bank and Postbank was a reaction to the expectation that foreign banks would enter the Dutch banking sector after 1992. NMB Bank was a rather small bank and wanted to increase its scale in order to be able to compete with larger foreign banks. NMB Bank's management expected many cross-border mergers and takeovers. The second merger, between NMB-Postbank and Nationale Nederlanden to create ING Group, was also driven by anticipatory reactions to internal market legislation. Finally, there was the merger between ABN Bank and AMRO Bank creating the giant ABN-AMRO Bank.

The mergers created a Dutch banking market having some characteristics that increase entry barriers. In particular, the combined effect of the Netherland's relatively small size and high degree of concentration makes it difficult for foreign financial firms to enter the Dutch banking market. However, the introduction of the euro is likely to change this situation by opening up possibilities for increased market integration, greater uniformity in market practices, and more transparency in pricing, as is confirmed by the postal survey we conducted among five Dutch banks.

Notes

1.   This paragraph is largely based on a 1996 case study of the Netherlands by Economic Research Europe (1997), (see below).
2.   A detailed discussion of these Directives can be found in Benink (1993), Zimmerman (1995), and Economic Research Europe (1997).
3.   This subsection is based on interviews we had with high-ranking officials of ING Group, including a member of the executive board.
4.   In this context see Becketti and Morris (1992), Fama (1985) and Sijben (1996).

References

Bank for International Settlements (1997), *67th Annual Report* (BIS, Basle).

Becketti, S. and C. Morris (1992), 'Are bank loans still special?', *Federal Reserve Bank of Kansas City Economic Review*, Fourth Quarter.

Benink, H.A. (1993), *Financial Integration in Europe* (Kluwer Academic Publishers, Dordrecht, Boston, London)

Boot, A.W.A. and S.I. Greenbaum (1995), *The Future of Banking* (Business Week Executive Briefing Service)

Brouwer, H.J. (1997), 'Uitzonderlijk goed jaar', *Bank- en Effectenbedrijf*, June, pp. 12-18.

Davis, E.P. (1994), 'Banking, corporate finance and monetary policy: an empirical perspective', *Oxford Review of Economic Policy*, 4, pp. 49-67.

Diamond, D.W. (1984), 'Financial intermediation and delegated monitoring', *Review of Economic Studies*, 51, pp. 393-414.

Economic Research Europe Ltd (1997), *The Single Market Review: Impact on Credit Institutions and Banking*, (Kogan Page, London)

Fama, E.F. (1985), 'What's different about banks?', *Journal of Monetary Economics*, 15, pp. 29-39.

Gardener, E.P.M. (1996), 'The future of traditional banking', *Revue de la Banque*, 4, pp. 186-98.

Gual, J. and D. Neven (1992), *Deregulation of the European Banking Industry (1980-1991)*, CEPR Discussion Paper, No. 703 (Centre for Economic Policy Research, London)

Gurley, J. and E. Shaw (1960), *Money in a Theory of Finance* (Brookings Institution, Washington DC.)

Haenen, H. (1994), 'Banken Blijven op Thuismarkt Steken in Consolidatie', *Het Financieele Dagblad*, Nov. 1.

Llewellyn, D.T. (1994), *Global Pressures on the Banking Industry*: paper presented at the European Banking Report Seminar, Rome, Nov. 30.

Llewellyn, D.T. (1997), 'Banking in the 21st century: the transformation of an industry', *Bulletin Economique et Financier*, Banque Internationale à Luxembourg,, 49, pp. 5-27.

McCauley, R.N. and W.R. White (1997), *The Euro and European Financial Markets*, BIS Working Papers, No. 41 (Bank for International Settlements, Basle)

Nederlandse Vereniging van Banken (1990), *Europa 1992 en de Nederlandse Bancaire Sector*, Amsterdam.

Schinasi, G. and A. Prati (1997), *European Monetary Union and International Capital Markets: Structural Implications and Risks*. Paper presented at an IMF seminar on EMU and the International Monetary System, Washington DC, March.

Sijben, J.J. (1996), 'Banks and the changed intermediation process', *Maandschrift Economie*, 60, Dec., pp. 456-77.

Sijben, J.J. (1997), 'De Euro, Bancaire Intermediatie en de Monetaire Politiek: Een Macro-Economische Visie', in *Intermediatie in Euro's* (Netherlands Institute for Banking and Stockbroking, Amsterdam, Oct. 28)

Swank, J. (1994), *Bank Behaviour and Monetary Policy in the Netherlands*: Ph.D Dissertation, Free University, Amsterdam.

Tamminga, M.K. (1991), 'Vijf molochs beheersen de financiële sector', *Het Financieele Dagblad*, Nov. 28.

Tsatsaronis, C. (1995), 'Is there a credit channel in the transmission of monetary policy? Evidence from four countries', in *Financial Structure and the Monetary Policy Transmission Mechanism* (Bank for International Settlements, Basle)

Zimmerman, G.C. (1995), 'Implementing the single banking market in Europe', *Federal Reserve Bank of San Francisco Economic Review*, 3, pp. 35-51.

10 Portugal

Paulo Soares de Pinho

1 INTRODUCTION

The aim of this chapter is to evaluate to what extent the Single European Act of 1986 affected the Portuguese banking industry and analyse the preparations made by this industry to face EMU. It is not a simple task. Being a highly regulated and protected market just ten years prior to the implementation of the Single Market legislation, the country's banking sector had to be deregulated at a very fast pace in order to allow for a smoother transition to the new European environment. Thus, in most cases, it is impossible to distinguish between the specific effects of the domestic deregulation of the early 1990s and the specific effects of the Single Market legislation.

There is, however, one point on which most observers do agree. Without the need to comply with the Single Market legislation, domestic banking deregulation would have been slower and most probably less extensive. Therefore, although their individual economic effects are indistinguishable, it is arguable that most domestic banking legislation passed between 1985 and 1992 had the Single Market in mind. And therefore, most of the economic changes that this market has recently experienced are either directly or indirectly a consequence of the Single Market Programme in banking.

2 MARKET STRUCTURE AND PERFORMANCE

2.1 Recent evolution

The Portuguese banking sector has undergone profound transformations during the last two decades. In 1975 all but three small foreign-owned banks were nationalised, entry into the market was banned, all interest rates were administratively set by the authorities, the opening of new branches depended upon central bank permission (which was sometimes denied), and private ownership of banking institutions was forbidden by the Constitution. The banks were entirely subordinated to the objectives of economic policy. The banking system in those days was divided into the following categories: three foreign banks, three special credit institutions, nine commercial banks and one investment bank. The latter, despite the official classification, had nothing to do with merchant banking, being a channel to finance industrial investment. The special credit institutions had the monopoly of mortgage lending and Caixa Geral de Depósitos (CGD), in particular, had the monopoly of all government agency and institution accounts, and payments to civil servants, pensioners, and many others.

In 1978, after a foreign payments crisis, the Government signed an agreement with the IMF which changed the shape of monetary policy, the main instrument of which became the imposition of credit ceilings. According to the expected GNP growth, a total ceiling was imposed on the economy. The major part of it was allocated to the Government to finance its borrowing requirements and the remainder was allocated to the productive sector through rationing. Because of the ceilings, most of the banks' funds were invested in public debt while only a small part was lent to business. In most cases, the banks were flooded with excessive liquidity earning very low yields. It should be noted that the larger corporations were all nationalised and massive political pressure was brought to bear to ensure that all the loss-making public units were getting all the money they needed. As a result, private companies faced great difficulties in finding loans and consumer lending was virtually banned.

This panorama led to a very inefficient, non-customer-oriented banking system. Profits dropped as a result of large operating costs, coupled with small margins for banks with a strong core of term deposits, excessive liquidity and bad loans to both nationalised and private companies. In 1984 ROE for the whole set of institutions was 4.2%, dropping to 0.3% in 1986 when heavy credit losses had to be recognised.

At the time Portugal joined the EEC in 1985, that panorama was mostly unchanged. Although a Constitutional amendment in 1984 had admitted the private ownership of banking institutions, only a few foreign-owned wholesale operations were then authorised and the first three new private retail banks only started to operate in 1986. Interest rate regulation persisted until 1990, with the administrative imposition of a minimum rate on time deposits (to encourage savings) which was progressively reduced and later removed, a maximum rate on demand deposits (to protect the less efficient institutions), and a maximum rate on loans (to prevent 'usury' associated with the excess demand resulting from the credit ceilings).

New foreign banks became progressively authorised but remained small. By mid-1989 the Government was still the owner of banks representing 85% of the market. In that year the (slow) privatisation process was initiated. This process, combined with the growing aggressivity of some private banks, caused the Government's market share to fall to about 45% in 1993. Throughout most of this period, not only was the banking charter subject to strict restrictions but branching expansion was highly constrained as well.

1985-1992 was thus characterised by a slow deregulation process, culminating with the first privatisation of a bank in 1989. Although there was a clear need for deregulating this highly protected market, it may be argued that without the need to comply with the Single European Act, the Government would have set a much slower pace. In particular, entry regulations, interest rates and branching restrictions could not persist after that date, forcing the authorities to soften the banks' adaptation to the new foreseen competitive environment. During this period market concentration declined smoothly and competition was far from fierce, although progressively increasing as a result of privatisations.

All these restrictions were abolished in December 1992 when a new banking law implementing the Second Banking Directive was passed and all banks had to comply with the 8% risk-asset solvency ratio. In a few words, those banks, which had lived under a highly regulated framework sustaining the existence of a virtual cartel where inefficiency went unpunished, holding substantial amounts of bad loans and maintaining excessive staff (a recurring problem, especially among the older institutions), suddenly found themselves operating under the same rules as all other European banks. Thus, in less than ten years they evolved from a highly protected framework to complete integration in the Single European Market for financial services. Therefore, it comes as no surprise that the results of the PACEC questionnaire (Gardener *et al.*, 2000) show Portugal as the country where the impact of the new legislation was ranked highest.

The results of this evolution are expressed in Table 10.1. The gradual elimination of entry restrictions pushed the number of banks up from 26 in 1987 to 46 in 1995. However, this impressive growth disguises the fact that most entrants, both foreign and national, remained small. In particular, several foreign-owned institutions focused on large and international corporations and never had more than two or three offices.

The year 1993 witnessed the highest growth in the number of banks. Although that should be expected to result from the 'banking passport', it is interesting to note that most new entrants that year were Portuguese-owned institutions that had been (for too long) on the Central Bank's waiting list for approval. Most notably, it was in 1993 that Chase Manhattan Bank announced its exit from the market. In the following years some of the new banks were created by existing institutions as specialised units in investment banking and mortgage or consumer lending. Thus, the rising figure for the number of banks does not show any particular change in the entry pattern by foreign institutions as a result of the SMP.

Table 10.1 Number of banks, branches and bankers, 1987-1998

Year	Banks	Branches	Bankers
1987	26	1,546	58,463
1988	27	1,598	58,394
1989	29	1,747	58,132
1990	33	1,982	59,162
1991	35	2,496	61,055
1992	37	2,840	60,772
1993	42	3,110	59,748
1994	44	3,548	58,610
1995	46	3,729	58,892
1998	57	4,354	56,467

Another problem with the above figures is that they do not account for the takeover activity in this market which led to the creation of banking groups consisting of several independent banks under one single management. Thus, the total number of independent units actually decreased between 1993 and 1999.

Even more impressive is the growth of the branch network, which more than doubled in that period. The gradual elimination of branching restrictions promoted a strong non-price competition, led by most of the large incumbents and a few newcomers. As a result, the country's coverage by the banking industry improved, although there is a notable tendency to concentrate new branches in the main cities. All banks in the country participate in a very efficient and technologically advanced ATM and POS system, Multibanco, which was easily accepted by the population and is used for a range of activities, including even the booking and payment of train reservations! Although some banks are trying to develop their own networks, offering privileged services to their customers, they are all still connected to Multibanco, to which all POS terminals are also connected. Some banks are already offering home-banking services via the internet and many already offer phone-banking facilities.

The number of bank employees rose until 1992, reflecting the needs of the new private and foreign banks which were trying to grow internally and had strong preferences for young employees without much banking

experience. However, after 1992, expansion policies came to depend upon
the acquisition of privatised institutions, therefore making the need for
new recruits less important. As a consequence of declining margins and
the exploration of potential synergies associated with acquisitions, banks
have been eliminating redundant activities. Thus, by controlling
admissions and taking advantage of normal and early retirements, banks
have been able to increase productivity by reducing total staff.

Today, the size of the Portuguese banking sector's assets is small by
European standards. In December 1998 total banking assets were about
219 million euros, of which 92 million were loans. Total deposits were
116 million euros, which results in a loan/deposit ratio of only 79%. This
figure is notably small by international standards. However, it is
interesting to note that in 1989, the last year of the credit ceilings system,
the ratio was only 48%.

2.2 Ownership structure and privatisations

The period 1985-99 witnessed an impressive change in ownership
structure as a result of the creation of new privately-owned Portuguese
banks, the entry of many reputable foreign institutions but, most
importantly, as a result of privatisations.

Figure 10.1

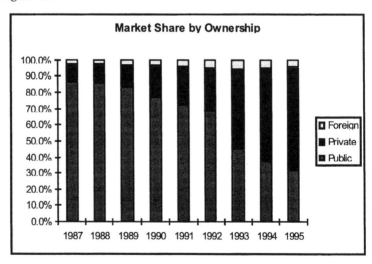

As may be seen from Table 10.1, the privatisation programme had a significant impact on the ownership structure of commercial banking. While in 1987 Portuguese-owned private banks represented about 10% of the total market, ten years later that figure rose to about 70%. On the other hand, foreign banks have generally remained small and, although their total share of the market doubled between 1990 and 2000, it has never exceeded 5% of deposits and about 7% of loans.

The banking market has always been dominated by Caixa Geral de Depósitos (CGD), which has consistently controlled about a quarter of this market. The giant CGD was given control of Banco Nacional Ultramarino (BNU), a former central bank in the Portuguese colonies which also acted as a commercial bank in the mainland. Together they account for about 30% of the market and there are no plans to privatise the group.

Today, the second largest banking group (accounting for about 20% of the market) is BCP/Atlântico. BCP (Banco Comercial Português) was the most aggressive and innovative among the new privately-owned institutions created in 1986. The bank based its expansion on a methodical market segmentation approach which led to the creation of different branch networks, each specialising in serving a specific market segment. In 1994 the bank was already among the top five institutions (in assets) and announced a hostile takeover bid for Banco Português do Atlântico (BPA), which had been privatised three years before. BPA itself invested in the privatisation programme and gained control of Banco Comercial de Macau (BCM) and União de Bancos Portugueses (UBP). After a complex and controversial process, BCP succeeded in its second takeover attempt in 1995, making it, in only ten years, the largest privately-owned banking group in the country, although not keeping UBP for itself.

The third largest group is the result of the association of three privatised banks. At the head is Banco Pinto & Sotto Mayor (BPSM), privatised in 1994, which was among the top five institutions. The new owner, António Champallimaud, negotiated with the Spanish bank Banco de Santander the controlling stake of Banco Totta & Açores (BTA), another member of the top five, which, after a troubled privatisation in 1989, had experienced frequent changes in ownership (being illegally acquired by the Spanish bank Banesto, later absorbed by Santander). Since BTA, in turn, had already acquired Crédito Predial Português (CPP), with this operation Champallimaud ended up controlling three banks accounting for about 19% of the market.

These are two of the most important concentration operations which significantly changed the structure of the Portuguese banking sector between 1993 and 1996. Other operations took place which grouped three or four institutions under one single management, although generally each one preserved its own legal identity. Figure 10.2 shows the evolution of the concentration indicator C4 'as if' the banks involved in the concentration operations have actually merged.

Figure 10.2

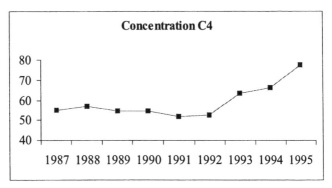

In 1996 the process was boosted again by the privatisation of Banco de Fomento e Exterior (BFE) which controlled Banco Borges & Irmão (BBI). The acquirer was Banco Português de Investimento (BPI), an investment bank created in 1985 which had already acquired Banco Fonsecas & Burnay (BFB). Today, this the fourth largest banking group in the country, followed by the privatised Banco Espírito Santo (BES) and the 'new' Banco Mello (which acquired UBP).

Three foreign-owned institutions existed before the 1975 nationalisations. Two of them pursued aggressive expansion strategies in the retail markets. Crédit Lyonnais Portugal was the most notable case. Although offering very high interest rates on deposits, and spending significant amounts on advertising in the early 1990s, it has been unable to change its market share (ranging between 0.7% and 1%) significantly. Similar attempts were made by Banco Bilbao Vyscaia which in 1991 acquired Lloyds Bank subsidiary in Portugal (then one of the oldest institutions in the country), Barclays Bank, Banque Nationale de Paris and Banco de Comércio e Indústria, which was taken over by the Spanish Banco de Santander. None of these institutions was able to secure a significant market share and most of them experienced losses in their years of greater aggressiveness. A similar attempt to enter the retail markets by the Spanish Banco Central Hispano in 1992 ended in 1994. After two consecutive years of heavy losses, this bank exited the market and made a strategic alliance with BCP.

All the other foreign banks in the country, including ABN-AMRO, Citibank, Deutsche Bank de Investimento (currently under direct control of Deutsche Morgan Grenfell), Generale de Banque and Bank of Tokyo have chosen to specialise in the large corporate market, which they serve with a reduced number of branches. Recently, Chemical Bank (Chase) sold its subsidiary to the BPSM group.

The Portuguese financial markets are dominated by the banks and thus even most non-bank competitors are controlled by them. Leasing and factoring companies are, in most cases, owned by banks and use their branches as a distribution channel. These institutions have been extremely important for the banking system because they have not been subject to the credit ceiling rules and have thus been a means of granting off balance sheet loans. The same occurs with most mutual fund management companies, consumer lending companies, asset management specialists and even brokerage firms, which are often completely integrated within banking groups.

A potential threat for the banking system is the Post Office's (Correios) intention to enter the banking market by establishing its own bank. So far it has used its branches to distribute banking products under private arrangements with some banking groups. However, its intention to establish its own bank is public and this institution is considering potential strategic allies with Portuguese banks. Correios and Caixa Geral de Depósitos have already announced a joint venture to run the Postal Bank.

Other potentially threatening non-bank competitors are the supermarket chains. One, Continente, has launched the credit card having the highest market share in the country, Visa Universo, co-branded with Banco Fonsecas & Burnay (BPI group). The success of this initiative has led Continente to create its own bank, Banco Universo, whose branches are located exclusively in Continente's stores. Another large distribution group, Jerónimo Martins, has chosen a different path by making a strategic alliance with BCP, resulting in a 50/50 ownership of a bank, Expresso Atlântico, which operates exclusively at the former's stores.

2.3 Banking performance

The progressive deregulation of the minimum rates on time deposits and maximum rates on loans had a positive impact on the net interest margin earned by the banking system, which in 1990 reached almost 6% of the earning assets (see Figure 10.3). However, the forces of deregulation, entry, and privatisation led to an increased competitiveness which continuously eroded banking margins throughout the first half of the 1990s. It is still too soon to evaluate to what extent the increased concentration may change this trend. In the first half of 1996 the decline in margins was small and banks were, for the first time, able to introduce significant changes in their pricing structure by introducing commission charges on banking operations which until then had been free.

Figure 10.3

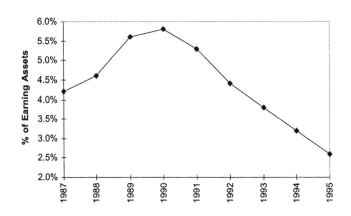

Net Interest Margin

It is important to note that the above figures disguise the fact that branch banks with extensive networks have been able to keep their margins above that average, while wholesale foreign banks are now well below it.

The high margins in the late 1980s did not translate into high performance because of high operating costs (2.6% of assets) and bad loans (6.5% of total loans). In this period banks recovered from the bad days of the early 80s and took advantage of the progressive flexibility (and later elimination) of the credit ceilings, reaching an average ROE above 11% (see Figure 10.4). Private and some foreign banks were then experiencing much higher ROEs while, on average, nationalised banks were showing a much lower performance.

As previously mentioned, the 1990s brought increased competition and eroded margins. To make matters worse, the 1993-94 recession lifted bad loans to about 8% of the total. ROE was able to stabilise at around

8.5% because of three factors: increased efficiency (operating costs progressively declined to 2% of assets); increased commission revenue; and capital gains associated with long positions in fixed income. In this period, foreign wholesale banks experienced the consequences of their specialisation in the highly competitive large corporate market and witnessed a sharp decline in their performance, while foreign retail institutions deliberately narrowed their margins as part of their aggressive pricing strategy which, together with a poor performance of their loan portfolios, brought them below the bottom line.

Figure 10.4

Return on Equity

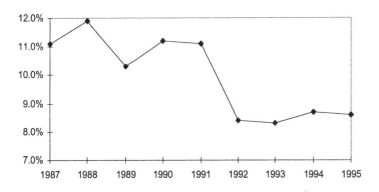

3   REGULATORY FRAMEWORK

3.1   Regulatory framework prior to the SMP

In 1987 the Portuguese banking sector was still under a very strict regulatory framework, the essential components of which were:

- most interest rates were set by the authorities
- new branches for existing banks depended upon Central Bank authorisation
- new banks had to be authorised by the Central Bank
- banks were subject to credit ceilings
- consumer lending was severely restricted

- only three special credit institutions were authorised to grant mortgage loans
- capital movements were controlled by the Banco de Portugal
- leasing and factoring were restricted to specialised companies
- there was no separation between commercial and investment banking
- there were no minimum solvency requirements.

The above restrictions were taken seriously by the authorities and, as previously mentioned, administratively-set interest rates were severely impeding the banks' income. In particular, entry restrictions were very strict and in 1987 there were only four Portuguese-owned private banks and nine foreign banks which had been authorised after the 1984 Constitutional Amendment authorised private ownership of banks.

Throughout the late 1980s, lending restrictions and high cash reserve requirements were maintained as the fundamental elements of monetary policy. Excess liquidity resulting from the former was partially invested in public debt and the remainder often ended up in deposits at the Central Bank.

In 1989 and 1990 several legislative changes were introduced aimed at smoothing the transition to the integration of the country's banking sector in the Single Market. The most important of these was the reshaping of monetary policy; it ceased to be based on credit ceilings, the abolition of which had long been demanded by the banks. The system was eliminated in March 1990 and replaced by 'recommended credit limits' which still had some limiting effects on the expansion of credit. In 1991 a system of indirect monetary control definitely replaced the ceilings system and the Banco de Portugal raised the required cash reserves to 17% (a few years later reduced to 2%) of total deposits and introduced a system to remunerate part of them. All required reserves had to be held at the Central Bank. By 1991 the last administrative interest rate limits were eliminated.

In September 1990 branching restrictions were lifted, although in a very original way. For every new branch they intended to open, banks had to purchase a certain amount of bad loans which had been transferred from the nationalised banks to a specialised company, Finangeste. And although entry restrictions remained in force as before, every new institution obtaining a banking charter in Portugal had to buy 900 million escudos worth of bad loans from Finangeste. This measure met with strong criticism from the European Commissioner for Competition as being 'against the spirit of the Single Market'.

With the Single Market in mind, a solvency requirement was imposed in 1990. A solvency ratio based upon Cooke's methodology was adopted which required a minimum of 4% in 1990, 6% in 1991 and 8% in 1992 and thereafter. This implementation of the Own Funds and Solvency Ratio Directives had a tremendous impact on Portugal's largely undercapitalised banking system, forcing the Government to inject large sums of capital into its banks. In this context, in every bank privatisation, a portion of the proceeds was used to increase the institution's capital. Consequently, in this period Portuguese banks benefited from a significant reinforcement of their capital base (see Figure 10.5).

Rules for harmonising provisions for loan losses were also introduced, in which it was required that all banks kept in their balance sheets 'provisions for general credit risks' not below 2% of total loans, while new rules for provisions for bad loans were based on the number of months each delinquent loan was overdue. Other prudential rules introduced in 1990 included a 'large exposures rule' limiting loans to a single customer to 0.4% of total equity and the total amount of large exposures to 8%. The banks' underwriting exposures were also limited.

Figure 10.5

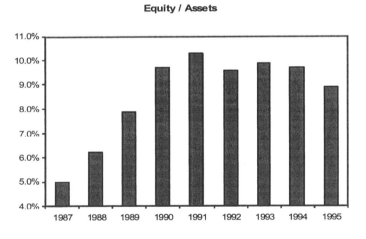

Equity / Assets

3.2 Main SMP legislation

In December 1992 the Government published what was meant to be the main piece of legislation for the banking sector. Generally designated as 'Lei Bancária' (banking law), Legal Decree 298/92 brought into

Portuguese law the main elements of the SMP Directives. Although entitled to delay it for two more years, the Government also introduced complete freedom of capital movements in January 1993.

With the new law, the 'universal banking' concept was adopted, putting an end to the distinction between banks and special credit institutions, which resulted in the entry of banks into the mortgage lending market, which in turn became ever more competitive. Banks also gained access to leasing and factoring lending, as well as to asset management and insurance distribution, while CGD had to be converted to bank status and lost all of its traditional privileges (at least in theory). In particular banks can, since then, attract the accounts of public sector entities.

The 'banking passport' concept was introduced by the new law, making the old entry restrictions completely obsolete. Since then, the Banco de Portugal has created no obstacles to the installation of the (few) EU banks that have made use of the 'passport', although it has continued to show extreme prudence when examining requests for bank charters from Portuguese citizens. These processes may still take more than a year before final authorisation is granted. The law also regulates the activity of branches of Portuguese banks in foreign countries and the activities of foreign branches in Portugal.

The new law regulates the prudential supervision activity of the central bank, Banco de Portugal, and incorporates the essence of the Own Funds and Solvency Ratio Directives. Most of the previously existing limitations to large exposures and provision rules were not affected by the new legislation, which introduced new restrictions on the banks' equity participations in financial and non-financial firms. The principle of consolidated-based supervision was acknowledged, as well as the own-country supervision rule.

A deposit guarantee fund was created in the context of the new law. However, it took some time to be implemented and it only guarantees a scaled fraction of deposits up to 8 million escudos.

3.3 Remaining barriers to the SMP

Portugal has fully implemented the SMP legislation and thus there are no remaining legal barriers to entry for European banks. However, there is a consensus that some other types of barriers still persist.

The experiences of foreign-owned institutions in Portuguese retail banking cannot be characterised as being completely positive. Two large Spanish-owned banks, Banco Central-Hispano and Banco de Santander (through its subsidiary BCI) suffered tremendous credit losses and showed an inability to control costs. The former was forced to abandon the market and the latter had to turn around its subsidiary and put it under Portuguese management. Among the French-owned banks, Crédit Lyonnais Portugal has suffered a similar fate and in 1999 it sold its retail banking activities to the Spanish bank BBVA, and Banque National de Paris was also forced to close down its retail activities. Among the foreign-owned retail banks only Barclays is currently in a stable situation, after spending a number of years in the red.

The poor performance of foreign banks in Portuguese retail banking has many possible explanations, among them the possible inability of foreign management teams to understand the specificities of Portuguese banks. These cultural barriers were discussed in Pinho (1996) and current evidence showing that foreign subsidiaries under Portuguese management are doing better in the retail arena (such as Barclays and BCI/Santander) only reinforces their relevance.

Other barriers which remain are the high cost of establishing *de novo* a retail network and the difficulty, for foreigners, in evaluating the credit risk of individuals and small/medium-sized corporate borrowers. These barriers apply to retail banking only, as some foreign banks have been very successful in the investment banking sector. Some invisible political barriers still remain, such as in the case of Banco Totta & Açores/Banco de Santander which is described below and is a good example of political interference in the acquisition of a Portuguese bank by a foreign entity.

4 IMPACT OF THE SMP

4.1 Bank strategies

The combined effect of privatisations, the entry of new private banks and the preparation for the Single European Market, significantly changed the competitive arena of the Portuguese banking industry. The new Portuguese-owned private banks, especially Banco Comercial Português, claim that their overall strategy, since they were founded, has always had the Single Market legislation in mind and that this has, accordingly, guided their strategies.

Public banks have always been non-market-oriented and are used to living under the umbrella of Government protection. Thus, the privatised institutions were forced into a complete strategic turnaround and had to become increasingly aggressive and competitive. As a consequence, bank marketing expenses soared and the early years of the 1990s witnessed a tremendous reshaping of the relationship between banks and their customers. In order to grow, banks made a greater use of both price and non-price competitive instruments, which resulted in declining margins (see Figure 10.3) and a tremendous growth in the branch network (see Table 10.1). Several institutions also made attempts to differentiate their products, both vertically and horizontally, which resulted in increased quality of service.

4.2 Mergers and acquisitions

The process of banking restructuring may be divided into three phases. In the first, the Government merged some of its institutions with the aim of diluting problem loans and excessive staff. In the second phase, the privatisation programme was initiated with no practical restrictions on the acquisition of banks by other banking entities. In the third phase, some privatised banks lacking the support of a stable shareholder base were acquired by other banks.

The acquisition of Banco Nacional Ultramarino by Caixa Geral de Depósitos consolidated CGD's position as head of the largest banking group in the country, controlling between 25% and 30% of the industry's activity. This group is supposed to remain within the public sector and is seen as a Government instrument of intervention in the banking and financial markets.

The first privatised bank was Banco Totta & Açores (BTA) in 1989. Initially lacking a stable shareholder base, the bank eventually fell under the control of the Spanish bank, Banesto. Although retaining the bank's Portuguese management team, Banesto was not accepted by the Government which accused it of violating the rules concerning foreign shareholder limits in BTA. This attrition, which eventually involved both Iberian Governments, was ended after Banesto's failure, rescue and, later, sale to Banco de Santander. The unofficial agreement stated that Banesto's shares should revert to Portuguese hands and stands as an example of the kind of political barriers which persisted after the implementation of the Single Market legislation.

The privatisation programme created a window of opportunity for banks willing to grow via acquisitions. In some cases, Portuguese-owned private banks were the acquirers of privatised institutions, as in the case of Banco Português de Investimento. The most surprising takeover occurred in 1995 when BCP announced a hostile bid for BPA. Its success led to the creation of the largest privately-owned banking group, second only to CGD. Later, Banco Pinto & Sotto Mayor successfully acquired BTA from Banco de Santander and became the head of the second largest private banking group. The combined effect of these acquisitions led by BCP, BPI and BPSM was a significant increase in market concentration, already depicted in Figure 10.2.

Although this takeover activity and increased concentration is sometimes attributed to the Single Market legislation, it is arguable that domestic factors have actually dominated it. Euro-optimists applauded this merger activity, arguing that 'large European-sized banks' were needed in the context of the Single Market. However, the resulting institutions, which are large by domestic standards, are relatively small when compared with medium-sized European banks. Actually, the largest Portuguese groups are smaller than the fifth largest Spanish bank. This fact, combined with the small level of internationalisation of Portuguese banks, leads to the conclusion that domestic factors, namely the opportunity created by the privatisation programme, were the true forces behind this merger activity.

4.3 Internationalisation

Although some banks claim that the volume of cross-border activities has increased as a result of the SMP, the level of internationalisation of Portuguese banks remains comparatively low. Most banks do not have any retail activities outside Portugal and limit their international activities to correspondent banking and a small presence in the most important financial centres (including off-shore) and countries with strong ties with Portugal. With few exceptions, no significant strategic changes have been detected resulting from the SMP.

Portuguese immigrants in France, Luxembourg and a few other countries have traditionally been an important target for some domestic banks. In particular BCP set up a new bank, together with the Spanish Banco Popular Español, with the aim of targeting both countries' immigrants in France. However, although the SMP legislation made immigrant remittances easier to handle, the other Portuguese banks did not increase their presence in these markets.

In the late 1980s, the large Government-owned banking group, Caixa Geral de Depósitos, made the 'political' decision to enter the Spanish retail market in a move which has not been replicated by any other Portuguese bank to date. This decision had the SMP as one of its main motivations, together with the political intention to 'show the flag' in the neighbouring country's market. The initial idea was that the SMP legislation would unify the Iberian market and thus the only chance for a Portuguese bank to remain a large and 'relevant' institution in the Iberian context would be to make a successful entry into the Spanish retail market. However, as described above, such unification is still in the distant future and, not surprisingly, CGD's performance in Spain is no better than Spanish banks' performance in Portugal.

Surprisingly for many, Mozambique is today's most important outside target for Portuguese banks, which clearly dominate that country's retail banking sector. Thus, taking advantage of opportunities for which they possess the relevant resources has been more important in the establishment of internationalisation policies than the SMP legislation which eliminates the legal barriers to entry in Europe but does nothing to remove other barriers perceived by Portuguese banks to be obstacles to their expansion into other European markets (PACEC, 1996).

4.4 Prices and margins

The SMP legislation did not affect all market segments within the Portuguese banking industry homogeneously. There is sufficient evidence to support the thesis that the banking passport was significantly more important for the large corporate segment than any other. Most foreign banks entered the market while avoiding the retail segment and concentrated on wholesale activities. The largest and safest companies immediately became their target, and price competition for that segment rapidly grew fierce. Thus, this segment achieved a 'perfect competition' scenario and it is arguable whether without the SMP legislation and the consequent entry by foreign banks, such a situation would ever have been achieved. Other segments of the banking market have also grown increasingly competitive although evidently not in such a perfect competition scenario. In the risky segments of the corporate market, margins have declined to a level that is, arguably, insufficient to cover expected losses.

As a consequence of the end of the restrictions in mortgage lending, all commercial banks entered this segment with the subsequent increase in both price and non-price competition which caused margins in this segment to drop significantly, varying from 100bp to 300bp.

Consumer lending restrictions were also lifted but, although most banks decided to enter this segment (traditionally viewed as among the riskiest), price competition is not as intense here as in other segments, the result of some lack of price consciousness by customers. Consequently margins are still high and exceed the historic levels of losses. One particular product, the credit card, is the object of intense non-price advertising, (leaflets, and so on) and some price competition via exemptions from annuity payments. However, commissions charged to retailers and interest rates on revolving credit are high enough to make this an exceptionally profitable product.

Because of the currently higher profitability of lending to individuals, banks have been making them their priority target. As a consequence we see a much higher growth of lending to individuals than to companies and a fast decline in the savings and solvency of families as a whole. This evolution is now degrading the average credit quality of individuals and it is likely that some myopia on the estimation of future losses may be artificially widening the perceived margins generated by these products. Regardless of what happens in the future, reported actual losses on consumer lending have consistently risen in both absolute and relative terms since 1990.

Deposit products have also been the object of increasing competition, especially for corporations which traditionally were not entitled to earn interest on current accounts. In the early 1990s high-yield current accounts were launched, supported by intense advertising campaigns. The leading banks were foreign-owned, failed to capture significant market share, and paid for their aggressiveness by having to bear heavy losses. Thus evidence has shown that retail deposit customers are not too price-sensitive and therefore such strategies will never succeed in achieving internally generated growth at a reasonable cost. An empirical analysis of this issue is performed by Pinho (1995b).

An empirical analysis by Barros and Leite (1996) concludes that competition increased after the implementation of the SMP legislation in both the deposit and credit markets. However, they found that banks with a strong presence in small rural markets have been able to keep higher average margins than institutions which focused on the urban areas. Since the latter have been the target of most of the entrants, it is arguable that the published numbers disguise a duality between competition in rural and urban areas. Thus, the large banks were able to survive in the intensely competitive urban arena of the early 1990s thanks to their profitable rural operations, and thus defeated the entrants, which were forced to drop their intense price competition strategies.

4.5 Costs and efficiency

Early studies on economies of scale and scope and productive efficiency of Portuguese banks are reviewed in Pinho (1995a) while new evidence is presented in Pinho (1997). Unfortunately, results for Portugal in the PACEC research are based on a small sample and provide unstable results, that is the technology 'changes' dramatically from one estimate to the next. Based on the comparison between the two Pinho studies, we conclude that the productive efficiency of Portuguese banks has been growing consistently since 1987 and that no special change in this trend has occurred since 1992. Thus, the progressive deregulation of the sector seems to have positively influenced bank costs and the implementation of the SMP legislation does not seem to have changed that trend. In both studies, Government ownership of banks is associated with lower efficiency, thus making the privatisation programme a key element in the detected improvement. In Pinho (1997) total factor productivity is also found to have increased from 1987 to 1994.

All studies, with the exception of PACEC, conclude that technology exhibits constant returns to scale for all but the smallest banks, where evidence of economies of scale is to be found. The study using most recent data, Pinho (1997), detects some technological change that, although not challenging the main conclusion, results in economies of scale being exhausted at a higher level of assets than was found in previous studies. Concerning economies of scope, results depend upon each author's classification of inputs and outputs. As an example, in Pinho (1997) small economies of scope are found for the joint origination of deposits and loans.

5   BANK PREPARATIONS FOR EMU

5.1 Introduction

Throughout the 1990s, the Portuguese authorities progressively adopted measures to ensure the country's participation in the first stage of EMU. The single currency became the major concern of economic policy, which was directed towards the reduction of inflation (and interest rates), Government deficit, and public debt. By 1995 it became clear that Portugal had excellent prospects of becoming a 'surprise' candidate for participation in EMU, and most economic agents, including banks, started to include the single currency scenario in their strategic planning. However, despite increasing confidence in the country's participation in the first stage of EMU, the banking sector took some time to initiate preparations for the impact of such a dramatic change on their operating environment. It was only in 1996 that, with the help of consultancy companies, banks started to make their plans to face EMU and by 1997 it could be argued that most institutions were ill-prepared and what preparations they had made were clearly behind schedule.

The discussion here of the impact of EMU will be divided into two broad areas: organisational and strategic. The following sections rely heavily on the results of personal interviews with bank managers and responses to a questionnaire prepared by the Institute of European Finance and the University of Cambridge.

5.2 Organisational impact

Most Portuguese banks assume that the major impact will occur in this category. It may indeed be easily argued that short-run (organisational) concerns dominate over those of the long run (strategic). Basically, the banks fear the costs associated with the complete reprogramming of computer systems, staff training, and marketing, as well as the complete restructuring of their foreign currency departments.

The number one concern is in the information systems area. Most institutions have been identifying the problems, generally with the help of consultants. In most cases, the EMU issue was handled together with the Y2K problem, which also required intensive reprogramming. All the country's ATMs belong to the same network, Multibanco, which is run by SIBS, an interbank company whose systems were prepared for EMU.

A substantial impact from EMU is also expected in the foreign exchange departments of banks. About 80% of total Portuguese trade takes place with EU partners and such trade generates a significant amount of bank commissions which, depending on the institution, may represent between 5% to 15% of total profits. In this context, a single currency will put an end to this most profitable activity and threaten the functions now performed by several hundred bankers. Although no lay-offs are expected as a direct result from EMU, it creates some pressure for an increase in early retirements.

Unlike their European counterparts, Portuguese banks did not make any particular efforts to produce information packages for their customers on EMU and its consequences on bank products and existing relationships, such as mortgage loans. Surprisingly, some banks also did not even make any staff training plans regarding the euro issue.

5.3 Strategic implications

Given the (so far) protected nature of the Portuguese domestic market, and the reduced level of internationalisation of local banks, the single currency is not expected to have a major impact on bank strategy. Although this is true on a general level of analysis, there are, however, some areas in which significant changes may occur.

The areas that most banks identify as strongly protected are small corporations and personal retail banking products, especially cheque accounts. In general, for all products and customer groups strongly dependent upon branches as a distribution channel, no serious threat is expected. The optimists among Portuguese bank strategists identify several market opportunities outside the Portuguese boundaries (although it should be expected that some European banks would detect the same sort of opportunities in Portugal). With a single currency, Portuguese banks expect to be able to sell savings products, and even mortgages, in other European countries, especially Spain. The distribution channels for this purpose will be based on database marketing through direct mail and phone calls. Despite the optimism, given the dimension of the different markets and the goodwill associated with some foreign bank brands, this increase in cross-border activities of European banks might be expected to be more harmful than advantageous to Portuguese banks.

The implementation of a single currency will make a decisive contribution towards the creation of a unified capital market in Europe. Thus, the large Portuguese issuers should be expected to rely increasingly on pan-European investment banks rather than on local institutions. Although this will reduce the role of local banks in the primary market of Portuguese equities, it will create opportunities for more efficient management of mutual funds and a reduced risk of international diversification of investments.

Given the above, a stronger segmentation of the corporate banking market is expected, with the large companies increasingly diversifying their sources of funding within Europe, and the small ones continuing to be a relatively captive market for the local institutions.

Portuguese banks expect EMU to have some impact on the distribution side of banking. Although the main role of the bank branch for the distribution of financial services is not under threat, banks expect a slight reduction in the relative importance of this channel. Both the number and individual size of branches should be expected to decline.

The distribution channels expected to gain relative importance in Portugal are those which still have a minor role in this market, namely direct mail, phone banking and internet banking. These relatively new channels are expected to play an increasingly important role in the distribution of a few financial services, although the banks see them more as complementary to the traditional branch rather than as substitutes. Current experience shows that these channels have been quite successful in the selling of new products to existing branch customers (cross-selling activities) rather than in the attraction of new ones. Thus, the traditional branch relationship is still seen as absolutely essential. The role of ATMs is also viewed as relatively protected, and even as having a small growth potential.

Products more likely to depend upon phone banking are customer deposits (as a complement to branch services), savings products, insurance policies and pension plans. Direct marketing will be used to sell credit cards, pensions and insurance products. Postal banking is expected to have a significant impact on the sale of retail banking products in rural areas with small branch coverage. The internet is not regarded as having a serious impact in the near future, although it may be useful to target a specific group of customers.

The international activity of Portuguese banks may be under serious threat. So far, expansion into other European markets has been dictated by two things: following Portuguese companies in order to provide them with international payments services and serving Portuguese immigrant communities. In both cases, a single currency will reduce or terminate the need for the commission-based services which have been the foundation for that expansion. Although the need for such an international presence by corporations is now reduced, immigrant communities may still, for a while, continue to constitute a captive market whose profitability will depend upon each bank's ability to innovate and adapt to the new circumstances through the design and sale of new financial products especially designed for them.

Portuguese banks do not expect to increase their presence in the other European markets as a result of EMU, except for large funding operations, an area in which a significant impact is expected. However, some increase in cross-border joint ventures and alliances is expected where France, Spain and the UK (especially in the field of investment banking) are the countries most likely to become the source of potential strategic alliances. Curiously, these are exactly the same countries that were mentioned as the most feared competitors, French banks being expected to erode the immigration market, Spanish banks being feared in some retail banking products, and UK-based institutions being considered a major threat in capital market activities as well as in the direct distribution of insurance, savings, mutual funds and pension products.

References

Barros, Pedro and António Leite (1996), 'Competition in Portuguese commercial banking', *Economia*, 20, pp. 7-30.

'Cruickshank Report' (March 2000), *Competition in UK Banking: A Report to the Chancellor of the Exchequer* (Stationery Office, London)

Gardener E.P.M., P. Molyneux and B. Moore (2000), *International Price Comparisons and the Competitiveness of UK Banking*, unpublished PACEC Ltd/IEF 1998 research summarised in Appendix E of the Cruickshank Report (*see above*)

Pinho, Paulo S. (1995a), 'Economias de escala e eficiência produtiva na banca Portuguesa: uma revisão da literatura' *in* P. Barros and P. Pinho (*eds*) *Estudos Sobre o Sistema Bancário Português* (Banco Mello, Lisboa)

Pinho, Paulo S. (1995b), *Dinâmica de Quota de Mercado e Instrumentos Competitivos no Mercado de Depósitos Português*, Working Paper 248, Faculdade de Economia da UNL.

Pinho, Paulo S. (1996), 'The cultural environment of Portuguese banking' in Leo Schuster, *Banking Cultures of the World*, (Fritz Knapp Verlag, Frankfurt)

Pinho, Paulo S. (1997), *Efficiency and Productivity Growth in Portuguese Banking*, (mimeo: available from the author).

11 Spain

José M. Pastor and Javier Quesada

1 INTRODUCTION

Well before Spain joined the Common Market, a group of economic sectors was concerned over how to adjust to the new conditions successfully. The financial sector in general, and especially the banking sector, was the clearest exponent of a rapid and continuing adjustment to the new atmosphere imposed by the new competitive panorama. This reaction accelerated over recent years as the Spanish banking system (SBS) became involved in multiple processes of change, namely the introduction and adjustment to new technologies, liberalisation, internationalisation, globalisation and deregulation. These processes were sometimes pushed by the authorities, following EC Directives, as well as by the banks themselves. Different strategies, including, among others, mergers and acquisitions and the establishment of cooperation agreements, were followed in order to adapt institutions to the new conditions imposed by the SMP.

As in many other economic sectors, the SMP imposed a double challenge on the SBS: the recognition of a much wider market and the fact that there would be new competitors from other European countries, all playing in a common field. Both circumstances were favoured by many deregulating decisions taken by the authorities and pushed by competition.

Although the SBS can now be considered a competitive sector, the situation was very different twenty years ago. In fact, it was not until the 1980s that the SBS started to change. Previously it had been subjected to strict regulations that involved the pricing of all banking products, and the geographical and functional limits of banks, as well as entry restrictions for new competitors.

This strict regulatory framework presented a serious obstacle to free competition for two reasons: first, it was an 'entry barrier' to foreign banks and, second, it was an 'exit barrier' because it precluded many non-performing banks from going into bankruptcy. The consequence of these circumstances was a lack of innovation processes proposed by private initiatives.

The situation described has changed substantially in the last fifteen years due to the SMP and to successive Directives. The aim of this chapter is to describe the main effects of the SMP on the SBS. Section 2 describes the impact on market structure and performance. Section 3 describes the regulatory framework, with emphasis on those deregulation processes that most affected the banks' behaviour and highlighting the main remaining barriers. Section 4 presents the areas in which the SMP had most consequences, differentiating, where possible, the effects caused by the SMP from the effects caused by generic trends common to all banking systems. Section 5 concludes the survey.

2   MARKET STRUCTURE AND PERFORMANCE

The SMP transformed the SBS into a completely different banking system. It started as a rigid and highly interventionist system with a domestic range, whereas the final stage implied a free market system increasingly integrated with international finance. The main significance of this liberalisation process was an increase in competition that led to a transformation in market structure and bank performance. These changes can be summarised in three elements: changes in the size and composition of the banking sector; the emergence of new competitors; and the presence of lower margins and rates of returns.

2.1 Changes in market size and composition

The removal of internal and external barriers has intensified banking firm competition on both sides of the balance sheet. This phenomenon forced banks to restructure their organisations in terms of employment and the size of their branch network. Also, it encouraged banks to expand operations into new national or international markets, and to consider merging with other banks.

When analysing the structure of the SBS by looking at the number of banks (Figure 11.1.i.a), one can appreciate the reduction in the total number of firms from 364 in 1985 to 307 in 1997. This is the result of two opposite forces. On the one hand there is a reduction in the number of savings and cooperative banks due to the many merger and acquisition processes that have taken place during the last two decades. On the other hand, the number of commercial banks has increased because fewer mergers have occurred and because the number of foreign banks has increased quite significantly. Regarding the presence of foreign banks, it must be pointed out that the degree of penetration is more or less important depending on the magnitude of reference used. So, in 1996 they represented 44% of the banks operating in Spain, 12% of total assets, 4.9% of total branches and 7.5% in terms of employees.

Figure 11.1(i) Evolution of the size of the SBS, 1985-1998 *(1985 = 100)*

a) *Number of banking firms*

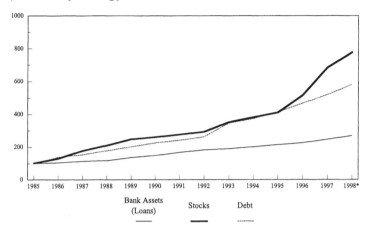

b) *Total assets in real terms*

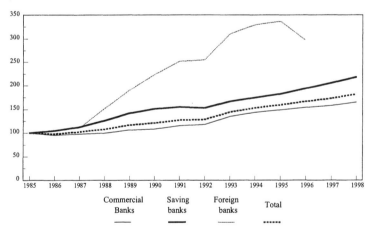

c) Number of branches

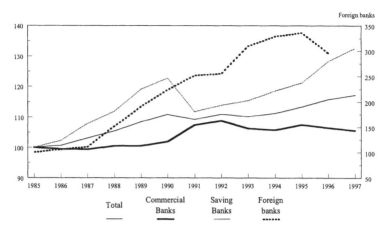

d) Number of employees

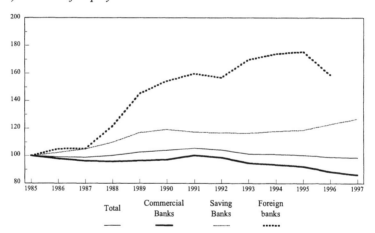

Source: Banco de España

Figure 11.1(ii) Evolution in the size of European banking systems, 1985-1995 *(1988= 100)*

a) Number of banking firms

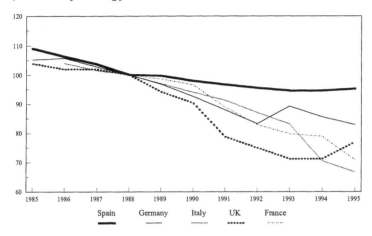

b) Total assets in real terms

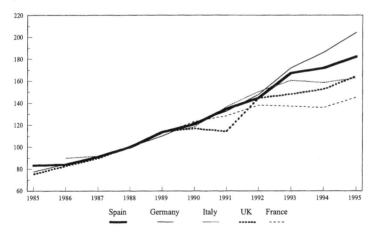

c) Number of branches

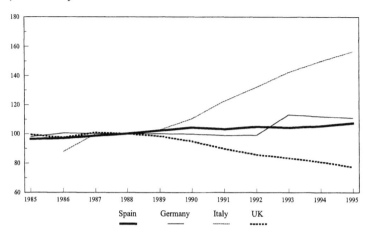

d) Number of employees

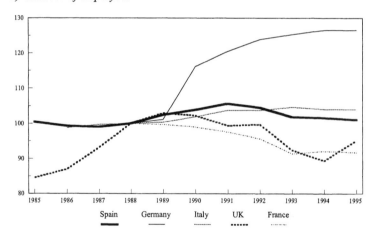

Source: Bank Profitability

Again, if we look at the structure of the SBS in terms of total assets (Figure 11.1.i.b), number of branches (Figure 11.1.i.c) and number of employees (Figure 11.1.i.d), the result is similar to the one described above, although there is a slightly different feature. Due to the different regulatory framework in the past, savings banks are oriented towards household banking and, for this reason, the number of branches and employees is higher when compared with that of commercial banks or, especially, with that of foreign banks. On the other hand, total employment in the complete banking sector is constant over the period, although for very different internal reasons. If we look at the number of employees of foreign banks we see a significant increase, which is due to their expansion in the domestic market. Spanish savings banks opened new branches in other regions and because of this the number of employees in savings banks increased, unlike the number of employees in commercial banks which decreased.

At an international level (Figure 11.1.ii) we see that, unlike other European countries, Spain has experienced a smaller reduction in the number of banking firms and a much more stable evolution in the number of employees and number of branches.

Summarising, the implementation of the SMP and the elimination of legal entry barriers did not seem to produce a massive entry of foreign banks into the SBS. Although the number of foreign banks has increased, the evidence is that this is not due to EU banks. The reason is that, in fact, many important implicit barriers still exist that do not allow banks to compete with each other on an equal basis. Among these implicit barriers, the density of the branch and ATM networks, and the fidelity of bank customers are the most important obstacles[1].

One way in which the SMP most greatly influenced the composition of the SBS was through the process of mergers and acquisitions. These M&As were carried out with the objective of increasing the size of banks and were, in many cases, favoured by government authorities. The central argument was that a bank of greater size would better meet the European challenge. The reasons behind this argument were the following:

- large companies have greater possibilities of exploiting existing economies of scale and scope
- mergers provide an opportunity to eliminate branch duplications as well as change management[2]
- only large banks have access to given markets and operations
- large banks are at less risk of being taken over by other companies, therefore mergers can be used as defensive strategies

- it is easier for a bank to gain international recognition and status when the company is large
- market power is usually greater for larger banks, both on the factor market and on the product and service market. Consequently, large banks should be able to get lower input and higher output prices
- many Spanish savings banks were concentrated mainly in local and regional markets. Given their limitation to expand beyond their geographical limits, mergers became the most convenient legal way of eluding this restriction. Savings banks made extensive use of M&As to expand their presence in other regions (see Figure 11.1.1.i.c)
- finally, some banks in the SBS used mergers to improve their capital adequacy ratio and benefit from a tax break.

Figure 11.2 presents the number of M&As between 1985 and 1997. As can be seen, there was a spectacular growth in their number, mainly at the beginning of the 1990s. Furthermore, the need to expand beyond their regional markets made mergers a much more attractive strategy for savings banks than for private commercial banks.

Figure 11.2 Number of mergers and acquisitions (accumulated values), 1985-1997

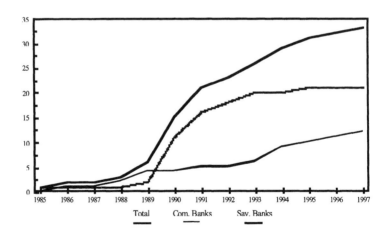

Source: Pérez *et al.* (1999)

Figure 11.3 Concentration ratios, 1985-1996

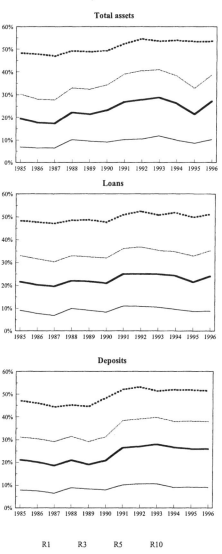

The explanation of why commercial banks used mergers less is due to their earlier possibility of having a national presence, which made mergers strategic instruments mainly for international expansion[3]. The direct consequence of the merger process was a substantial increase in the concentration of the SBS during the nineties. To analyse this phenomenon, Figure 11.3 represents the market share of the one, three, five and ten largest banks using three different variables: total assets, loans and deposits. Sector concentration grew fundamentally from 1990 but the relevant question is whether market power increased with the increase in concentration.

In banking literature the relationship between performance and market structure has generated two competing hypotheses (see Berger, 1995 and Maudos, 1998). On one hand, the traditional hypothesis proposes that market concentration lowers the cost of collusion between firms and results in higher than normal profits. On the other hand, the efficiency structure hypothesis postulates that the most efficient firms obtain greater profitability and market share and, as a consequence, the market becomes more concentrated. Some authors (Maudos, 1988) have tested these two hypotheses and obtained results that support the efficiency hypothesis[4]. Based on these results, and on the fact that margins have decreased significantly, we can conclude there has been an increase in competition during the period analysed.

2.2 Emergence of new competitors

Increased competition in the SBS brought about by the SMP should not be assessed by considering only the number of new foreign banks but by other aspects, such as competition from non-bank financial intermediaries. Banks face not only other banks but also other financial intermediaries that compete in the same market.

This process of disintermediation channelled directly loanable funds from savers to borrowers without any reflection on the banks' balance sheets. Thus the role of banks is concentrated on small and medium-size customers, depositors as well as borrowers, relying on their efficient role as producers of information and monitors of the risk of loans to non-financial firms. Large depositors and borrowers go directly to the capital markets, so bypassing the banking system.

The intensity of this process of disintermediation led to a decrease in importance of bank assets and liabilities and gave rise to a fall in the degree of banking in the economy, in spite of the growth of the financial system as a whole. Figure 11.4 shows how bank assets (loans) have increased less than other financial assets.

Figure 11.4 Bank v. non-bank financial assets, 1985-1998 *(1985 = 100)*

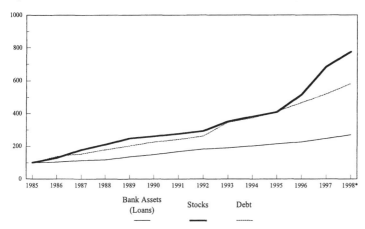

Source: Banco de España

2.3 Changes in performance

Without a doubt, greater competition brought about a positive impact on the real economy. More specifically, this episode introduced incentives for the creation of new financial products, it contributed to the improvement in the quality of the already existing products and services, and it forced companies to reduce the prices of their operations.

However, competition can also produce undesired effects, such as the emergence of new risks for banks. Basically, there are two reasons to support such a statement. First, increased competition induces banks to adopt riskier strategies in order to restore margins. Second, the existence of more competitive markets makes the survival of less efficient firms more difficult.

Under these circumstances, and given the importance of banking institutions, the role of the supervisory authority is crucial. Its mission is not only to prevent bank failure, but also to ensure that, if the collapse of one bank occurs, this does not contaminate the rest of the system through systemic risk thereby minimising the consequences on the real economy. In this respect, the EU has implemented some prudential legislative measures (see Table 11.1).

Evaluating whether there has been an increase in risk in the SBS caused by the SMP is a very difficult question. Traditionally, the loan losses ratio has been taken as a pertinent measure of risk. However, this magnitude is contaminated by economic shocks and it cannot be taken as a good indicator of risk management. Thus, in order to check if the increase in competition raised risk within the SBS, we use Pastor's (1999) results. He obtained a measure of risk management efficiency purged by a set of economic factors.

Table 11.1 Prudential legislative measures

Prudential legislative measures	Implemented in national law
Consolidated Surveillance Directive (83/350/EEC)	1985
Consolidated Accounts Directive (86/635/EEC)	1991
Own Funds Directives (89/299/EEC and 92/16/EEC)	1993
Solvency Ratio Directive (89/647/EEC)	1993
Large Exposures Directive (92/121/EEC)	1993
Deposit Guarantee Directive (94/19/EC)	1996

Figure 11.5 Loan losses ratio and risk management efficiency, 1986-1995

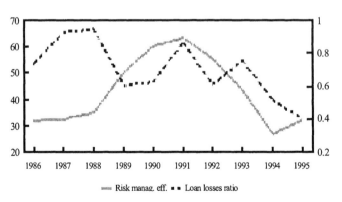

Note: Risk management efficiency (l.h.axis); loan losses ratio (r.h.axis)
Source: Pastor (1999)

Figure 11.5 shows the two definitions of risk. If we look at the loan losses ratio, we observe a decrease, although with some fluctuations, so we can conclude that there has been a decrease in risk. However, if we look at the value of risk management efficiency represented on the left-hand side of Figure 11.5, it indicates the opposite. Risk management efficiency is defined as the portion of bank loan losses that are produced by internal factors. The picture shows that the proportion of bank loan losses produced by internal factors fluctuates around 40%. However, the situation is very different if we break down the total period into sub-periods. Thus, during the period 1985-91 risk management efficiency is continuously increasing. However, after 1991 this proportion begins to decrease. This was the consequence of an increase in default rates brought about by the intensity of competition in the loan market. Hence, it appears that the higher competitive environment has contributed positively to an increase in the banking system's risk.

2.4 Changes in margins and returns

Concerning the impact of competition on the performance of banks, the evolution of margins has been quite satisfactory (see Figure 11.6). Margins and returns were reduced without causing a serious problem to the system between 1985 and 1997 although there were exceptions caused by moral hazard questions. We can take this reduction as positive evidence of a considerable intensification of competition. Commercial and savings banks managed to accommodate the reduction of margins through a corresponding abatement of operating costs.

Under the new competitive conditions, the capacity of banks to maintain or even improve their market share must be attributed increasingly to their efficiency and less to the market power they may enjoy[5]. The most important entry barriers that still exist are those built by banks themselves using strategies of differentiation in services (see Section 3.2 below). Conversely, those barriers originating in exogenous factors, that is legal, technological or cultural barriers, have become much less meaningful. When we compare the return on equities (ROE) of the SBS with that of other countries, we do not find substantial differentials. Moreover, the rate of decrease of ROE was higher in Spain than in many other countries (see Figure 11.7 and Table 11.2).

In 1994 only Italy, France and Germany had smaller ROEs. What this means is that, although the high margins that prevailed in Spain looked very profitable for foreign banks, in reality higher operating costs and higher capital ratios did not permit higher profit ratios[6].

Figure 11.6 Margins, 1985-1997

a) Net interest income

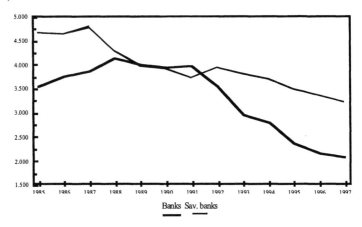

b) Operating profit

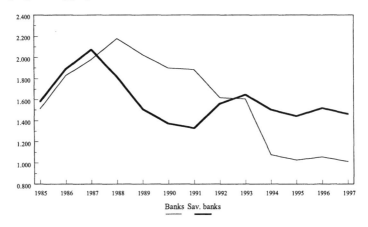

Source: Banco de España

Figure 11.7 Profitability (ROA and ROE), 1985-1996

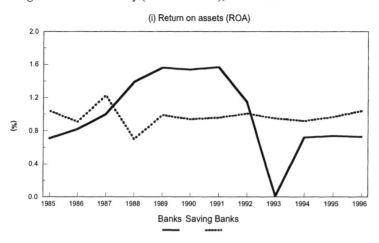

(i) Return on assets (ROA)

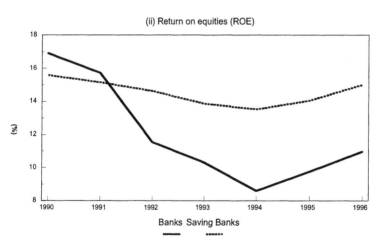

(ii) Return on equities (ROE)

Source: Banco de España

Table 11.2 Return on equities, 1990-1994

	1990	1991	1992	1993	1994
UK	11.9	8.9	8.2	14.2	14.9
Ireland	11.7	13.2	16.4	13.0	14.6
Luxembourg	9.4	7.7	11.7	15.0	13.2
Greece	17.5	19.1	16.4	12.7	11.3
Portugal	18.7	20.5	15.6	8.7	10.7
Netherlands	9.6	8.7	8.7	11.0	10.6
Belgium	9.2	7.8	8.9	10.7	10.4
Spain	*15.6*	*14.2*	*11.2*	*9.2*	*10.3*
Germany	6.4	6.5	5.6	7.1	6.4
France	9.2	7.4	4.2	2.8	1.4
Italy	11.2	8.5	4.6	4.8	0.7
EU	10.9	8.1	5.5	7.4	5.5

Source: Bank Profitability

3   REGULATORY FRAMEWORK

The existing regulatory framework looks very different from the environment that prevailed ten years ago. However, notwithstanding the important efforts made by Spanish authorities to homogenise the legal framework, there is still a long way to go. In this section we review the most relevant measures of deregulation already introduced, as well as the protective barriers that still remain. To do so, we use the results of a postal survey carried out by Economic Research Europe Ltd (1997) which appraises how Spanish bankers have perceived all these changes.

3.1 Main deregulation processes

The processes of harmonisation and deregulation were so wide in scope that it would be very arduous to list all the measures that were adopted. Therefore, in this section we will concentrate on those deregulatory measures that, due to their transcendence or to their repercussions, have had the most important effects on the SBS:

* the elimination of legal distinctions between commercial and savings banks
* the deregulation of interest rates
* the liberalisation of capital movements (Art. 67 of the EEC Treaty)

* the Own Funds Directive (89/299/EEC) and Solvency Ratio Directive (89/647/EEC).

3.1.1 Elimination of legal distinctions between commercial and savings banks

Although savings banks are quite important in the SBS, with a market share of over 50% in deposits and close to 40% in loans, they have traditionally been submitted to a much stricter regulatory framework than commercial banks. In many aspects, this was a competitive disadvantage. The legal distinctions between commercial and savings banks can be summarised as follows:

* *obligatory investment coefficients*: savings banks, which can be conceived as regional public banks, were forced to invest large proportions of their assets in public debt. This not only mean a loss of freedom with respect to asset allocation, but also meant that savings banks could not achieve a high level of profitability because the rates of return on these public securities were far below market rates
* *liquidity coefficient*: the different framework regulating commercial and savings banks also affected reserve requirements. This coefficient was used by monetary authorities as an instrument of monetary control. The reserve ratio reached 22% in the mid-1980s, and was considered a tax on bank deposits, which lowered bank profitability.
* *branch expansion limitation*: until 1988, both commercial and savings banks had their branch networks limited by bank regulation. This constraint was particularly severe for savings banks which, by law, had limited expansion beyond their own region. This legal limitation did not allow savings banks to diversify their activities on a regional basis so they were, and still are, institutions with an extremely regional market. This phenomenon creates serious problems for many savings banks when they face a very low demand for banking services.

3.1.2 Deregulation of interest rates (Article 67 of the EEC Treaty)

Although in 1985 the main bases for free competition were already established by the SMP, competition between banks was, until the end of the decade, more 'potential' than 'real'. The level of interest rates on loans and deposits had been kept fairly stable and was quite similar among banks. The liberalisation processes encouraged by the SMP did not produce any significant effect until the end of the 1980s. Although there was no specific EU legislation with respect to interest rate regulation, this element could be considered as one of the most crucial issues that distorted competition.

Since the early 1950s, interest rates on bank loans and deposits had definite limits. This situation resulted from the years of reconstruction after the Spanish Civil War. The government, in order to encourage investment for the development of the industrial sector, fixed the level of interest rates. However, this situation lasted longer than was necessary. By the late 1980s, following a period of high inflation, this regulation should have disappeared.

The removal of the limits on interest rates was the most visible deregulation measure. Once started, the process of liberalisation extended to other areas of the banking sector and fairly quickly transformed the SBS into an extraordinarily competitive environment. At the end of 1989 Banco de Santander, one of the largest banks in the country, introduced a 'new' demand deposit with high remuneration. The rapid reaction of the other banks resulted in a general increase in deposit interest rates. This fight for new deposits characterised a period of extraordinary competition among banks which was called the 'battle for liabilities'.

A period of high interest rates followed. Later, banks lost their objective of fighting for deposits, no matter how high the cost, and deposit interest began to decrease. By 1994, this product had almost completely disappeared from the market and interest rates were back to their initial levels. But competition did not cease. It moved from the liability to the asset side. Thus, at the beginning of 1992, when interest rates were completely deregulated, Banco de Santander again introduced a new product. It was a modality of mortgage loan with a variable interest rate defined as a margin over MIBOR. This new mortgage meant a substantial decrease in interest rates. As in the case of deposits, other banks reacted very quickly to this aggressive strategy. Banks fought for mortgage loans held by customers at other banks, offering similar products at good prices. As a result, there was a sharp decrease in financial margins and revenues.

Respondents to the questionnaire revealed their perception of the legislation in terms of its impact on their organisation and practices. As can be observed in Figure 11.8, deregulation of interest rates was the most important element for Spanish bankers. Almost 60% of the participants considered it to be of critical importance, giving it a score of 100%, with an average score of 84% overall.

Figure 11.8 Level of importance of legislation in terms of impact on your organisation and its practices

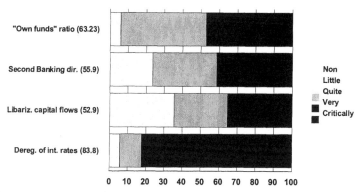

Note: 0 = none; 25 = little; 50 = quite; 75 = very; 100 = critically.
Source: Economic Research Europe Ltd

3.1.3 Liberalisation of capital movements (Art. 67 of the EEC Treaty)

Freedom of capital movements was another cornerstone of a completely integrated European market. Spain formally lifted administrative controls in 1992 but the effects of the liberalisation had been anticipated by all the markets years before. Respondents to the questionnaire were asked about the influence caused by the liberalisation of capital movements (Article 67) on their organisations. Almost 70% reported that liberalisation of capital movements was considered a positive change. However, although the effect is positively valued by the respondents, only 11.7% recognised a critical impact on their organisation and practices. The global score is also small, at 52.9%.

3.1.4 Second Banking Coordination Directive (89/646/EEC)

The Second Banking Coordination Directive is one of the key elements in the liberalisation process of banking services established by the SMP. It offers a comprehensive framework for the regulation of the banking sector and solves some of the problems left by the First Banking Directive. The Second Directive includes references to the conduct of banks, and deals with the structure of the sector and with prudential regulation. Essentially, it eliminates some of the most important barriers that still remained. The modifications that were introduced can be summarised as follows:

- it establishes a unique licence that eliminates the need to be authorised by the host country to conduct operations
- it introduces the principle of home country control so that EU bank branches are not subject to the host country's regulatory supervision: the home country supervisory authority is responsible for the control of its banks. However, some control remains in the host country, such as liquidity supervision and the controls derived from the operation of monetary policy. There are also some articles (19/4 and 21) which make foreign banks subject to host country laws in the case of 'the general good'.

Although the Second Banking Coordination Directive was introduced in 1988 and became a Directive a year afterwards, only much later (1994) was this regulatory framework enacted in Spanish law. Respondents to the questionnaire were asked about the significance of the Second Banking Coordination Directive. Their responses are also shown in Figure 11.8. Only 5.8% considered the significance of this regulation to be critically important for their organisation, and 35.3% regarded it as very important. These results corroborate that the increase in competition coming from foreign banks was not very important.

3.1.5   Own Funds Directive (89/299/EEC) and Solvency Ratio Directive (89/647/EEC)

The main objectives of the Own Funds Directive were the attainment of a certain level of harmonisation of the different definitions of own funds and also of a given degree of confidence in the comparability of the solvency ratios. Meanwhile, given the definition contained in the Own Funds Directive, the aim of the Solvency Ratio Directive was the harmonisation of the minimum requirements for all credit institutions in the EU. The Solvency Ratio Directive calculates the solvency ratio as a weighed sum of risk-adjusted assets, fixing the minimum level at 8%.

The existing levels of capital adequacy were quite high in Spain before the implementation of the SMP. The banking crisis of the late 1980s had encouraged supervisory authorities to fix high capital requirements so that, when the Directives became effective, Spain already held capital ratios higher than those of other European countries.

The results of the postal questionnaire corroborated this assertion. Respondents were asked about the legislative impact of the Own Funds and Solvency Ratios Directives on their organisation and practices. Figure 11.8 shows that only 11.7% considered this regulation critically important in their organisation and 35.3% regarded it as very important.

3.2 Remaining barriers to the SMP

The preceding sections have shown that the processes of deregulation and homogenisation were quite important for the SBS. More specifically, the SMP exercised greater influence in some areas, such as interest rate deregulation, than in others, such as the entry of foreign banks. A partial explanation of this unequal outcome could be the consequence of a different temporal lag required for the effects of SMP to be totally visible. However, it is true that this disparity can also be explained by the persistence of barriers that hinder the full benefits of the SMP. In this section we briefly outline some of the legal barriers still existing in the SBS Apart from barriers that are specific to the banking sector, there are other (horizontal) barriers that obstruct the aim of the SMP, such as taxes and labour regulations.

3.2.1 *The concept of 'general good'*

The SMP assumes legal homogeneity between EU countries, and at the same time it precludes governments' ability to apply specific policies that are not permitted by Community laws. Nevertheless, this loss of independence is not complete because national governments can annul those sections of the SMP that go against the concept of the 'general good'. Traditionally, the European Court of Justice resolves all conflicts between national laws and Community laws. To this end, the European Commission has produced a document which defines the concept of 'general good'. This document establishes, very clearly, those cases in which the host country can apply the case of 'general good' with respect to a EU bank.

The Spanish authorities have not yet used the concept of 'general good' to prevent the entry of foreign banks. It is conceivable that the existence of horizontal barriers common to all the sectors and the presence of specific obstacles that prevent foreign banks from penetrating SBS explain why the clause has not been utilised.

3.2.2 *Remaining barriers in the banking sector*

The main barriers that still prevail in the SBS are:

- limitations on opening new branches: in April 1994, the limitation on foreign banks with respect to the expansion of the branch network was eliminated. Nevertheless, this limitation still operates on new banks on a temporary basis. These constraints establish an actual barrier for new banks, both national and foreign, to penetrate the banking market

- collective investment funds or mutual funds: institutions are restricted to the use of derivative products traded in Spanish financial markets
- capital markets: the SMP assumes the use of EU capital markets by credit institutions, however prior authorisation is required in Spain
- housing subsidies: for a long time, Spanish Governments have operated broad and generous programmes that provide grants and subsidies for housing. These programmes usually include maximum limits on housing prices, grants, and interest subsidies. Although applicants are free to choose the institution to provide the mortgage loan, there is a group of selected banks that collaborate in the programme. This phenomenon can distort free competition and make the entry of foreign banks into the mortgage market very difficult, and even unattractive.

Figure 11.9: Extent to which trade barriers faced by organisations from other EU countries have been removed in the last 3 years

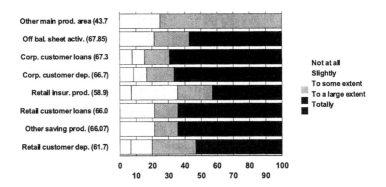

Note: 0 = not at all; 25 = slightly; 50 = to some extent; 75 = to a large extent; 100 = totally
Source: Economic Research Europe Ltd

Figure 11.9 shows how respondents value the importance of the removal of barriers in other EU countries. Except for retail insurance products, Spanish respondents give equal value to all the other areas. Approximately 60% of the respondents consider the removal of barriers to be complete or quite substantial, and almost none of them consider the removal to be non-existent.

3.2.3 Implicit barriers

In addition to legal barriers, there are certain implicit obstacles that hinder rapid integration into a single market. In the case of Spain, the existence of a highly dense network of branches and ATMs can discourage the entry of foreign banks, even in the presence of legal protection.

Certainly, limitations on the opening of new branches and on the provision of mortgage subsidies (see Section 3.2.2) constitute obstacles to the free entry of other EU banks into the SBS. Nevertheless, even if these barriers completely disappear, the current position of banks holding highly developed commercial networks (see Table 11.3) will prevent European banks from penetrating the retail banking segment without great difficulty.

Table 11.3 Implicit barriers: branches and ATMs per 1000 inhabitants and km², 1995

	Branches/ population	*Branches per km²*	*ATMs/ population*	*ATMs per km²*
Austria	0.5812	0.0559	0.4205	0.0404
Belgium	1.8057	0.5998	0.3605	0.1197
Denmark	0.4237	0.0514	0.2068	0.0251
Finland	0.3156	0.0048	0.4740	0.0072
France	0.4576	0.0489	0.3930	0.0420
Germany	0.5390	0.1234	0.4372	0.1001
Greece	0.1427	0.0113	0.1291	0.0103
Ireland	n.a.	n.a.	0.2566	0.0133
Italy	0.3571	0.0692	0.3713	0.0719
Luxembourg	0.8683	0.1377	0.4561	0.0723
Netherlands	0.4353	0.1640	0.3551	0.1338
Portugal	0.3487	0.0375	0.3716	0.0400
Spain	*0.9245*	*0.0718*	*0.6804*	*0.0529*
Sweden	0.2936	0.0063	0.2663	0.0057
UK	0.1813	0.0439	0.3574	0.0865

Source: Bank Profitability (OECD) *and* Blue Book of Means of Payments (European Monetary Institute)

An extensive and intensive branch network is clearly the main instrument required for competing in the retail market. Small savers are more sensitive to the physical proximity of a bank than to interest rate differentials. Highly sophisticated bank services will be less in demand by this type of small customer. In fact, their deposits and/or loans are not large enough to benefit from economies of scale.

In the light of what has just been said, some time will have to pass before all the benefits arising from the SMP can be effective. The time required for competition to force a decrease in fees and commissions in the Spanish retail market could be even longer.

4   IMPACT OF THE SMP

Numerous economic benefits are traditionally attributed to the SMP: price reductions, output increases, improvements in efficiency, higher quality of banking services, larger consumer surpluses, the possibility of exploiting scale economies, and so on. However, many of these benefits would be generated without the SMP. In fact, many countries that are not members of the EU have been experiencing these processes without being involved at all in the SMP. So the relevant and difficult question is how to separate the consequences of the SMP from those of other natural processes, such as the globalisation of economies. This section presents an overview of the main impact of the SMP.

4.1 Bank strategies

There is clear evidence that Spanish banks changed their strategies to quite an extent during the 1980s. Many of the new procedures were aimed at internal competition, specifically between national commercial banks and savings banks, the adoption of which was independent of the SMP. However, other strategies were designed especially to face the SMP. For this reason it is particularly difficult to isolate the influence of the SMP on Spanish banks.

The postal survey carried out by Economic Research Europe Ltd (1997) identifies the most influential factors in bank behaviour. Firstly, technical change, a higher degree of competitiveness, and the process of liberalisation are the main driving forces in the transformation of the banking sector. This is as true for Spain as well as for all other EU countries. Secondly, the SMP is considered to be a factor of reduced importance for bank strategies. Thirdly, competition arising from non-bank institutions is more significant for bank behaviour than the presence of competitors from other EU countries. Consequently, it seems than the SMP has not been considered a crucial issue by Spanish bankers.

However, the SMP has induced new strategies in many product areas. These innovations have been less important in retail banking (see Figure 11.10), for example those introduced in insurance products, in loans and in mortgages. It seems as though social or cultural barriers, together with the costs of establishing new networks, remain serious barriers to cross-border trade in the retail product sector. As in other European countries, the most pronounced changes took place in off-balance-sheet activities and corporate loans.

Figure 11.10: Extent to which strategy has been revised in response to SMP for certain product areas

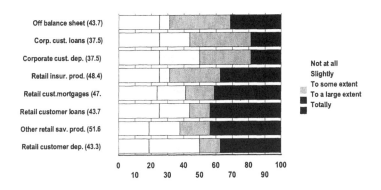

Note: 0 = not at all; 25 = slightly; 50 = to some extent; 75 = to a large extent;
        100 = totally
Source: Economic Research Europe Ltd

4.2 Internationalisation

Another important effect of the SMP is the internationalisation of bank activities. Figure 11.11 shows that the level of trade between Spanish banks and other EU markets has increased slightly. As far as particular products are concerned, the largest increase in cross-border trade has been concentrated in other retail saving products, retail customer deposits, corporate customer loans, and off-balance-sheet activities. Conversely, there has been very little increase in cross-border trade in retail insurance, suggesting that Spanish banks are attempting to consolidate the bancassurance segment as a new domestic product rather than moving abroad to new EU markets.

Figure 11.11: Extent to which your organisation's trade with other EU countries has changed over the last three years

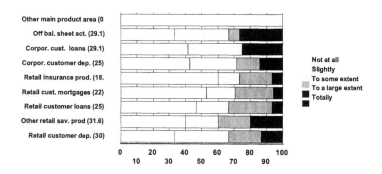

Note: 0 = not at all; 25 = slightly; 50 = to some extent; 75 = to a large extent;
     100 = totally
Source: Economic Research Europe Ltd

Table 11.4 Postal survey results: impact of the SMP in several areas

| | International-isation[1] | | Price, Cost and Margins | | | | | |
| | | | Loan margin[2] | | Deposit margin[3] | | Efficiency and scale econ.[4] | |
	Sp	EU	Sp	EU	Sp	EU	Sp	EU
Totally	0	1	9	0	0	0	0	6
To a large extent	31	36	67	16	52	13	13	14
Slightly	23	54	25	54	39	68	42	44
Not at all	42	7	0	30	0	19	22	30

Notes:[1]Extent to which the SMP has been responsible for any reported changes in the level of trade that your organisation does in other EU countries
[2]Extent to which the SMP has been responsible for any reported changes in the loan margin
[3]Extent to which the SMP has been responsible for any reported changes in the deposit margin
[4]Extent to which the SMP has been responsible for any reported reductions in the costs of supplying services in other EU countries
Source: Economic Research Europe Ltd

However, compared to other EU banks, the SBS shows a lower degree of internationalisation of wholesale banking and a higher degree of internationalisation of retail bank activities. This finding may reflect the fact that Spanish bankers do not consider expanding into other EU markets through the opening of networks to be excessively costly. Results of the postal survey reveal that Spanish respondents do not consider the effects of the SMP on the internationalisation of banks to be very important. Moreover, they consider that SMP has had comparatively less impact in Spain than in the EU as a whole (see Table 11.4).

4.3 Prices, costs and margins

Evidence on the SBS indicates that increase in competition has had a strong impact on the price of loans and on the cost of deposits. In fact, interest rates on deposits increased greatly from 1989 to 1994. Meanwhile, the interest rate on mortgages and corporate loans suffered a large decrease. The direct consequence of these impacts was a strong decrease in margins (see Figure 11.12.i.a.). However, it seems that it is much more difficult for banks to reduce their operating expenses (see Figure 11.12.ii.a). Figure 11.12.i.a shows a large reduction in margins for private commercial banks and, to lesser extent, for savings banks. This lower reduction in margins for savings banks may be due to the fact that they are facing an environment that is less competitive than that faced by commercial banks because their customers show a high degree of fidelity and a low sensitivity to interest rates.

Spanish price reductions and operating expenses reductions have been larger than in other EU countries (Figures 11.12.i.b and 11.12.ii.b) although they differ according to products. Mortgage and corporate loan rates have experienced a larger reduction than rates on retail personal loans[7]. It would be interesting to know to what extent the decrease of margins can be attributed to the SMP. Evidence shows that deregulation of interest rates is not the only factor with a strong impact on the SBS (see Figure 11.8) but it is also the fact that respondents attribute these price reductions largely to the SMP.

Figure 11.13 represents the variations of loan and deposit rates. Spanish bankers consider that there has been a larger effect derived from changes in loan prices than from those in deposit prices. Moreover, respondents attribute price changes to the SMP. In short, it seems that the SMP was the main cause of bank price competition. However, a great part of the price reductions perceived by bankers, even though they are supported by data, could be reflecting the reduction of the inflation rate, together with a given monetary and fiscal policy mix, so we must be cautious with their interpretation. In fact, there is evidence[8] that loan rates and money market rates move together very closely. The slight divergence between these two interest rates largely reflects risk premiums. Accordingly, there is not much room left for additional loan price reductions for those firms which borrow in financial markets. Conversely, there are more possibilities of lower rates for those firms borrowing from banks through traditional channels.

Figure 11.12(i) Net interest income, 1985-1997

a) Spanish banking system (1985=100)

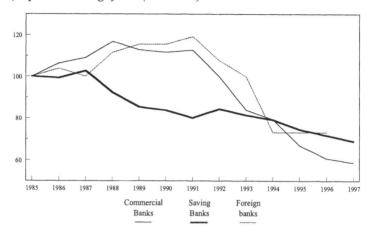

b) European banking systems (1988=100)

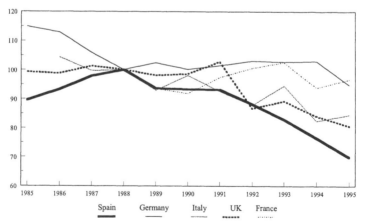

Source: Banco de España *and* Bank Profitability.

Figure 11.12(ii) Operating expenses, 1985-1997

a) Spanish banking system (1985=100)

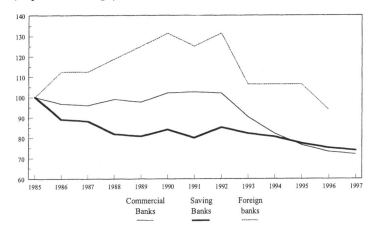

Commercial Saving Foreign
Banks Banks banks

b) European banking systems (1988=100)

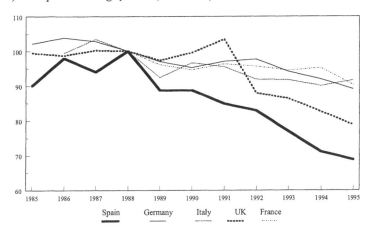

Spain Germany Italy UK France

Source: Banco de España *and* Bank Profitability.

Figure 11.13 Changes in prices and impact of SMP: Spain v. EU

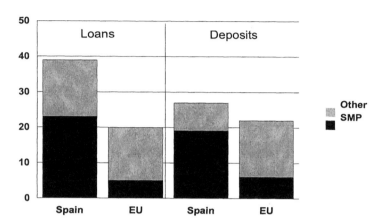

Note: 50 = large decrease; 25 = small decrease; 0 = no change
Source: Economic Research Europe Ltd

4.4 Efficiency and scale economies

Another important expected theoretical effect of the SMP is an improvement in bank efficiency[9] and scale economies. In fact, more competition should bring about greater cost control, increasing outputs and, therefore, more efficiency. On the other hand, the larger market size caused by the SMP should allow firms to experience cost reductions induced by scale economies. However, previous findings in banking literature, for Spain in particular, suggested that the potential reduction in costs arising from efficiency gains are much larger than those provided by scale economies (see Berger and Humphrey, 1991).

Figure 11.14 shows the trend of efficiency calculated as the deviation of minimal cost over actual cost[10]. During the period under analysis, savings banks were more efficient than commercial banks. Moreover, it seems that the adjustment process to deregulation did not significantly affect bank performance.

There are not significant scale economies (Figure 11.15) and, because of this, there is not much room for cost cutting by means of merely increasing bank size. These results are also in agreement with traditional findings: potential cost savings from improving efficiency are much more significant than those brought about by scale economies. More specifically, by reducing the inefficiency levels, savings banks could reduce their total costs by 7% and commercial banks by 12%. Meanwhile, scale economies could bring about a reduction in costs of around 3% in commercial banks and 4% in savings banks respectively.

Figure 11.14 Cost efficiency, 1985-1997

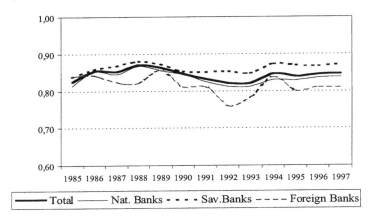

Source: Pérez et al. (1999)

Figure 11.15 Scale economies

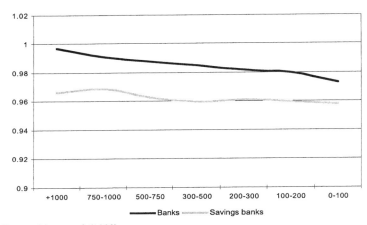

Source: Pérez *et al.* (1999)

All these results suggest that the increase in market shares brought by mergers only resulted in slight scale economies. This effect could be due to the fact that most Spanish banks are still concentrated in the domestic market and they lack the international exposure that might bring about the real benefits of scale economies.

5 CONCLUSIONS

The SBS, as many other economic sectors, has had to react to the new competitive atmosphere created by the liberalisation process of the SMP. This is a common feature shared by all the EU banking systems. However, since Spain had been submitted to a much more restrictive regulatory framework than other banking systems, the change was more drastic and visible.

The main effect of the liberalisation process was the increase in competition that changed the size and composition of the market as well as its performance in margins and prices. Unexpectedly, the implementation of the SMP did not produce a massive entry of foreign banks into Spain, although it did encourage a large number of mergers and acquisitions, increasing substantially the concentration of the SBS. However, it seems that the SBS has become riskier since 1991, when competition began in the loan market. Margins have decreased as a consequence of competition and returns on equities are one of the lowest in Europe.

Numerous economic benefits are traditionally attributed to the SMP. However, many of these changes would have happened without the SMP so the relevant and difficult problem was to separate the consequences of the SMP from those of other natural processes. To solve this problem and answer other questions we carried out a postal survey of bank managers. The survey reveals that technical change and competition from non-bank institutions are the most influential factors for bank behaviour. In contrast, the SMP has not been considered a crucial issue by Spanish bankers. It mainly influenced off-balance-sheet activities and corporate lending. Similarly, Spanish banks did not significantly increase their presence in other EU banking systems, specially in wholesale banking.

Evidence on the SBS indicates that the increase in competition had a strong impact on loan prices and on financial costs. Spanish price reductions have been, in general, larger than in many other EU countries, although they differ according to products. Evidence shows that the deregulation of the interest rate is not the only factor with a strong impact on the SBS but it is also the fact that respondents attribute these price reductions largely to the SMP.

Another important expected effect of the SMP is the improvement in bank efficiency and scale economies. The final report suggests significant scale economies experienced in 1990 and 1991, and diseconomies for the remaining years. All these results suggest that, although there has been an increase in the size of the market as a consequence of the SMP, banks do not exploit the potential cost reductions implicit in scale economies. This is because most Spanish banks are still concentrated in the domestic market and they lack the international exposure that might bring about the real benefits of scale economies. With respect to the opinion of Spanish bankers on the influence of the SMP on scale economies and efficiency, the results of the postal survey show that they do not consider the SMP to be crucial. These results are very similar to those obtained for all of the EU countries.

Many of the questions presently left unanswered will be analysed in future studies taking a longer perspective on the period of adaptation to the SMP. As always, these conclusions should be considered valid until new evidence is available.

Notes

1. Past interest rate regulation prevented banks from offering competitive prices therefore branch expansion was the only method of attracting new deposits. As a consequence, Spain became one of the most overbanked economies in the world. Given the high density of existing branches, as well as the high degree of fidelity of depositors to their own banks, new banks had to compete for deposits by raising them on the interbank market and concentrating on the segment of loans to non-financial firms.

2. Pastor (1996), and more recently Pérez *et al.* (1999), offer evidence on the degree of scale economies in the SBS. The general conclusion is that there are not important scale economies, thereby weakening the argument in favour of mergers.

3. The particular legal form of ownership of savings banks in Spain makes it impossible for a commercial bank to take over a savings bank. However, a savings bank can purchase a private commercial bank.

4. Molyneux *et al.* (1994) also tested the hypothesis for the Spanish banking system. Their results support the structure-conduct-performance hypothesis, the opposite result to Maudos (1998). There are some reasons that could explain this different result. First, the period covered by Molyneux *et al.* is 1986-89 while that of Maudos is 1990-93, a much more deregulated period. Secondly, Molyneux *et al.* used a narrower definition of geographical area than Maudos and, thirdly, they used market share as a proxy of efficiency.

5. See Smirlock, 1985. Vennet (1994) found an increase in market power in the case of Spain that is very difficult to match with the evolution of margins. However, Maudos (1998), with more a more recent data set,

obtained the opposite results.

6. On this issue, see Pérez and Quesada (1991), Pastor *et al.* (1994 *and* 1995), and Pérez *et al.* (1995 *and* 1999).
7. See Economic Research Europe Ltd. (1996), Figure 4.1.
8. See Economic Research Europe Ltd. (1996), Table 4.3.
9. We refer to efficiency as a general concept, different from the concept of X-efficiency, see Leibenstein (1966 *and* 1976).
10. The efficiency has been calculated using the stochastic parametric approach. We have estimated a translog cost function, where the error term is composed by the disturbance and by the inefficiency component.

References

Banco de España, *Boletín Estadístico*.

Berger, A.N. and D.B. Humphrey (1991), 'The dominance of inefficiencies over scale and product mix economies in banking', *Journal of Monetary Economics*, 28 (1), pp. 117-48.

Berger, A.N. (1995), 'The profit-structure relationship in bankinng: test of market-power and efficient-structure hypotheses', *Journal of Money, Credit and Banking*, 27 (2), pp. 404-31.

Confederación Española de Cajas de Ahorros (CECA), *Anuario Estadístico*.

Consejo Superior Bancario (CSB), *Anuario Estadístico de la Banca Privada*.

Economic Research Europe Ltd (1997), *The Single Market Review: Impact on Credit Institutions and Banking*, (Kogan Page, London)

Farrell, M. (1957), 'The measurement of productive efficiency', *Journal of the Royal Statistical Society*, Series A, 120 (3), pp. 253-81.

Leibenstein, H. (1966), 'Allocative efficiency vs. X-efficiency', *American Economic Review*, 56, pp. 392-415.

Maudos, J. and J.M. Pastor (1995), *Prestación de Servicios Bancarios en las Cajas de Ahorro Españolas: Cajeros Automáticos Versis Oficinas*, Instituto Valenciano de Investigaciones Económicas, Working Paper IVIE WP-EC 95-14.

Maudos, J., J.M. Pastor and J. Quesada (1997), 'Technical progress in Spanish banking: 1985-94' in J. Revell (*ed.*) *The Recent Evolution of Financial Systems*, (London, Macmillan)

Maudos, J. (1998), 'Market structure and performance in Spanish banking using a direct measure of efficiency', *Applied Financial Economics*, 9, pp. 191-200.

Molyneux, P. *et al.* (1994), 'Market structure and performance in Spanish banking', *Journal of Banking and Finance*, 18, pp. 433-44.

Molyneux, P. and W. Forbes (1995), 'Market structure and performance in European banking', *Applied Economics,* 27, pp. 155-59.

Pastor, J. M. (1999), 'Efficiency and risk management in Spanish banking firms', *Applied Financial Economics* (forthcoming)

Pastor, J. M. (1996), 'Eficiencia económica, técnica, asignativa y de escala en los bancos y cajas de ahorro españoles', *Cuadernos de Información Económica*, March.

Pastor, J.M., F. Perez and J. Queseda (1995), 'Are European banks equally efficient?', *Revue de la Banque*, 6, pp. 324-33.

Pastor, J.M., F. Perez and J. Queseda (1994), 'Indicadores de eficiencia en banca', *Revista Vasca de Economía (EKONOMIAZ)*, 28 (1), pp. 78-99.

Perez, F., J.M. Pastor and J. Queseda (1995), *Efficiency Analysis in Banking Firms: an International Comparison*, Instituto Valenciano de Investigaciones Económicas (IVIE), Working Paper WP-EC 95-18.

Pérez, F. *et al.*, (1999), *Sector Bancario Español (1985-1997): Cambio Estructural y Competenci*, Caja de Ahorros del Mediterráneo.

Pérez, F. and J. Quesada (1991), *Dinero y Sistema Bancario: Teoría y Aplicaciones al Caso Español*, Espasa-Calpe.

Smirlock, M. (1985), 'Evidence on the (non)relationship between concentration and profitability in banking', *Journal of Money Credit and Banking*, 17, pp. 69-83.

Stigler, G.J. (1976), 'The Xsistence of X-efficiency', *American Economic Review*, 66, pp. 213-16.

Vennet, V. (1994), 'Concentration, efficiency and entry barriers as determinants of EC bank profitability', *Journal of International Financial Markets, Institutions and Money*, 4 (3-4), pp. 21-46.

12   United Kingdom

Edward P.M. Gardener and Philip Molyneux

1   MARKET STRUCTURE

As in other European countries, the UK banking market has undergone substantial change over the last twenty years, mainly driven by domestic deregulation as well by various other forces that have changed the supply and demand characteristics of the financial services industry (Molyneux *et al.*,1996). Compared to its main European counterparts the UK has a relatively small number of banks. As Figure 12.1 illustrates, the total number of authorised banking institutions has fallen from around 600 in 1985 to just over 460 in 1998. It also shows the decline in the number of mutual building societies over the same period.

Figure 12.1 Number of banks and building societies, 1985-1998

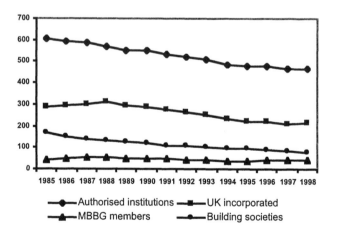

Source: Banking Business: An Abstract of Banking Statistics (1999), Volume 16, Table 1.04, p. 6 (British Bankers' Association, London); Annual Abstract of Banking Statistics 1996, Volume 13, Table 1.04, p. 7; Housing Finance, No 44, November 1999, Table 31, p. 71, (Council of Mortgage Lenders, London)

The decline in the total number of banks is attributable to foreign banks that already had UK operations acquiring relatively small UK investment banks, as well as a modest consolidation in the domestic retail banking market. Table 12.1 shows that during the second part of the 1990s the decline in the number of UK incorporated banks has been greater than for foreign banks. This reflects the growing consolidation trend in the domestic market. A decline in the number of non-European banks (particularly Japanese banks) has been counteracted by the increased presence of European institutions, whose number increased from 79 to 109 between 1993 and 1999. Table 12.1 illustrates these trends and shows that the total number of foreign banks operating in the UK fell from 255 to 247 between 1993 and 1997. Foreign banks typically do little sterling-denominated business, focusing mainly on wholesale foreign currency activity relating to investment banking activity.

Table 12.1 also illustrates the number of banks and subsidiaries of the main UK retail banks, otherwise known as the major British banking groups (MBBG). These banks dominate sterling-denominated banking business in the UK. The MBBG includes 11 major banks, along with their subsidiaries. Four of these were formerly mutual building societies that converted to bank status: Abbey National (converted in 1989), Alliance and Leicester (1997), Halifax (1997) and Woolwich (1997). The MBBG and the building societies are the major players in the retail banking market.

During the 1990s, UK banks and building societies engaged in a significant reorganisation. This is characterised by the decline in branch numbers that has occurred, especially since 1990. Figure 12.2 shows the trends in branch and ATM numbers in the UK since 1985 and illustrates that during the 1990s, while branch numbers were declining, the introduction of ATMs at branches and in 'remote' locations grew significantly. Although not shown in the diagram, there was also a substantial growth in EFTPOS terminals, from 4,640 in 1993 to 8,984 in 1997, further reflecting the trend to supplement traditional with new distribution channels[1].

The reason for the shift from branches to other means of financial service delivery mainly relates to the desire of UK retail financial service firms to improve operating efficiency as well as customers' increasing demands to access banking services outside the traditional, rather limited, banking hours.

Table 12.1 Number of banks in the United Kingdom, 1993-1999

	1993	1994	1995	1996	1997	1998	1999
Number of authorised institutions of which:	508	486	481	478	466	468	449
UK incorporated	253	232	224	220	212	214	202
European authorised institutions	79	97	102	103	105	105	109
Incorporated outside the European Economic Area	176	157	155	155	149	149	138
(a) Channel Islands and Isle of Man institutions	26	27	41	34	41	(a)	
(b) MBBG members and their banking sector subsidiaries (included above)	39	37	37	40	41	44	43
(c) BBA member banks (included above)	328	318	307	306	311	337	327

Note: Lists of authorised institutions are published by the Bank of England

(a) Those institutions (including branches of some UK banks and representative offices) which have opted to join the UK banking sector. With effect from end-September 1997, Channel Islands and Isle of Man institutions were no longer considered part of the UK banking sector.

(b) Major British banking groups (MBBG) in 1999 included the following: Abbey National Group, Alliance & Leicester Group, Bank of Scotland Group, Barclays Group, Halifax plc, Lloyds TSB Group, Midland Group, National Westminster Group, Royal Bank of Scotland Group, Standard Chartered Group, Woolwich plc.

(c) As at end-March.

Source: Banking Business: An Abstract of Banking Statistics (1999), British Bankers' Association, Vol 16, Table 1.04, p. 6.

Figure 12.2 Number of branches and ATMs, 1985-1998

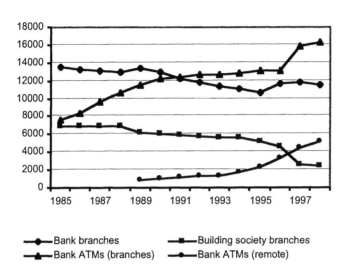

Notes: Branch and ATM/cash dispenser numbers are for MBBG (parents only) and exclude data on smaller banks. The bank data include Abbey National (from 1989 onwards), Bank of Scotland, Barclays, Lloyds, Midland, National Westminster, Royal Bank of Scotland, TSB, Alliance and Leicester (from 1997 onwards), Halifax (from 1997 onwards) and Woolwich (1997 onwards).
Source: Banking Business: An Abstract of Banking Statistics (1999), Volume 16, Tables 5.02 and 5.03, pp. 52-3 (British Bankers' Association: London); Annual Abstract of Banking Statistics 1996, Volume 13, Table 5.02, p. 52.

Together with the general decline in branch numbers, the restructuring of the system has also led to a fall in bank and building society employment, as shown in Figure 12.3. The fall in staff employed is particularly noticeable for retail banks where it fell by around 75,000 between 1990 and 1996. The increase in employment after 1996 is attributable to building society conversions to bank status. In addition, Figure 12.3 also reveals that there has been a modest increase in employment by foreign banks since 1996, reflecting the booming capital markets activity of foreign-owned investment banks in London.

Figure 12.3 Employment (000s) in the UK banking sector, 1990-1998

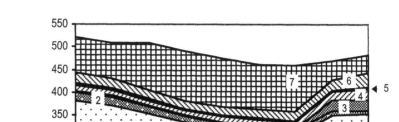

Notes: Employment figures relate to banks that are members of the British Bankers' Association. In 1997 the incorporation of all banking subsidiaries of members (which were not previously members) resulted in a marked increase in the total staff numbers for BBA members.

Source: Banking Business: An Abstract of Banking Statistics (1999), Volume 16, Table 5.01, p. 50 (British Bankers' Association: London); Annual Abstract of Banking Statistics 1996, Volume 13, Table 5.01, p. 64.

A clearer picture of employment trends at the top UK retail banks is given in Figure 12.4. This shows that Barclays, NatWest and Lloyds (now LloydsTSB) have been the most aggressive at reducing staff numbers during the 1990s. Surprisingly, the other main banks have maintained relatively stable employment levels over the same period. It is also interesting to note that of the 300,000 plus staff employed by the MBBG in 1998, around 60% were female, of which over 60,000 were part-time workers; this compares with only 2,200 part-time male employees. Throughout the 1990s there has been a gradual increase in the number of part-time staff employed in the banking sector, mainly in the retail sector. Again, the decline in employment numbers and the increase in part-time employment are indicators of the main banks' desire to improve their operating efficiency.

Figure 12.4 Number of staff (000s) employed by major banks, 1985-1998

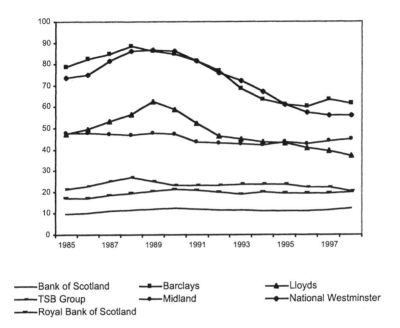

Bank of Scotland   Barclays   Lloyds
TSB Group   Midland   National Westminster
Royal Bank of Scotland

Source: Banking Business: An Abstract of Banking Statistics (1999), Volume 16, Table 5.01, p. 50 (British Bankers' Association: London); Annual Abstract of Banking Statistics 1996, Volume 13, Table 5.01, p. 64.

2   FINANCIAL STRUCTURE

The balance sheet structure of the UK banking system differs from that of many other European markets mainly because of the significant presence of foreign banks. The latter primarily engage in foreign currency denominated (eurocurrency) business and undertake only modest sterling banking operations. In contrast, the UK banks primarily engage in sterling-denominated activity. Given the important presence of foreign banks this means that a substantial proportion of total balance sheet activity is foreign currency orientated. This can be seen in Figure 12.5 which shows that foreign currency business is at least as important as sterling activity in the banking sector's balance sheet. Similarly, Figure

12.6 also illustrates the importance of foreign currency deposits in the UK system.

Figure 12.5 UK banking sector asset structure, 1985-1998 *(£billions)*

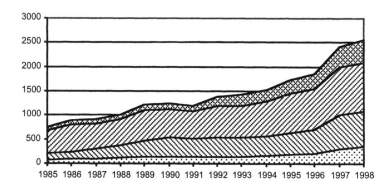

□ Total other assets
▣ Foreign currency market loans and advances
◨ Sterling advances
□ Sterling market loans

Source: Banking Business: An Abstract of Banking Statistics (1999), Volume 16, Table 1.01, p. 3 (British Bankers' Association: London); Abstract of Banking Statistics 1996 , Volume 13, Table 1.01, p. 2

As already mentioned, the UK banking sector's balance sheet has a high foreign currency component because of the significant presence of foreign banks mainly undertaking wholesale foreign currency money and capital markets business in London. Foreign bank presence in the domestic banking sector is minimal: the most noticeable foreign operators in the retail market are the specialist credit card providers such as MNBA and GE Capital. If one considers the assets share of the banking system in 1998, UK-owned banks account for 45% of the total, followed by other European-owned banks (29%), US banks (8%) and then Japanese banks (5%)[2]. The share of other European banks has increased significantly since 1990 when it stood at around 11%, whereas the assets share of Japanese banks has fallen (mainly because of retrenchment related to problems in their domestic market) and the share of US banks has remained relatively constant.

Figure 12.6 UK banking sector liability structure, 1985-1998 *(£billions)*

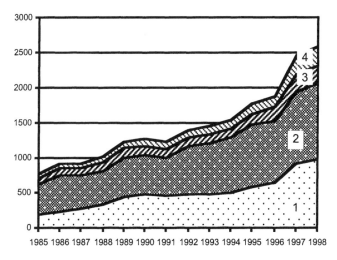

1 Sterling deposits   2 Foreign currency deposits
3 CDs and short-term paper   4 Other liabilities

Source: Banking Business: An Abstract of Banking Statistics (1999), Volume 16, Table 1.01, p. 3 (British Bankers' Association: London); Annual Abstract of Banking Statistics 1996, Volume 13, Table 1.01, p. 2

The large increase in the presence of continental European banks has, to a certain extent, been brought about by continental European banks acquiring UK merchant banks, such as Dresdner Bank's purchase of Kleinwort Benson and Swiss Bank Corporation's (now part of Union Bank of Switzerland) acquisition of S.G. Warburg in 1995. In addition, many large European banks have moved the headquarters of their capital markets operations to London, as well as building up substantial private banking and asset management businesses in London during the latter half of the 1990s. It is difficult to say whether the increased presence of European banks in the UK has been a direct result of the SMP although there must be a presumption that it has had some effect in promoting foreign bank establishment (and growth). This is because the introduction of the single banking licence and the reduction in barriers to cross-border banking and capital markets business brought about by the legislation has made it easier for EU banks to conduct cross-border activity, especially in capital markets areas[3].

Figure 12.7 MBBG sterling lending to UK residents (billions), 1985-1998

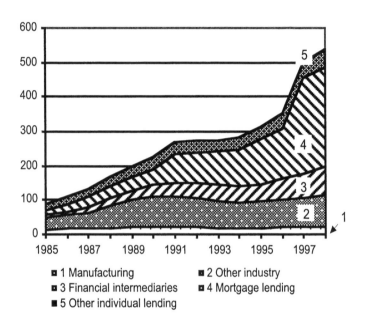

Source: Banking Business: An Abstract of Banking Statistics (1999), Volume 16, Table 2.08, p. 17 (British Bankers' Association: London); Annual Abstract of Banking Statistics 1996, Volume 13, Table 2.09, p. 25.

The MBBG dominates sterling business in the UK and the make-up of its lending business is shown in Figure 12.7. The figure shows that during the 1990s there has been substantial growth in domestic mortgage lending relative to other types of lending. This is the case even when one takes into account the conversion of various building societies into banks from 1996 onwards. The relatively low level of lending to the manufacturing sector is also noticeable and this has raised policy concerns about inadequate bank funding available to small and medium-sized enterprises (SMEs)[4]. Although not shown, individual sterling deposits comprise around 55% of MBBG non-bank sterling deposits, followed by company deposits (17%). Throughout the 1990s the proportion of individual sterling deposits as a percentage of total sterling deposits has increased. This trend reflects the growing focus of UK banks on retail banking activity at the expense of corporate and investment banking business. The success of LloydsTSB in generating spectacular profitability, driven mainly by retail banking, has encouraged all the top UK banks to emphasise this business area. The (relatively) low funding cost of retail deposits, coupled with the healthy margins generated through mortgage and other consumer lending, has encouraged the main banks to prioritise retail banking/financial services and to de-emphasise other areas. (For example, NatWest and Barclays significantly reduced their investment banking operations because of poor performance at the end of 1997).

Figure 12.8 Net lending for consumer credit, 1985-1998

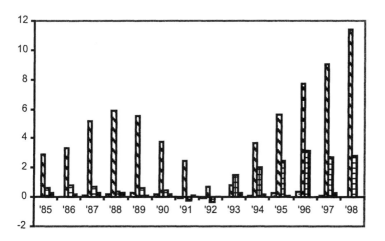

◘ Building societies ◘ Banks ◙ Specialist lenders ■ Others

Source: Banking Business: An Abstract of Banking Statistics (1999), Volume 16, Table 4.06, p. 46 (British Bankers' Association: London); Annual Abstract of Banking Statistics 1996, Volume 13, Table 4.06, p. 60.

The main UK banks have been particularly aggressive in competing with building societies and other specialist lenders in the consumer credit and mortgage areas. Figures 12.8 and 12.9 illustrate net lending trends in these two sectors over the last fifteen years. The cyclical nature of the two areas is clearly evident: rapid growth in consumer and mortgage lending up to 1988-1990 then a decline during the UK's recession and an increase thereafter. In fact, the boom in credit expansion in the late 1980s, prior to the early 1990s recession, has strong similarities with the credit trends that have been experienced in the UK during the late 1990s! The two figures also show that banks dominate net lending for consumer credit, and by 1997 and 1998, because of the building society conversions, they were also the main new lenders in the mortgage area.

Figure 12.9 Net mortgage lending, 1985-1998 *(£billions)*

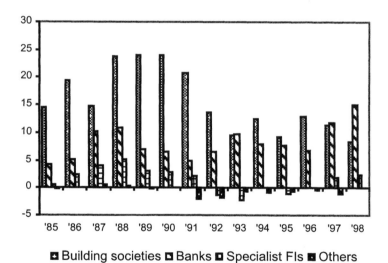

□ Building societies □ Banks □ Specialist FIs ■ Others

Source: Banking Business: An Abstract of Banking Statistics (1999), Volume 16,
    Table 4.05, p. 45 (British Bankers' Association, London): Annual Abstract of
    Banking Statistics 1996, Volume 13, Table 4.05, p. 58.

3   MARKET CONCENTRATION AND COMPETITION

The UK banking market, like many other European systems, is relatively concentrated with the top four banks accounting for 25% of all banking sector assets and 49% of UK banking and building society assets. The level of concentration, as illustrated in Figure 12.10, has fallen slightly during the 1990s, a trend contrary to concentration developments in many other European markets (see Economic Research Europe, 1997).

Figure 12.10   Percentage share of top four banks' assets, 1985-1998

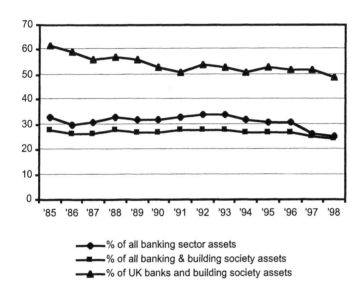

Notes: The top four banks are defined as Barclays, National Westminster, Midland and Lloyds TSB. Assets for Lloyds TSB pre-1994 are obtained by summing assets of Lloyds Bank and TSB. The share of these banks falls substantially as a proportion of all banking sector assets in 1997 because of building society conversions to bank status.

Source: Banking Business: An Abstract of Banking Statistics 1999, Volume 16, Table 1.01, p. 3 and Table 3.01, p. 26; Annual Abstract of Banking Statistics 1996, Volume 13, Table 1.01, p. 2 and Table 3.02, p. 39; Housing Finance, No. 44, Table 32, p. 71 (Council of Mortgage Lenders: London)

However, while the market share of the top banks has fallen overall, this conceals the concentration trends in specific market segments. For example, Bowen *et al.* (1998) find that the market share of the top three mortgage providers increased from 34% in 1992 to 43% in 1997; the figures for the top four firms was 39% and 50% respectively. In addition, 12 mortgage providers were found to account for 80% of the domestic mortgage market. The same authors also found the retail deposit market to be quite concentrated, with the top four banks having 45% of the market in 1997, although this level of concentration had remained roughly the same throughout the 1990s. The area that stands out as being the most concentrated is banking services to SMEs where the top four suppliers have 83% of the market[5].

Growing regulatory concerns about excessive concentration, coupled with historically high UK bank profitability, led to the recent UK Government report on competition in UK banking, the so-called Cruickshank Report[4], which examines a broad range of issues relating to competitive conditions in the UK banking market. However, the main focus is on three main areas: money transmission services; services to retail customers; and services to small and medium-sized enterprises (SMEs). Overall, the report finds that there are important limitations to competition in various key markets and the current regulatory environment is inappropriate to deal with this. Recommendations are therefore made for a major overhaul of bank regulation in order to improve competition and innovation in UK banking.

One area that comes in for particular criticism is the market for money transmission services where 'profound competition problems and inefficiencies' were found to exist. The report argued that money transmission services are dominated by a handful of major banks and the current arrangements restrict entry and result in high costs to retailers for accepting credit and debit cards, as well as excessive charges for cash withdrawals (up to six times their cost). Money transmission services were also found to be 'cumbersome and inflexible' and slow to adapt to the new demands of e-commerce.

In the supply of retail banking services it was found that competition had increased in the mortgage, personal loan, and credit card areas, although the prices charged by new entrants so far had only a limited impact on established bank pricing. In addition, the dominant role played by the major banks in the current account market was believed to restrict competition in many other product areas. Significant barriers to switching current accounts remain. The report voiced concerns about the inadequate representation and redress for consumers in the event of disputes. It also referred to 'significant information problems', citing the fact that consumers were rarely aware of the terms and conditions of the products they bought.

The market for SME banking services was found to be much less competitive than the retail sector. Problems associated with switching current accounts, financial product information, representation and redress were found to be acute. The market for SME services is much more concentrated than the retail sector and entry barriers were found to be high. (It is noticeable that the building societies that converted to banks have not entered the SME market in any significant fashion). Money transmission costs for UK SMEs was also found to be very high on an international basis and access to risk capital for high growth firms was perceived to be limited.

Taking together the report's findings on retail and SME banking services, a broad range of recommendations are made including:

- strengthening the current arrangements for customer redress and representation, including the establishment of a new Financial Services Consumer Council
- improving customer information by publishing, via the Financial Services Authority (FSA), a broad range of benchmark retail and SME services according to price (providing both regional and UK prices)
- various initiatives to improve the flow of equity finance to high growth SMEs

and, more controversially,

- recommending that, until UK merger law is reformed, the Government should refer all mergers between financial suppliers to the Competition Commission if the merging firms have 'material shares of the market'
- calling for a Competition Commission inquiry into banking for SMEs.

An important theme throughout the report is the highly concentrated nature of the UK current account and SME markets, as well as the structure of the domestic payments system. All these areas, the report argues, are characterised by high entry barriers as well as limited price and non-price competition. The large market shares held by a handful of banks is put as a major reason for the high profitability of UK banks during the 1990s. Market structure and adverse competitive outcomes are most pressing in the SME market. As the Cruickshank Report states, 'the competition problems are so significant that a change in market structure may be the only way of achieving an effectively competitive marketplace. The only mechanism for delivering such a change...is action following a complex monopoly reference to the Competition Commission'.

Overall, the report argues that there is substantial scope for increased competition as well as the opportunity for competing banks to make adequate returns, even in the provision of basic banking services. The recommendations, although unpalatable to the main UK banks, go a long way to promote more effective competition in the UK banking market. The authorities, of course, must also balance the need to promote competition against the imperatives of prudential regulation. However, there is little doubt that new technologies, such as the internet and other types of electronic payments systems, create substantial opportunities for opening up the UK market.

4   NEW SERVICES AND NEW ENTRANTS

The range of services offered by UK banks has expanded over the last decade or so to encompass a broad range of retail and corporate banking services. Up until 1986 commercial banks were restricted from owning stockbrokers and could not be members of the London Stock Exchange. The famous Big Bang reforms of 1986 that ended the legal separation between broking and jobbing firms, allowed UK banks to acquire securities firms. This encouraged them to offer a wider range of both retail and wholesale securities business to their clients. At the same time, the 1986 Building Societies Act liberalised various activities for the building societies sector which allowed them to compete more effectively in traditional banking areas, such as in the unsecured consumer lending area. This also encouraged the main banks to compete more aggressively in the retail mortgage market.

During the late 1980s the main strategic focus of UK banks was to maximise market share, with less emphasis on shareholder returns and efficiency criteria. This resulted in the banks prioritising balance sheet growth in key areas such as consumer and mortgage lending, as well as dedicating substantial capital resources to building their securities operations. Most of the top banks offered insurance products and services to their clients but this was mainly through tie-ups with major insurance companies. In fact, the 1986 Financial Services Act that reorganised the UK's regulatory structure for investment services stipulated that banks had either to offer one supplier's insurance products or had to act as broker and quote a range of products from competing insurers. After the 1986 Act, of the main banks only NatWest chose to be a broker whereas all the other banks chose to provide insurance services from a sole supplier.

While this legislation, as well as the 1987 Banking Act, aimed to establish a new regulatory structure for financial service provision in the UK, it also led to a gradual breakdown in demarcation lines between different financial service business areas. Previously banks, building societies and insurance companies mainly competed in separate markets, although the banks had made some inroads into the mortgage sector since the abandonment of the building societies' cartel in the early 1980s, and a handful had modest insurance operations. Competition in the retail financial services sector from 1986 onwards, therefore, intensified, especially between banks and building societies. In securities business, NatWest and Barclays significantly bolstered their operations by acquiring investment banking/securities firms with an avowed strategy to build major investment banking operations to compete with the top US houses, a strategy that was to culminate in failure and the sale of the bulk of these operations by the end of 1997.

In general, therefore, banking business in the second half of the 1980s was characterised by growth and product diversification strategies in the light of the new regulatory environment. The change in the regulatory environment also mirrored various developments at the EU level. The 1988 Second Banking Directive legislated for a universal banking model as part of the SMP and therefore UK developments were pretty much in line with these developments. It is difficult, however, to say how much regulatory developments at the EU level impacted on UK legislation, especially since legislation like the 1986 Big Bang had pre-empted the new EU rules. It was the case, however, that the UK was moving to a regulatory framework that permitted banks to provide a universal range of financial services.

Throughout the latter part of the 1980s, UK banks continued to expand in both traditional and non-traditional areas, although the 1987 stock market collapse and the recession that ensued in the late 1980s and early 1990s forced the major firms to review their strategies. Out went the 'growth for growth's sake' strategy and in came the era of efficiency drives and shareholder value. Lloyds Bank (now LloydsTSB) was the most aggressive in formulating a strategy that aimed to double its share price every three years.

All the main banks, because of the poor returns posted in the recession years, began to focus much more on ways to improve their returns, especially to shareholders. This meant prioritising high return areas by directing capital to businesses that generated the best risk-adjusted return on capital and cutting costs, and downgrading or jettisoning poor performing businesses. Again, Lloyds was the first major bank to announce that it did not intend to build significant investment banking operations. It also reduced its international banking activity and stated that it would focus mainly on domestic (especially) retail financial services. Barclays and NatWest continued to pursue a universal domestic financial service strategy, with an emphasis on building substantial investment banking operations. While some of the top banks in the late 1980s suggested that they would consider pursuing a broad-based European strategy, by the time the UK recession ended in 1992 all decided to concentrate on their domestic activities (although Barclays and NatWest did have European ambitions in the investment banking arena).

Table 12.2 provides a snapshot of the evolution of services offered by certain banks over the last forty years. The table clearly illustrates the broadening of retail financial service provision over the period.

While UK banks continued to expand the range of retail services on offer, they also began to sever their links with insurance companies and other firms. Traditionally most banks and building societies acted as distribution channels for insurance companies' products. Banks began to realise that they could generate better returns by doing this themselves. Only LloydsTSB had a long-established in-house insurance operation so others began to pursue a more aggressive bancassurance strategy, (see Genetay and Molyneux, 1998). This, of course, forced some insurers to consider their options and by the mid-1990s some had set up their own banks, as shown in Table 12.3.

The attractive returns being posted by the retail financial service divisions of the main UK banks, as well as the exceptional performance of LloydsTSB throughout the 1990s, was also, perhaps, a motivating factor encouraging non-financial service firms to enter the domestic retail banking market. As can be seen in Table 12.4, various supermarkets have also entered into banking offering limited, yet attractive, deposit and loan services.

As the Cruickshank Report notes, these new entrants have acted as a stimulant to competition in the retail market, although they have had little impact on the pricing behaviour of the major banks so far. This lack of price impact is put down to costs associated with customer switching, lack of price transparency in the market for retail financial services, and general customer inertia. The recommendations proposed by Cruickshank, and discussed above, aim to address these issues.

Table 12.2   Services offered by banks, 1960s-1990s

Personal Banking			1960s	1970s	1980s	1990s
Credit Card	Barclays		Y	Y	Y	Y
	Lloyds-TSB			Y	Y	Y
	Midland			Y	Y	Y
	Halifax				Y	Y
	Woolwich				Y	Y
Mortgage	Barclays			Y	Y	Y
	Lloyds-TSB				Y	Y
	Midland			Y	Y	Y
	Halifax		Y	Y	Y	Y
	WoolwichB		Y	Y	Y	Y
Real Estate	Barclays					
	Lloyds-TSB				Y	
	Midland					
	Halifax				Y	Y
	Woolwich				Y	Y
Insurance						
Life	Barclays		Y	Y	Y	Y
	Lloyds-TSB				Y	Y
	Midland				Y	Y
	Halifax					Y
	Woolwich					Y
Non-Life	Barclays				Y	Y
	Lloyds-TSB				Y	Y
	Midland					Y
	Halifax					Y
	Woolwich					Y
Asset	Barclays		Y	Y	Y	Y
Management	Lloyds-TSB				Y	Y
	Midland			Y	Y	Y
	Halifax					Y
	Woolwich					Y

Y = Service offered.
Relative position of bank by size of total assets:
    Barclays, 1; Lloyds-TSB, 4; Midland, 6; Halifax, 5; Woolwich, 9

Source: Bowen, Hogarth and Pain (1998), The recent evolution of the UK
        banking industry and some implications for financial stability, Table 12,
        p.271 in *The Monetary and Regulatory Implications of Changes in the
        Banking Industry,* BIS Conference Papers, Volume 7, March 1999, pp
        251-94.

Table 12.3 Insurance companies offering banking services

	Prudential Banking	Standard Life Bank	Legal & General Bank	Scottish Widows Bank	Sun Bank (Sun Life of Canada)
Start date	October 1996	January 1998	July 1997	May 1995	1994*
Current a/c	No	No	No	No	No
Savings a/c	Yes	Yes	Yes	Yes	Yes
Telephone	Yes	Yes	Yes	Yes	Yes
Postal	Yes	Yes	Yes	Yes	Yes
Branch	No	No	No	No	No
Personal loans	Yes	In future	No	Policy loans only	No
Credit cards	No	No	No	No (group issues)	Yes
Mortgages	Yes	No	Yes	Yes	Yes
Business services	No	Savings a/c	No	Savings a/c	Savings a/c with cheque book, loans**
Deposits (as at)	£958m (Dec. 1997)	£1,000m (Sep. 1998)	£200m (Dec. 1997)	£400m (Sep. 1998)	£460m (Dec. 1997)

Notes: *Opened as Confederation Bank; ** Sun Bank also undertakes asset leasing activities for personal and business customers.

Source: Bowen, Hogarth and Pain (1998), The recent evolution of the UK banking industry and some implications for financial stability, Table 17, p. 274 in *The Monetary and Regulatory Implications of Changes in the Banking Industry*, BIS Conference Papers, Volume 7, March 1999, pp. 251-94.

Table 12.4 Supermarkets offering banking services

	Tesco Personal Finance*	Sainsbury's Bank**	Marks & Spencer
Start date	February 1997	February 1997	Late 1980s
Current a/c	No	No	No
Savings a/c	Yes	Yes	Long-term savings products only
Telephone	Yes	Yes	No
Personal loans	Yes	Yes	Yes
Credit cards	Yes	Yes	Yes
Mortgages	No	Yes	No
Personal insurance	Home and travel	Home	No
Business services	No	No	No
Deposits (as at)	£600mn (March 1998)	£1,500mn (February 1998)	n.a

Notes: *Tesco has a 49% stake in Tesco Personal Finance, a joint venture with Royal Bank of Scotland. ** Sainsbury has a 55% stake in Sainsbury's Bank, a joint venture with Bank of Scotland.

Source: Bowen, Hogarth and Pain (1998), The recent evolution of the UK banking industry and some implications for financial stability, Table 18, p. 275 in The Monetary and Regulatory Implications of Changes in the Banking Industry, BIS Conference Papers, Volume 7, March 1999, pp. 251-94.

In addition to the new entrants into the banking markets, many traditional and non-traditional suppliers of retail financial services are developing internet banking operations but, as in the rest of Europe, the take-up has been relatively slow. Typically, the internet is used most often as an additional channel to meet the requirements of more sophisticated bank customers and, as such, the market is relatively small. Around 2% of bank customers use on-line banking services in the UK. Table 12.5 gives an indication of internet banking penetration in the UK, with Barclays being the biggest provider.

Table 12.5 Number of internet banking customers in the UK

Barclays	380,000
First Direct	120,000 (*source*: First Direct)
Nationwide	90,000 (*source*: Nationwide)
Lloyds/TSB	67,000 (*source*: Report and Accounts)
Egg	60,000 (*source*: Prudential interim figures)
Royal Bank of Scotland	45,000 (*source*: Royal Bank of Scotland)

Source: Financial World, Special Report, October 1999, p. 22

In the majority of cases, however, UK banks still appear to regard the internet as little more than a means to a marketing end. Most banks have some kind of Web presence but the functions provided are limited and there is little integration with back-office and other bank systems. Few banks regard internet services as a core business area. Other evidence suggests that UK banks are still prioritising the development of call centres and phone-based banking services at the expense of internet delivery because they believe PC penetration is, as yet, too low to justify a major strategic focus. Others, such as HSBC, are focusing on developing the main alternative delivery channel, interactive TV. Given that satellite TV penetration is higher than PC penetration in the UK (and also in many other European countries), banking services developed through these channels may grow much faster than internet banking, especially when broadcasters switch to digital channels in the near future.

So far we have mainly discussed developments in the retail financial services sector and that is because this sector has experienced the most noticeable changes. This contrasts with banking to SMEs where the top four banks dominate the market and there has been little change on the supply side throughout the 1990s. It is noticeable, for instance, that none of the building societies that converted into banks during the 1990s have targeted this market segment. Of course this could be because they do not have, or cannot quickly acquire, the expertise to compete in this market segment. It could also be the case that switching costs are so high for SME customers that these 'new' banks do not feel that they would be able to attract a large enough client base to make the offering of SME services worthwhile. It could also be that retail financial services are perceived as more profitable. Whatever the reasons, there are concerns that this sector of the market is not as competitive or innovative as it should be, hence the recommendations of the Cruickshank Report to refer this area to the UK Competition Commission for further scrutiny.

Finally, in the investment banking business sector, Barclays and NatWest have had to scale back substantially their activities as the poor returns generated by this business area acted as a drag on profitability throughout most of the 1990s. Between 1994 and 1997 both banks were posting return on equity of over 20% on their domestic banking activity compared with single figure returns from investment banking. This had such an adverse impact on investor sentiment that it forced the two banks to sell off the bulk of their investment banking arms at the end of 1997, although Barclays retained its large asset management operations (Barclays Capital). The aim of these two banks to create global investment firms was just too costly a strategy to pursue, especially given the strength of their main competitors such as Goldman Sachs, Merrill Lynch and Morgan Stanley Dean Witter.

Rather than concentrating on investment banking, these and the other top UK banks have recently focused on building their asset management and private banking arms. This is mainly because this business requires little regulatory capital (unnecessary if one holds third-party assets) and it generates relatively stable fee- and commission-based income. Because of the low capital cost, a successful asset management and/or private banking operation can significantly boost shareholder returns.

5 BANKING PERFORMANCE

UK banks have been among Europe's best performing financial firms during the second half of the 1990s. This is because they have benefited from the buoyant domestic economy and have also managed to maintain relatively high interest margins, unlike banks in continental Europe where margins have mainly fallen. In addition, costs have been reduced (although some banks like LloydsTSB have been much more successful than Barclays and NatWest in improving cost efficiency) and provisioninghas fallen dramatically. Taking these factors together, this has resulted in a sustained increase in banking sector profits from 1993 onwards.

Table 12.6 shows the trend in net interest margins for a handful of UK banks during the 1990s. One can see that the main banks have been able to sustain margins around the 4% level. While interest income declined as a proportion of total income during the second half of the 1980s and the recession years of the early 1990s, it increased from 1993 onwards, exceeding 60% between 1996 and 1998. Non-interest income as a source of total income fell over the same period. This is shown in Figure 12.11.

Figure 12.11 Income of major British banking groups, 1985-1998 (*% of gross income*)

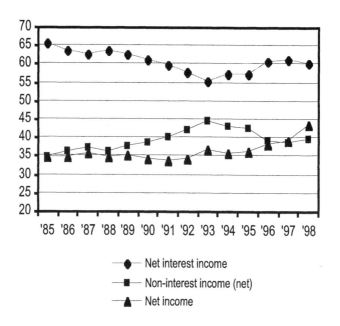

Note : Figures from 1996 onwards cover the expanded MBBG, including Alliance & Leicester, Halifax and Woolwich.

Source: Banking Business: An Abstract of Banking Statistics (1999), Volume 16, Table 3.08, p. 36 (British Bankers' Association, London); Annual abstract of Banking Statistics 1996, Volume 13, Table 3.06, p. 45.

Table 12.6 Net interest margins (domestic business) UK retail banks, 1990-1998

Bank	1990	1991	1992	1993	1994	1995	1996	1997	1998
Barclays	3.9	3.8	3.9	3.8	4.1	4.2	4.3	4.5	4.4
LloydsTSB					4.1	3.6	3.5	3.7	3.8
Midland	2.8	2.6	2.8	2.8	2.9	3.0	2.8	2.7	2.5
NatWest	4.5	4.3	3.9	3.7	3.6	4.4	4.3	4.4	4.3
Royal Bank of Scotland	3.1	2.7	2.7	2.7	2.6	2.4	2.3	2.2	2.3
Woolwich							2.3	2.2	2.2

Source: Banking Business: An Abstract of Banking Statistics (1999), Volume 16, Table 3.07, p. 35 (British Bankers' Association, London)

In fact the trends in interest and non-interest income simply reflect the cyclical characteristics of the domestic economy. When in recession, demand for loan products is depressed so banks (consciously or unconsciously) depend more on non-interest income as a source of income. When the economy grows, then demand for loan products increases thus helping to boost interest income's share of total income.

On the cost side, the main banks have been, on average, successful at reducing their cost to income ratios from around 65% in 1994 to 57% in 1998. Staff costs as a proportion of total income have also declined to around 30% of gross income. In addition, the net costs of provisioning have dramatically fallen since 1992, acting as a strong boost to overall profitability. Cost trends for the MBBG are shown in Figure 12.12.

Figure 12.12 Costs of major British banking groups, 1985-1998 (*% of gross income*)

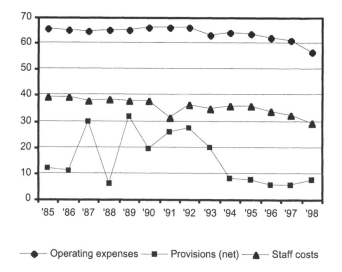

Note : Figures from 1996 onwards cover the expanded MBBG, including Alliance
& Leicester, Halifax and Woolwich
Source: Banking Business: An Abstract of Banking Statistics (1999), Volume 16,
Table 3.08, p. 36 (British Bankers' Association, London); Annual Abstract of
Banking Statistics 1996, Volume 13, Table 3.06, p. 45.

Figure 12.13 Profits of major British banking groups, 1985-1998 (*% of gross income*)

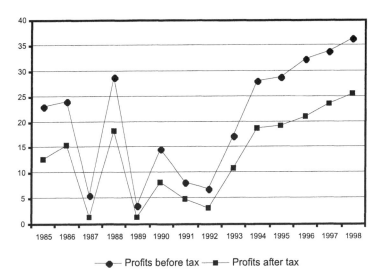

—●— Profits before tax —■— Profits after tax

Note: Figures from 1996 onwards cover the expanded MBBG, including Alliance & Leicester, Halifax and Woolwich

Source: Banking Business: An Abstract of Banking Statistics (1999), Volume 16, Table 3.08, p. 36 (British Bankers' Association, London); Annual Abstract of Banking Statistics 1996, Volume 13, Table 3.06, p. 45

As already noted, high margins, lower costs and buoyant economic conditions feeding loan demand have fed through into a sustained increase in profitability from 1992 onwards, as shown in Figures 12.13 and 12.14. It is interesting to note the variation in performance among the major banks as shown in Table 12.14. The dip in returns generated by Barclays and NatWest in 1996 and 1997 is mainly attributable to the poor performance of their investment banking operations. It is also interesting to note the exceptional performance of LloydsTSB from 1995 onwards. In fact, shareholders in UK banks increasingly benchmark performance against that of LloydsTSB. That is one reason why NatWest (one of the poorest performers) recently lost its independence after being acquired by Royal Bank of Scotland in February 2000: shareholders were dissatisfied with the returns it had been generating compared with some of its major competitors.

Figure 12.14 Pre-tax profits of major UK banks (%), 1985-1998

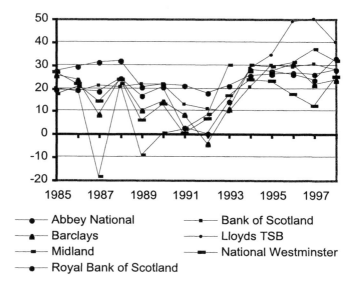

—•— Abbey National   —■— Bank of Scotland
—▲— Barclays   —•— Lloyds TSB
—■— Midland   —■— National Westminster
—•— Royal Bank of Scotland

Source: Banking Business: An Abstract of Banking Statistics (1999), Volume 16, Table 3.06, p. 33 (British Bankers' Association, London); Annual Abstract of Banking Statistics 1996, Volume 13, Table 3.04, p. 41.

6 CHANGING REGULATORY ENVIRONMENT

The regulatory environment in the UK banking and financial services industry has changed dramatically since the mid-1980s. In general, new legislation has covered three main areas. First, a range of regulatory changes have been sought to reduce demarcation lines between different types of financial service firms, especially between banks and building societies, as well as between commercial and investment banking business (Big Bang). Second, the UK has also implemented EU legislation into domestic banking law, facilitating the introduction of the single banking licence and harmonising prudential regulation for both commercial banks and investment firms. Finally, the most recent legislation has been put in place to transfer regulatory responsibility for the whole financial system to a 'super' regulator, the Financial Services Authority, following the Labour

Government's announcement that it was making the Bank of England independent for monetary policy purposes. The major regulatory developments, as well as other significant events, are shown in Table 12.7.

Changes governing the regulatory treatment of the building society sector have probably had the biggest impact. Ironically, reforms that have been put in place to improve the competitive stance of the mutual sector vis-à-vis commercial banks has led to a systematic decline of the former. This is because most of the largest building societies, as outlined above, embraced demutualisation, leading to a shift of assets from the mutual to the commercial banking sector. While the mutual sector has declined in relative importance, those societies that converted still mainly undertake mortgage business: their balance sheet structures have not changed dramatically.

Table 12.7 Building society demutualisation

	Conversion to bank status		Merger with bank	
	Institution	*Rank in building society sector*	*Institution*	*Rank in building society sector*
1989	Abbey National	2		
1995			Cheltenham & Gloucester	6
			Leeds Permanent*	5
1996			National Provincial	6
1997	Alliance & Leicester	4	Bristol and West	7
	Halifax	1		
	Woolwich	3		
	Northern Rock	5		

Notes: * Merger with Halifax that subsequently became a bank.
Source: Bowen, Hogarth and Pain (1998), The recent evolution of the UK banking industry and some implications for financial stability, Table 15, p. 273 in *The Monetary and Regulatory Implications of Changes in the Banking Industry*, BIS Conference Papers, Volume 7, March 1999, pp. 251-94.

Having said this, however, the Cruickshank Report notes that the mortgage sector is one of the most competitive segments of the UK banking market. This it attributes partly to these conversions but more importantly to new insurance company entrants, such as Standard Life Bank, that offer highly competitive services. The same report (Appendix E) also notes that competitive conditions in the UK mortgage market compare favourably with those of North America, France and Germany.

Another area where the change in legislation has had a big impact is in the restructuring of the domestic merchant banking industry. Prior to the 1986 Big Bang reforms, investment banking and securities business were dominated by UK-owned banks, mainly partnerships operating in the City of London. Independent UK firms like Morgan Grenfell, Kleinwort Benson, S.G. Warburg and others dominated domestic business.

Big Bang allowed commercial banks to become members of the London Stock Exchange and the legal separation between stockbroking and jobbing firms (those operating on the floor of the exchange) was abandoned. This led to a frenzy of domestic and foreign commercial banks, as well as the main US investment banks, acquiring domestic securities firms. The merger and acquisition frenzy faltered, to a certain extent, after the 1987 stock market crash, although Deutsche Bank acquired Morgan Grenfell in 1989. It recommenced after the UK recession, particularly from 1995 onwards, and by the beginning of 2000 there were hardly any significant independent UK merchant banks.

Investment banking and securities business in the UK is now dominated by the major US 'bulge bracket' firms, as well as various Swiss and German universal banks.

The gradual structural deregulation relating to commercial banking, investment banking, securities business and insurance now means that financial firms have the choice of being universal operators. In the domestic banking market all of the commercial banks and building societies offer a full range of financial services to their customers. Even new operators, like Egg (the internet banking arm of the insurance company Prudential), offer banking, insurance and various investment services.

The 1997 decision by the government to create a single financial services regulator, the Financial Services Authority, is another clear reflection of the ongoing universalisation of the UK banking industry.

Table 12.8 Major changes in the UK regulatory environment, 1986-1998

Date	Regulatory event	Effects
1986	Big Bang: London Stock Exchange abolishes fixed minimum commissions and single capacity trading	
1986	Building Societies Act (came into effect in January 1997): (a) Increased potential for commercial lending by allowing building societies to provide other services relating to house purchase and finance (b) Provisions made for building societies to convert from mutual to corporate status (c) Limits imposed on wholesale funding: building societies are not able to obtain more than 20% of their funding from money market sources (although this could be raised to 40% by statutory instrument) (d) Building Societies Commission created to supervise building societies	Lending limits: Class 1 lending: 90% of assets Class 2 and 3 combined: 10% of assets Class 3 lending: 5% of assets Definitions: Class 1: advances secured on first mortgage to owner-occupiers of residential property Class 2 (non-class 1): wholly secured loans Class 3 (unsecured loans): interests in estate agencies, broking and other subsidiary activities
1987	Banking Act	Strengthened Bank of England's regulatory powers. New legislation created a single category of authorisation, requiring institutions to be able to satisfy 'fit and proper' tests. Deposit protection fund increased to protect 75% of retail deposits up to a maximum of £20,000

Jan. 1988	Building societies' wholesale funding limit: (a) Wholesale funding limit raised to its maximum ceiling of 40% (b) Unsecured lending limit per capita increased from £5,000 to £10,000	Some societies had had difficulties competing in the mortgage market with the 20% limit; this problem was overcome by increasing the limit to 40%
1989	Second Banking Co-ordination Directive (2-BCD) adopted by EC member countries	Main effect was to give a 'passport' to a bank authorised in one member state to open a branch or do business in another member state without further authorisation
1990–93	Building societies' lending limits: (a) Limits on Class 2 and Class 3 lending combined increased from 10% (1990) to 17.5% (1991) to 20% (1992) to 25% (1993) (b) Limits on Class 3 lending increased from 5% (1990) to 7.5% (1991) to 10% (1992) to 15% (1993)	Building societies able to take on more unsecured lending
1992	Second Consolidated Supervision Directive (implemented 1993): replaced 1983 Consolidated Supervision Directive	Extended range of institutions subject to requirement of consolidated supervision and extended range of activities covered by consolidated supervision
1993	Large Exposures Directive: UK implementation of the Directive on the monitoring and control of large exposures of credit institutions	
April 1995	Capital Adequacy Directive (CAD) introduced: amended in December 1995	Set minimum capital requirements for market risks in trading books of banks and investment firms

Date	Event	Description
July 1995	Deposit protection scheme: Credit Institutions (Protection of Depositors) Regulations amended in the UK Deposit Protection Scheme to meet the requirements of EU Deposit Guarantee Schemes Directives.	Increased the maximum level of protection for an individual depositor from 75% of £20,000 to 90% of £20,000 (or ECU 22,222 if higher). This brought the Scheme into line with the Building Societies Investor Protection Scheme
1996	Introduction of gilt repo market	
1996	Real Time Gross Settlement (RTGS) went live	
1996	Investment Services Directive introduced	Purpose was to provide a single European 'passport' for investment firms and make changes in access to regulated markets
1996	Sterling liquidity: new system for measuring sterling liquidity introduced for large UK banks	Prior to this, most banks in the UK were supervised on the 'mismatch' approach whereby assets and liabilities are allocated on the maturity ladder and limits are set on the size of the mismatch in various time bands. This approach was less suitable for very large banks whose balance sheets were characterised by highly diversified retail deposit bases. For large banks it is more suitable for them to hold an adequate stock of liquid assets
1996	Capital Adequacy Directive 2 (CAD-2): amendment to the Capital Adequacy Directive 1995 implemented end-1998	Provision made for banks to use a measurement system for market risks similar to that in CAD, but also to use their own internal value at risk models as determinant of supervisory capital for market risks (including commodities)

1997	Chancellor announces Bank of England independence: supervisory responsibilities to be transferred to the Financial Services Authority.
	Building Societies Act	Building societies' powers extendedto compete with the banks
1998	Bank of England Act	Legally establishes monetary policy independence for the Bank of England
Mar 2000	Cruickshank Report on 'Competition in UK Banking'	(a) Recommends reform of payments system through establishment of a new licensing/regulatory body to be known as PayCom (b) Refers bank services to the SME (small and medium-sized enterprises) sector to the Competition Commission under a complex monopoly reference.

Source: Adapted from Bowen, Hogarth and Pain (1998), The recent evolution of the UK banking industry and some implications for financial stability, Appendix 1, pp. 293-4 in *The Monetary and Regulatory Implications of Changes in the Banking Industry*, BIS Conference Papers, Volume 7, March 1999, pp. 251-94.

7 IMPACT OF THE SMP

The main EU legislation implemented into UK law as part of the SMP includes the following Directives:

- Second Banking Co-ordination Directive (and the related Solvency Ratio and Own Funds Directives)
- Second Consolidated Supervision Directive
- Large Exposures Directive
- EU Deposit Guarantee Schemes Directive
- and the Investment Services and CAD Directives.

In terms of the impact of this legislation, the Second Banking Co-ordination Directive was expected to have a major influence in reducing barriers to cross-border trade in banking services, thus facilitating greater EU-wide activity by national banks. The single banking licence made it easier to establish within the EU and the harmonisation of prudential rules meant that no jurisdiction would have any unfair competitive advantage in terms of bank prudential supervision. The Directive formed the cornerstone of the SMP for commercial banks and other credit institutions, and was implemented into UK law by the start of 1993. Afterwards there followed similar legislation for the securities industry in the form of the Investment Services Directive and Capital Adequacy Directives, although these took longer to agree upon at EU level because of prolonged debate about harmonising capital requirements for firms that did both commercial banking and securities business.

ERE (1997) investigates the influence of the pre-1993 legislation on the UK banking market and generally finds that it had little impact. This may, of course, have been because the UK economy experienced a recession between 1990 and 1992, and the main banks were focusing primarily on domestic rather than European issues. The limited impact of the legislation on domestic bank strategy might also have been a consequence of the fact that the banking market had already been substantially deregulated. Whatever the reasons, it is clear that the landscape of the UK banking industry barely altered as a consequence of the SMP. To illustrate this it is useful to highlight some of the main findings of the ERE (1997) study. For example, in a survey of UK banks, 88% of respondents stated that the SMP had had no impact on loan pricing in the domestic market. Strangely, evidence from the same survey found that only 39% of the same respondents said the SMP had no influence on deposit rates. (These findings, however, are probably explained by the very small changes in loan and deposit margins over the survey period). Irrespective as to whether one looks at the evidence on retail or wholesale banking, the influence of EU legislation in the UK market is, at best, 'very slight'. Compared with virtually all the other EU countries, the SMP legislation appears to have had one of its least impacts in the UK.

While the SMP appears to have little impact on the domestic banking market, ERE (1997) reveals that it did at least encourage UK banks to expand, albeit in a limited fashion, their EU branch networks. It also facilitated greater cross-border trade by UK banks in off-balance (mainly derivatives) business, investment management services, and other corporate and wholesale activities. This presumably was because the single licence and freeing up of capital controls across the whole of the EU allowed UK commercial and investment banks to expand their businesses more readily throughout continental Europe. This goes both ways nowadays as EU banks have significantly increased their presence in London post-1992, selling wholesale and investment banking services, as well as private banking and asset management activity, back into the EU.

In general, the main finding of the ERE (1997) study was that the SMP had its greatest impact at the investment banking and wholesale end of the market, and this was true across the whole of the EU. From a strategic perspective, UK banks recognised that the elimination of capital controls and the single licence facilitated cross-border business, but mainly in wholesale banking business areas. The barriers to cross-border establishment and provision in retail banking were perceived as being just too great, especially since the top UK commercial banks had had bad experiences of foreign retail banking (especially in the US market) and they did not want to make the same mistakes again. Overall, the SMP had only a marginal impact on the domestic UK banking system and, for whatever reasons, did not provide sufficient impetus to encourage any UK banks to embrace a EU-wide strategy.

Throughout the rest of the 1990s the top UK banks focused on adding shareholder value by reducing costs and growing their domestic retail financial services operations. By the beginning of 2000, only HSBC had a major overseas presence, in particular because of its historical connections with the Far East and Hong Kong. It added to its substantial US operations by acquiring the Safra banking empire in 1999, and also acquired Crédit Commercial de France, the seventh largest French bank, in March 2000. This reflected HSBC's desire to build its private banking and asset management businesses, a strategy being followed by many global banks as these areas require little regulatory capital and tend to generate stable returns (and relatively high returns on capital invested).

While rumours abound about pan-European deals between UK banks and banks in the Netherlands, Germany and Spain, none have, so far, materialised. However, at least the SMP set the groundwork for the establishment of an integrated European banking market. The impetus and rationale for cross-border deals between UK and EU banks is likely to accelerate as we move towards the introduction of the single currency at the retail level on 1 January 2002. Of course, the impetus for such deals would be further encouraged if the UK were to join EMU, but we will have to wait and see if this happens.

8 CONCLUSIONS

So far we have shown that the changing features of the UK banking system have mainly been a consequence of the changing market environment and also a result of various domestic regulatory reforms. While the SMP appears to have influenced the strategic positioning of UK-based banks in relation to cross-border provision of wholesale banking services, there appears to have been little material impact on the domestic commercial banking scene. European banks from outside the UK have no significant presence in retail financial services or banking to SMEs. Although the presence of continental European banks in the UK has grown post-SMP, their activities are almost solely confined to wholesale investment banking and securities activities based in the City of London. Strong domestic securitisation trends in the corporate sectors of countries like Germany have also been a factor.

As has been noted above, the SMP appears to have facilitated greater pan-European opportunities for banks that concentrate on wholesale investment banking and securities activities rather than those dedicated to mainstream domestic commercial banking activity. One could argue that it is the London-based US 'bulge-bracket' and other investment banks that have most readily embraced the opportunities afforded by a pan-European market.

The same can probably be said about strategic positioning in the context of EMU. The introduction of the single currency from the 1 January 1999 and the creation of a single European monetary policy have acted as a strong fillip to create an integrated European capital market. The recent spate of alliances between major European stock markets and derivatives exchanges is clearly a precursor to full integration. In addition, it is difficult for the eurozone to sustain more than 20 derivatives exchanges trading contracts based on almost identical bond contracts, especially when one considers that the US can sustain only five such exchanges, so integration is gradually occurring in capital markets business and the money market is already integrated. Also, portfolio constraints that restricted institutional investors in the eurozone from investing in foreign currency assets (for example, EC legislation which dictates that insurance companies have to hold a certain percentage of their assets in the same currency denomination as their liabilities) have been blown away with the introduction of the euro. This means that institutional investors that were typically overweight in domestic bonds and underweight in both domestic and foreign equities, have substantial portfolio restructuring opportunities, further boosting EMU-wide capital markets activities.

Many analysts also forecast that increased capital market integration would promote company listings. Growing pressures on state-funded pensions would also encourage the investment habit throughout the eurozone, further boosting capital market activity. Given that this perception of the impact of EMU on capital markets business appears to have been accepted by the investment banking community, it is hardly a surprise that the main UK-based investment banks all espouse some form of European strategy. EMU, and its precursor the SMP, has certainly had a bigger impact on investment banking than on the traditional commercial banking sector.

While EMU has afforded various wholesale banking opportunities to the main UK commercial banks, the same cannot be said on the retail side. Unlike in many other European countries, there has not been a major consolidation trend. Consolidation in the Italian, French and Spanish banking markets appears to be (mainly) defensive, strengthening one's domestic market position against the threat of foreign take-over and also building a base to expand into the eurozone, although few have done so. Many deals, of course, are aimed at building domestic scale in order to reduce overlapping costs and boost performance. In the smaller eurozone countries, the lack of domestic merger opportunities because of the already highly concentrated nature of the domestic market is forcing the major banks to acquire cross-border, as witnessed by the spate of Dutch-Belgian and pan-Nordic deals. Many of the pressures to consolidate in anticipation of the threats and opportunities posed by EMU appear to have been less present in the UK banking market up until recently. First, UK commercial banks have been among the best European bank performers in terms of return on equity since 1996. Interest margins have remained relatively high throughout the 1990s thus helping to sustain profitability. There has been little perceived threat of foreign acquisition because of the good performance of UK banks and subsequent high market valuations. Profitability has been strongly driven by the retail financial services business and this is where the main banks have strategically focused. Given that few eurozone commercial banks and/or banking markets appear to be able to generate the same level of returns, the UK banks have shunned European expansion, believing that any substantial acquisition is likely to destroy shareholder value.

The domestic UK banking market is relatively concentrated and the competition authorities are unlikely to agree to a merger between any of the top four banks. In addition, only one bank, the Royal Bank of Scotland, has a major strategic alliance with a eurozone bank and none espouse any major European ambitions in their strategy. As such, the main institutions have continued to focus on domestic retail financial services business, expanding more rapidly into insurance, as illustrated by LloydsTSB's acquisition of Scottish Widows in 1999. NatWest also attempted to go along the same route, as is reflected in its (failed) bid for the insurer Legal & General.

Concern about NatWest's bancassurance strategy, among other things, prompted the hostile bid battle between Bank of Scotland and Royal Bank of Scotland for NatWest. Royal Bank of Scotland succeeded in acquiring NatWest in February 2000. The deal was not referred to the competition authorities because the Scottish bank's share of the total UK domestic banking market was modest compared with NatWest's. This bid battle, plus the critical Cruickshank Report which almost certainly rules out any deal between the top banks, is forcing banks to revise or reconsider potential pan-European (or at least part-European) strategies. While there is still potential for a limited number of large domestic bancassurance deals, the start of 2000 has witnessed substantial market rumours about mergers between some of the main UK banks and similar institutions operating in the eurozone.

Although it has come to UK domestic banks later than some other European countries, it now seems that the constraints imposed by both the market and regulators will force the major institutions into eurozone deals. This will almost certainly happen before the euro is introduced as a retail currency in January 2002. The full impact of EMU on UK bank strategy has hardly been realised. Current forces, however, suggest that irrespective of whether the UK is 'in' or 'out' of the eurozone, the main banks are almost certainly going to engage in substantial cross-border eurozone deals within the near future.

Notes

1. See European Central Bank: 'The Effects of Technology on EU Banking Systems', July 1999, Table A4 for EFTPOS trends in EU banking.
2. See Bank of England Statistical Abstract (1999) Part 1; compiled from Tables 3.2, 3.2.1 to 3.2.6, pp. 40-53 for data on the asset share of foreign banks in the UK banking market. Also see Bowen, Hogarth and Pain (1998), 'The recent evolution of the UK banking industry and some implications for financial stability' (Table 14, p. 272) in *The Monetary and Regulatory Implications of Changes in the Banking Industry*, BIS Conference Papers, Volume 7, March 1999, pp. 251-94.
3. The ERE (1997) study notes that the SMP legislation had the largest impact in the capital markets and wholesale banking areas in facilitating cross-border activity.
4. Policy concerns about funding to SMEs are a central theme of the UK Government report 'Competition in UK Banking: a Report to the Chancellor of the Exchequer' published in March 2000 and chaired by Don Cruickshank. The report recommends that the UK banks be referred to the Competition Commission because of the possibility of a complex monopoly existing in the provision of banking services to the SME sector. The top four UK banks account for 83% of the SME market.
5. See footnote 4.

References

Bank of England (1999), *Statistical Abstract Part 1*, (Bank of England, London)

Bowen, Hogarth and Pain (1999), 'The recent evolution of the UK banking industry and some implications for financial stability' in *The Monetary and Regulatory Implications of Changes in the Banking Industry*, BIS Conference Papers, Vol. 7, pp. 251-94.

British Bankers' Association (1996), *Annual Abstract of Banking Statistics, Vol 13*, (BBA, London)

British Bankers' Association (1999), *Banking Business: An Abstract of Banking Statistics, Vol. 16*, (BBA, London)

'Cruickshank Report', (March 2000) *Competition in UK Banking: A Report to the Chancellor of the Exchequer*, (Stationery Office, London)

Economic Research Europe Ltd (1997), *The Single Market Review: Impact on Credit Institutions and Banking*, (Kogan Page, London)

European Central Bank (July 1999), *The Effects of Technology on EU Banking Systems*, (ECB, Frankfurt)

Financial World (October 1999), 'Will a computer in every home ruin your channel delivery strategy?': Special Report, (Chartered Institute of Bankers, London)

Genetay, Nadege. and Philip Molyneux (1998), *Bancassurance*, (Macmillan, London)

Housing Finance (1999), No. 44, November, (Council of Mortgage Lenders, London)

Molyneux, Philip, Yener Altunbas and Edward Gardener (1996), *Efficiency in European Banking*, (John Wiley, Chichester)